The Marshall Plan

Between 1948 and 1951, the Marshall Plan delivered an unprecedented $12.3 billion in U.S. aid to help Western European countries recover from the destruction of the Second World War, and forestall Communist influence in that region. *The Marshall Plan: A New Deal for Europe* examines the aid program and its ideological origins, and explores how ideas about an Americanized world order inspired and influenced the Marshall Plan's creation and execution. The book provides a much-needed re-examination of the plan, enabling students to understand its immediate impact and its political, social, and cultural legacy. Including essential primary documents, this concise book will be a key resource for students of America's role in the world at mid-century.

Michael Holm is Lecturer in History at Boston University.

For additional documents, images, and resources please visit *The Marshall Plan* companion website at: www.routledge.com/cw/criticalmoments

Critical Moments in American History

Edited by William Thomas Allison, Georgia Southern University

A full list of titles in this series is available at www.routledge.com/Critical-Moments-in-American-History/book-series/CRITMO. Recently published titles:

The Marshall Plan

A New Deal for Europe

Michael Holm

Routledge
Taylor & Francis Group

NEW YORK AND LONDON

First published 2017
by Routledge
711 Third Avenue, New York, NY 10017

and by Routledge
2 Park Square, Milton Park, Abingdon, Oxon, OX14 4RN

Routledge is an imprint of the Taylor & Francis Group, an informa business

© 2017 Taylor & Francis

The right of Michael Holm to be identified as author of this work
has been asserted by him in accordance with sections 77 and 78 of
the Copyright, Designs and Patents Act 1988.

Library of Congress Cataloging in Publication Data
CIP data has been applied for

ISBN: 978-1-138-91570-1 (hbk)
ISBN: 978-1-138-91571-8 (pbk)
ISBN: 978-1-315-69008-7 (ebk)

Typeset in Bembo and Helvetica Neue
by Florence Production Ltd, Stoodleigh, Devon

Contents

Series Introduction

Welcome to the Routledge *Critical Moments in American History* series. The purpose of this new series is to give students a window into the historian's craft through concise, readable books by leading scholars, who bring together the best scholarship and engaging primary sources to explore a critical moment in the American past. In discovering the principal points of the story in these books, gaining a sense of historiography, following a fresh trail of primary documents, and exploring suggested readings, students can then set out on their own journey, to debate the ideas presented, interpret primary sources, and reach their own conclusions—just like the historian.

A critical moment in history can be a range of things—a pivotal year, the pinnacle of a movement or trend, or an important event such as the passage of a piece of legislation, an election, a court decision, a battle. It can be social, cultural, political, or economic. It can be heroic or tragic. Whatever they are, such moments are by definition "game changers," momentous changes in the pattern of the American fabric, paradigm shifts in the American experience. Many of the critical moments explored in this series are familiar; some less so.

There is no ultimate list of critical moments in American history—any group of students, historians, or other scholars may come up with a different catalog of topics. These differences of view, however, are what make history itself and the study of history so important and so fascinating. Therein can be found the utility of historical inquiry—to explore, to challenge, to understand, and to realize the legacy of the past through its influence on the present. It is the hope of this series to help students realize this intrinsic value of our past and of studying our past.

William Thomas Allison
Georgia Southern University

Figures and Tables

FIGURES

TABLES

Acknowledgments

This book began from the conviction, in the words of one of the most influential public intellectuals of the twentieth century, that "what rules the world is ideas because ideas define the way reality is perceived." Too often historians of American foreign relations have been uncomfortable with this reality, uncomfortable with ideas as significant factors in policy-making. This belief in the power and importance of ideas informed much of my doctoral research at Boston University and this book is, in many respects, a narrow spinoff of my earlier work on the impact of American ideology on foreign policy during the 1940s. As a result this volume, to a considerable extent, bears the mark of those esteemed intellectuals who have shaped my professional development thus far. Debating the power of ideas in mid-twentieth century U.S. foreign policy with brilliant minds such as Bill Keylor, Andy Bacevich, and David Mayers has been the experience of a lifetime. We may often have disagreed and pushed each other—sometimes perhaps to the brink—but they have all taught me to be a better critic, a better scholar, a better teacher, and, I hope, a more eloquent thinker. I have learned much from them but I would like to believe that, at times, my thinking may have challenged their perceptions of what constitutes and inspires America's role in the world as well. If so, that is what the intellectual endeavor is all about. It is about the exchange of ideas to refine, recalibrate, and force new and interesting ways and prisms through which to perceive reality.

The debt I owe to these gentlemen is immeasurable, as are the personal and professional ones that I have incurred to Boston University's Louis Ferleger, Erik Goldstein, and Cathal Nolan for their constant and unwavering support of my academic pursuits. I owe much to my students as well. During my years of teaching history and international relations at Boston University, I have been fortunate to encounter cohort after cohort of remarkably gifted young individuals, all of whom, in one form or another, have been subjected to my research and my ideas in classroom discussions and through reading and writing assignments. The enthusiasm that so many of them brought, and continue to bring, to the classroom, their engagement, commitment, and pursuit of knowledge—all of it I find wonderfully inspirational. The list is too long to complete in full but a special thank you goes to Tyler Snyder, Liz Kelley, Samuel Baker, Natalie Armacost, Natalie Kaufman, James Klimas, Briana Vessells, Morgan Barry, Katie Rice, Annie Frantel, Tessa Steinert-Evoy, Aura Lunde, Elizabeth Cameron, Cristina Inceu, Colin Rosenow, Kristin Wagner, Hannah Cohen, Erin Shyr, and especially Marissa Comeau. Marissa took three of my courses on U.S. history at Boston University before graduating in the spring of 2015. Already as a student she demonstrated exceptional writing skills and, in conversations with me, Marissa several times voiced an interest in pursuing a career as an editor for an academic publishing house. As I began writing this book I therefore, quite naturally, turned to Marissa to enlist her assistance. She was the first to read through the present book manuscript and she provided the first round of edits. Her sharp pen and insightful mind helped turn the first draft into an actual book. I could not have completed this without her. Marissa, I am forever grateful. I hope we get to work together again.

The opportunity to publish my first book with Routledge as part of the Critical Moments in American History series has been made all the easier by the incredible level of support I received from the start of the process. Early on, series editor Bill Allison pushed me to think about the Marshall Plan beyond the traditional narrative as did the anonymous reviewers who, with the critic's potent pen, forced me to shift vantage points and think differently about my approach to the Marshall Plan as well as the inclusion of primary sources. At Routledge, I owe a great debt also to Genevieve Aoki and Dan Finaldi. Both worked dutifully and patiently with me, answered questions quickly and showed a real dedication to the project. Their support of the manuscript, in the acquisition of sources, and their incredible knowledge made this process smoother than I could have hoped for or even imagined. I cannot thank them enough for having taken on and backed this book with such dedication throughout the entire process. Such a level of help means the world, especially to a first-time author.

Finally, to Judy, my fellow troublemaker—as always—thank you for your love, and patience throughout this last year of research and writing. Your support of my work nourishes me and keeps me healthy in ways you could not ever imagine. Your dedication to your own work, likewise, provides me with an inspiration that I will never be able to express in words. Lastly, but not least, your tolerance of me in my moments of frustration says everything about your remarkable personality and your heart. Know J, that I am forever grateful. PLY.

Boston
April, 2016

Timeline

1945

February
Roosevelt meets Stalin and Churchill at Yalta.

April
President Franklin Roosevelt dies. Harry S. Truman becomes the 33rd President of the United States.

April
Truman receives the first reports laying out the desperate situation in Western and Central Europe. Poverty, destruction, starvation, and despair dominate in the nations of America's former allies and enemies.

May–August
VE Day in Europe in May following Nazi Germany's surrender and VJ day in August following Japan's surrender.

July–August
Truman meets Stalin and Clement Attlee (Churchill is defeated in an election in the middle of the Conference and replaced by Attlee) in Potsdam in Germany to finalize the future of Germany. Germany is to be occupied and divided into a U.S., Soviet, U.K., and French zone. The capital of Berlin, deep inside the Soviet zone, is similarly divided.

August
In accordance with wartime agreements, the U.S. suspends Lend-Lease aid to its allies. Instantly the socio-economic crises worsen in Great Britain and France.

Fall
Great Britain receives a loan of $3.75 billion from the U.S. (approved by Congress in 1946). Negotiations over terms demonstrate the U.S. determination to bring Britain's position as the world's premier power formally to an end.

1946

January
The Soviet Union rejects participation in the Bretton Woods agreements.

February
George Kennan writes the Long Telegram laying out the need for U.S. containment policy.

March
Delivering a speech in Fulton, MO, Winston Churchill declares that an Iron Curtain has descended across Europe.

September
U.S. Secretary of State James Byrnes announces in Stuttgart that the United States is committed to Germany's recovery and independence. The speech is a strong rebuttal to Soviet and French ambitions.

November
Following elections to the French Assembly, the Communists emerge as the largest party. Only a coalition of other parties prevents the French Communist Party from taking control of the government. The strong Communist performance is mirrored elsewhere in Western Europe as well.

1947

January
U.S. Senate unanimously confirms George C. Marshall as James Byrnes' replacement as U.S. Secretary of State.

March
After Great Britain in February informs the U.S. it can no longer continue its support mission to Greece, President Harry S. Truman presents the Truman Doctrine to the U.S. Congress. In his speech he calls for U.S. aid to Greece and Turkey and, in strongly ideological language, presents the Cold War as a battle between ways of life.

April
Marshall attends a Foreign Ministers Conference in Moscow. His unproductive meetings make clear to the Americans that the Soviet Union is prepared to allow Europe to collapse.

April
Marshall delivers radio address after his visit to Moscow. He informs the American people of the terrible conditions in Europe and insinuates that action will need to be taken.

May
Communists are ousted from governments in Italy and France.

May	Undersecretary of State for Economic Affairs Will Clayton presents an alarming report about the conditions in Europe to Marshall.
June	Marshall speaks to Harvard Alumni. He proposes U.S. aid to European nations if the European powers can unite and agree on requests and distribution.
June–July	British Foreign Secretary Ernest Bevin meets with French Foreign Minister Georges Bidault in Paris to discuss Marshall's Harvard proposal. They decide to invite Soviet Foreign Minister Vyacheslav Molotov to a meeting to discuss the matter further but, unable to agree, Molotov walks away from the conference and from Marshall Aid in early July.
July	Stalin orders Eastern European leaders not to participate in the Conference on the Marshall Plan.
Summer–Fall	The privately organized Committee for the Marshall Plan is created as a lobby group to convince the American public and politicians of the ERP's importance.
September	In response to the Marshall Plan, the Soviet Union forms the Cominform, an organization run by Moscow, which forces its neighbors further under its control. Andrei Zhdanov condemns the Marshall Plan and U.S. foreign policy as imperialistic.
September	First proposal for aid from the Europeans is finalized.
Fall	The Truman Administration prepares, and Congress approves, an interim aid package until the Marshall Plan, now formally called the European Recovery Program, can be finalized.
November–December	Another conference of foreign ministers is held in London. Marshall is once again disappointed by the Soviets' unwillingness to compromise over German recovery.
December	President Truman presents the Marshall Plan to the American public in advance of Congressional discussions.
1948	
January–February 8	The Senate Foreign Relations Committee hold public hearings on the Marshall Plan. Marshall testifies on January 8.
February–March	Congressional debates begin on the Marshall Plan. It comfortably passes House and Senate.
February–March	The coalition government in Czechoslovakia is ousted and replaced with a Communist government loyal to Moscow.
March	In response to the lurking Soviet threat, the United Kingdom, France, Belgium, Luxembourg, and the Netherlands sign the Brussels Pact, a security treaty to protect Northwestern Europe against outside aggression.
April	After Congress passes the Marshall Plan, President Truman signs the bill into law. Paul Hoffman is appointed Administrator of the Economic Cooperation Agency (ECA), the agency created to implement the plan. Averell Harriman is appointed special representative of the ECA in Europe. The ECA will set up offices in all Marshall Plan recipient countries.
April	The Organization for European Economic Cooperation (OEEC) is founded by the European powers. Its purpose is to ensure a collaborative European approach to Marshall Aid.
April	In Italy, the Christian Democrats defeat the Communist Party thereby ending Moscow's last realistic chance of a Communist ballot box victory in Europe. The CIA plays an important role in the election's outcome.
June	At the London Conference, representatives from the United States, Great Britain, France, and the Benelux countries commit to granting West Germany greater political autonomy.

June	The Western powers announce plans for a new Deutsche Mark to supplant the former German currency which had become worthless. The Soviets refuse to participate.
June	The Soviet Union seals off highway and railway access to the Western zones of Berlin. The city possesses food and fuel supplies for less than six weeks. In response President Truman launches the Berlin Airlift. For the next 11 months, U.S. and British cargo planes will bring tons of food and fuel to West Berlin's citizens. The Berlin incident further commits the United States to Western Europe's survival.
Summer–Fall	Marshall Aid begins to flow into the 16 Western European nations that are part of the program.
November	Harry S. Truman defeats Republican challenger Thomas Dewey to win a second term as president. The Democrats regain control of both houses of Congress.

1949

January	Harry Truman accepts Marshall's resignation as Secretary of State. He appoints Dean Acheson to succeed him.
January	Truman's Inaugural Address lays out the Point Four program. The program aims to make the Marshall Plan's ideals and visions available to the underdeveloped world.
April	The United States and its European partners create NATO.
May–October	Germany is divided. In the eastern half of the country, the German Democratic Republic is under the control of German Communists and greatly reliant on Moscow. In the western part, the Federal Republic of Germany emerges as a liberal Democracy and part of the West.
September	Under pressure from the United States, Great Britain is forced to devalue the pound by 30 percent as exports slow down.

1950

May	Robert Schuman presents the Schuman Plan leading to the establishment of the European Coal and Steel Community. The goal is economic and political unity in Europe.
June	Communist North Korea attacks the U.N.–created and –supported Republic of Korea in the South. In response, the U.S. and the U.N. go to war to stop Communist aggression. In Europe, American aid increasingly shifts from economic toward military assistance.
September	Truman appoints George C. Marshall Secretary of Defense
December	Truman announces the redeployment of U.S. troops to Europe to bolster NATO.
December	Marshall Aid to Great Britain ends.

1951

April	France, West Germany, Italy, Belgium, and the Netherlands form the European Coal and Steel Community. Great Britain rejects becoming a member.
October	The Mutual Security Agency absorbs most ECA operations in Europe.
December	The Marshall Plan officially comes to an end.

1952

March	President Truman decides not to run for a third term as president.
November	After prolonged infighting in the Republican Party, General Dwight Eisenhower, a non-establishment candidate is nominated for president. He overwhelmingly wins the general election bringing an end to the GOP's isolationist roots.

1953

March	Joseph Stalin dies.
June	The Korean War comes to an end.

Introduction

"My plans for visiting Harvard now seem to be definitely squared away . . . I will not be able to make a formal address, but would be pleased to make a few remarks . . . and perhaps a little more."[1] Rarely, if ever, has a public address of such magnitude by an American statesman been prefaced so modestly. The "little more" to which recently appointed Secretary of State George Catlett Marshall referred in this personal note to Harvard University President James B. Conant on May 28, 1947, would go on to outline what would ultimately become the European Recovery Program (ERP), the Marshall Plan in global parlance.

Marshall would formally propose the ERP at Harvard a week later. Between 1948 and 1952, the program made the United States the principal benefactor of Europe's post-World War Two recovery. During this four–year period, grants and loans totaling close to 13 billion dollars flowed across the Atlantic in the form of goods, development projects, and other assistance programs. It would play a vital role in addressing the difficulties Washington's Western European partners faced as they dug out from the destruction of Adolf Hitler's six-year onslaught. Great Britain, Ireland, France, Italy, the Tri-zone (the later Federal Republic of Germany), Belgium, the Netherlands, Luxembourg, Portugal, Greece, Turkey, Norway, Sweden, Denmark, Iceland, Austria, and Switzerland—16 nations in all—benefited from American aid to help cement what Marshall, in his 12-minute Harvard address, called "the rehabilitation of the economic structure of Europe." As he explained it that day in Cambridge, "Europe's requirements for the next three or four years of foreign food and other essential products—principally from America—are so much greater than her present ability to pay that she must have substantial additional help or face economic, social, and political deterioration of a very grave character." The picture the Secretary of State painted of Europe was one of nations facing insurmountable debts, weak currencies, widespread unemployment, barely functioning infrastructures, and collapsing industries and agriculture. Marshall saw no alternative to the United States stepping in to prevent "hunger, poverty, and chaos." It was an effort intended to "provide a cure rather than a mere palliative." At the same time, he made it clear that the program would not be for everybody. Any "government that is willing to assist in the task of recovery will find full co-operation. . . . Any government which maneuvers to block the recovery of other countries cannot expect help from us."[2] In response to Marshall's address, Soviet leader Joseph Stalin first feigned interest in the proposal and then abruptly withdrew, forcing his satellite countries across Eastern Europe—some against their will—to follow suit. His denunciation of the Marshall Plan as American economic imperialism and a plan to infiltrate foreign countries divided Europe in two. The Iron Curtain that former British Prime Minister Winston Churchill had described a year earlier was now a reality. As a result, the Marshall Plan would be a New Deal for Western Europe only.

In American national memory, the Marshall Plan is recalled as the ultimate act of good will: an economic mission that saved Europe from hunger, despair, and Communism. It continues to instill pride. It represents the good Cold War America, the one that existed before the death knell sounded in Vietnam. In 2000, the Brookings Institution collected surveys from 450 members of the American Historical Association to determine the Federal Government's most significant legislative achievements. They overwhelming selected the effort to "rebuild Europe" after the Second World War. Along the same lines, a recent History News Network poll voted Marshall's Harvard speech the most important document in American history, well ahead of the Federalist Papers, Thomas Paine's *Common Sense*, Abraham Lincoln's "Emancipation Proclamation," Martin Luther King Jr.'s "I Have a Dream" speech, and the Fourteenth Amendment to the U.S. Constitution, which provides the right to citizenship, due process, and equal protection under the law.[3] While unscientific, this poll conducted by a popular history site frequented by both scholars and citizens with an interest in the past is nonetheless telling. As Al Gore told historian Arthur Schlesinger, Jr., whom the Vice President in May of 1994 summoned to the White House for advice on his own upcoming speech to that year's graduating class at Harvard, "the only Harvard commencement speech anybody remembers was Marshall's in 1947." It is remembered because the Marshall Plan is part of the national mythology. Its very name, historian William Hitchcock correctly asserts, attains a "talismanic quality."[4] So does its namesake: the aid program to Western Europe made a legend of George Marshall and cemented his name in

American national folklore. So synonymous is Marshall's name with the European Recovery Program that few non-specialists today seem to recall that he had served as the United States Army Chief of Staff and was instrumental in masterminding the greatest enlargement the U.S. military had ever undertaken. He also played an essential role in the preparation and launch of the U.S. Army and Army Air Forces' D-Day invasion of Normandy in 1944. Marshall was the man President Franklin Delano Roosevelt refused to deploy to Europe during the war because his military knowledge and skills were deemed too important. As the President bluntly told Marshall, "I didn't feel I could sleep at ease if you were out of Washington."[5] The British Prime Minister Winston Churchill considered Marshall as, simply, the organizer of victory. It is perhaps the only example of an official whose crucial role in "the good war" is overshadowed in our national recollection by later achievements.

Reverence has historically been the dominant feeling towards the Marshall Plan in both donor and recipient countries. Public opinion echoes the sentiment expressed by ERP official Charles Kindleberger that "Marshall Plan dollars saved the world." Beneficiaries certainly concurred. British Foreign Secretary Ernest Bevin called it "a life line to sinking men," an act that "brought hope where there was none." Franz Blücher, the West German Vice Chancellor considered it "the first fact by which Germany was reintroduced into the family of nations. . . . Without the Marshall Plan we wouldn't have been able to survive."[6]

The European Recovery Program's positive legacy is further underlined in the way it outlived its own era. Every passing anniversary inspires new essay collections, books, and conference papers on both sides of the Atlantic, with the vast majority praising it.[7] As it has become mythologized over time, the plan has emerged as a source of inspiration for politicians, journalists, philanthropists, and some economists. Quick to highlight Europe's rise from ruin to prosperity during the second half of the twentieth century, advocates remain fond of proposing Marshall Plans for Asia, Latin America, Africa, and the Middle East; for individual countries such as Egypt or Greece; for specific cities such as Detroit; even for the developing world as a whole. Economist and Dean of Columbia University's Business School, Glenn Hubbard, decries the ineffective way in which twenty-first century Africa aid is channeled through local governments and NGOs rather than the local business sector, saying that the ERP "made loans to European businesses, which repaid them to their local governments, which in turn used that revenue for commercial infrastructure—ports, roads, railways—to serve those same businesses." Calling for a renewed Marshallesque commitment, Hubbard expresses the familiar view that traditional "Aid to Africa has not [worked]. An African

Marshall Plan is long, long overdue." As British historian Niall Ferguson wrote on the sixtieth anniversary of Marshall's speech, when "critics lament the allegedly modest sums currently spent by the American government on foreign aid, they often draw an unfavorable contrast with the late nineteen forties" and the Truman era.[8]

★   ★   ★

Despite the near unanimous praise that the Marshall Plan enjoys in popular memory, scholars of American politics and economic history have been far more divided about its actual impact and the motivation behind it. While the earliest accounts, some written while the ERP was still in its final years, echoed the beliefs of Churchill and Bevin that Marshall Dollars were crucial for Europe's economic revival, later interpretations have questioned both its practical achievement and the noble aspirations of the program. The assessment of the ERP's economic influence on the ground, for example, has been significantly lowered, while analyses of Europe's productive capabilities and performances by the time American aid finally began arriving, have been comparably upgraded. This thesis, most persuasively advocated by British economic historian Alan S. Milward, contends that local initiatives undertaken prior to the arrival of Marshall Aid were the principal drivers of Europe's economic boom between 1948 and the financial crises of the 1970s. The total ERP package, he points out, equaled less than three percent of the recipients' combined national income and less than a fifth of their gross investment. The Marshall Plan was "on a scale between insignificant and slight," too small to have had any serious economic impact overall.[9]

While subsequent historians have shared Milward's interest in the Marshall Plan's impact on the ground, the majority of scholarship continues to focus on the motivation behind it. In this context, the ERP is part of a long-running intellectual feud about the origins of the Cold War and about the causes and consequences of U.S. diplomacy more generally. Between the 1960s and the end of the Cold War, diplomatic historians engaged in a fierce debate over these issues, which tore apart their field. The ferocity of academic debates often goes unnoticed outside the journals and conference halls where it commonly takes place. College students habitually assume that assigned books and journal articles more or less present the final word on the subjects they encounter. The debate over the origins of the Cold War provides the most telling rebuttal of such presumptions. As one scholar who was right in the middle of it recalls, the disagreements over who was responsible for the Cold War were capable of "eliciting torrents of impassioned prose, of inducing normally placid professors to behave like gladiators at scholarly meetings, of provoking calls for the suppression of unpopular points of view, [and] threats of lawsuits."[10]

It is useful to briefly highlight the main points of the four major schools of thought that engaged in academic infighting on this issue. Not only will this clarify that, despite its veneration, the Marshall Plan has generated considerable debate and even raised questions that go to the heart of contemporary American foreign policy. It is also valuable because, in spite of the detailed and impressive scholarship, it will make clear that, in many respects, these arguments have not really taken us far toward a historical understanding of what Americans think of the United States' role in the world on the long axis of American history or the Marshall Plan's location on that axis.

The so-called orthodox or traditionalist Cold War school of thought traces its origins to the writings of George Frost Kennan. Kennan was a senior diplomat at the U.S. Embassy in Moscow as the Second World War came to an end and a firsthand witness to Stalin's postwar policies in Europe.

In February 1946, he fired the parting shot in the debate over U.S. policy in Europe when, in a lengthy cable to the State Department, he drafted the first comprehensive analysis of the Soviet Union's ambitions in Europe. Written at a time when Communist governments loyal to Moscow were seizing power across Central and Eastern Europe, Kennan's 5,500-word "Long Telegram" explained that the "Kremlin's neurotic view of world affairs" came from an intense sense of "insecurity." From Kennan's perspective, a combination of old Russian imperial ambitions and Marxist ideological visions was at the heart of this westward expansion. As he informed the Secretary of State, the United States needed a greater commitment to contain this emerging threat of Communism in Europe.[11]

This assessment of the situation in Europe became the hallmark of orthodox Cold War scholarship. Their principal conclusion was that Soviet aggression in Europe and the Middle East, Stalin's unilateral unwillingness to pursue amicable relations with the West, and his rejection of normal diplomacy after 1945, all forced the Cold War upon the United States.[12] Among the most forceful voices were officials directly or indirectly involved in the preparation and execution of the Marshall Plan. The State Department's Herbert Feis and Joseph M. Jones, for example, presented the ERP as both a balanced and necessary measure to counter Soviet postwar ambitions in Europe and secure stability in the Western world as well as a benevolent and idealistic act that rescued beleaguered allies from socio-economic collapse. While orthodox scholarship did not ignore the potential economic benefits to the United States, these were

George Frost Kennan

A United States diplomat and historian, George Frost Kennan (1904–2005) was a career Foreign Service Officer in Europe from 1926 to 1953. He was stationed at the U.S. Embassy in Moscow at the end of the Second World War and during the early years of the Cold War. He later became Ambassador to the Soviet Union until Moscow declared him *persona non grata* and forced his resignation in 1952. One of the architects of U.S. Cold War policy, his two most important writings—a top secret 1946 diplomatic cable known as the "The Long Telegram" and the 1947 *Foreign Affairs* article, "The Sources of Soviet Conduct," famously known as the "X" article—laid out the need for a U.S. policy to "contain" the Soviet Union's advances in Europe.[1]

"The main element of any United States policy toward the Soviet Union," Kennan argued, "must be that of a long-term, patient but firm and vigilant containment of Russian expansive tendencies." He called for counteracting "Soviet pressure against the free institutions of the Western world" through the "adroit and vigilant application of counter-force at a series of constantly shifting geographical and political points, corresponding to the shifts and maneuvers of Soviet policy." This approach he anticipated, would "promote tendencies which must eventually find their outlet in either the break-up or the gradual mellowing of Soviet power." In 1947, the newly appointed Secretary of State George Marshall made Kennan head of the State Department's Policy Planning Staff (PPS), where he went on to play an important role in the creation of the European Recovery Program. Kennan was, however, a realist in foreign policy, and he split with the Truman administration over its more ideological and militaristic policies including the 1947 Truman Doctrine and the creation of NATO in 1949, both of which he deemed unnecessarily hostile and counter to the kind of behind-the-scenes diplomacy that he was a master of. After the Soviet acquisition of the atomic bomb and the fall of China to Communism in 1949 exposed the weaknesses of containment policy, Paul Nitze replaced Kennan as head of the PPS in early 1950. Kennan would continue to serve in a series of government positions. After his retirement from government service, he went on to become one of the nation's foremost public intellectuals on U.S.–Soviet relations.

Note

1   X (George F. Kennan), "The Sources of Soviet Conduct," *Foreign Affairs*, 25, 4 (July, 1947), 566–582.

consistently downplayed. If anything, they presented America's role in the world as innocent. In Jones' view, the Marshall Plan ushered in an era in which U.S. policy changed for the better and accomplished extraordinary deeds.[13]

By the early 1960s, American scholars more skeptical of U.S. motivations in the world began dismissing these lofty orthodox conclusions. The revisionist school most commonly associated with the rise of the New Left traces its origins to William Appleman Williams' 1959 book, *The Tragedy of American Diplomacy*. Rooting their beliefs in former Secretary of State John Hay's turn-of-the-century Open Door Notes, which were intended to ensure American access to the traditionally European-dominated areas in China, revisionists charged that economic interests and the collaboration between business interests and power politics always dictated U.S. foreign policy. In pursuit of profit, the upper echelons of the political system and the business elite in the United States—those whose privileges depended on economic growth—advocated overseas economic expansion and involvements around the world. Far from being a benevolent measure, the Marshall Plan was part of a political ploy intended to bolster American exports, ensure American predominance in Europe, and promote the establishment of an American empire.

Williams inspired a cadre of followers who came to view President Harry Truman as an "enthusiastic and militant advocate of America's supremacy in the world" and U.S. foreign policy as tragically misguided.[14] Since the expertise of Williams' disciples was in U.S. foreign policy rather than Soviet or Eastern European affairs, revisionists focused their efforts on what they considered aggressive U.S. initiatives. The Soviet Union, they concluded, was merely reacting to events rather than shaping them. Historians such as Walter LaFeber and Gabriel Kolko considered every policy initiative, from the Second World War Lend-Lease aid to the Marshall Plan, blatant examples of U.S. international economic hegemony. In Kolko's view, the ERP would have been introduced with or without a Soviet threat because its ultimate goal was to preserve America's access to foreign markets. More recent revisionist-leaning historians, such as Arnold Offner and Carolyn Eisenberg, similarly insist that these financial ambitions made Washington unreceptive to Soviet security concerns in Europe. In their view, Washington reneged on every wartime commitment made to Stalin, particularly over the contentious issue of Germany's future. Since the ERP targeted the revival of an economically and democratically strong Germany, the aid program was a dagger pointed directly at the Communist world. As such, responsibility for the Cold War and the division of Europe lay not with Stalin but with Washington for its refusal to cooperate and its constant search for profit.[15]

In the early 1970s, an alternative interpretation known as Cold War post-revisionism emerged from the hyperbolic orthodox-revisionist fracas. Tempered by the Vietnam War and Watergate, inspired by the détente policies which, by then, had begun to ease Cold War tensions, and frustrated by the increasingly counter-productive academic debate, post-revisionists sought a less emotional angle of interpretation. Championed by John Lewis Gaddis, William Taubman, and other younger diplomatic historians, a general consensus emerged that while Stalin and the Soviet Union remained principally responsible for the Cold War, the Truman Administration's aggressive rhetoric and exaggerations of the Communist threat had helped spark the conflict's outbreak.[16] While post-revisionists conceded that economics was a key weapon in the U.S. national security state's arsenal, they insisted that Washington introduced economic measures for political gains, not the other way around as revisionists insisted. The Marshall Plan, Gaddis believed, was a vehicle for the U.S. to "seize both the geopolitical and the moral initiative in the emerging Cold War."[17] This search for a more neutral synthesis caused these historians to overemphasize pragmatic decision-making and traditional concerns of national interest. In post-revisionist scholarship, a lack of mutual trust and poor communication was largely to blame for the Cold War. Even if Soviet conduct in Eastern Europe caused the conflict, it was perpetuated by American actions in the West.

Emerging in the late 1970s, corporatist scholarship challenged the three earlier schools of thought by placing greater emphasis on the role of non-state actors in U.S. foreign policy. Most commonly associated with the historian Michael J. Hogan, corporatism explained America's role in the world as a collaborative effort between Washington and influential non-governmental groups.[18] According to this view, banks, industries, organized labor, and agriculture—the key components of the capitalist system—formed "a pattern of interpenetration and power sharing" with the foreign policy apparatus. Corporatists considered the European Recovery Program part of a Washington-coordinated transnational strategy to not only rescue the European economies, but to Americanize that continent's financial and productive functionalities. The goal was to "equip participating countries with American production skills, fashion American patterns of labor-management teamwork . . . [while] maximiz[ing] the chances for economic integration and social peace."[19] Although they shared some conclusions with the revisionists, corporatists rejected indicting American diplomacy wholesale. Whereas Hogan did not consider the ERP an altruistic rescue operation, his classic work on the program, nonetheless, deemed the plan both effective and necessary for Western Europe's survival. Rather than create an aggressive U.S. empire as revisionists claimed, corporatists largely believed that the ERP instead helped cement what the Harvard scholar Charles Maier defined as "consensual American hegemony."[20] Corporatists acknowledged that U.S. influence in Europe grew as a result of the Marshall Plan, but only to the extent that its Western European partners were willing to accept.

★   ★   ★

Although these four schools of thought disagreed on whether the policies launched after 1945 were principally inspired by national security, access to markets and strategic resources, the development of an American empire, or the preservation of the capitalist system, each couched their argument in very conventional interpretations of international relations. While they differed on the definition, each considered national interest to have been the principal driver of U.S. postwar policy. In terms of the Marshall Plan the view that national interest caused the American aid operation continues to dominate contemporary analyses by historians and political scientists. If less impassioned, the continuing debate among scholars since the end of the Cold War borrows liberally from all of the four approaches described above to identify a series of overlapping and mutually reinforcing factors as the root cause of the ERP.

First, the Marshall Plan reflected a shift in American global strategy. The Second World War's exposure of American vulnerability led Washington to the national security conclusion that Europe could not be dominated by one or more totalitarian powers. Second, and closely related, the interwar experience in Europe showed that poverty and desolation provided breeding grounds for this kind of totalitarianism. If Europe proved unable to recover after 1945, that scenario might repeat itself. While the war had permanently destroyed and discredited the political ultra-right, European Communist parties on the ultra-left now threatened postwar stability in France, Italy, Greece, Tri-zone Germany, and elsewhere. The antidote was a united and democratic Europe, the prerequisite for which was economic recovery. Third, the United States was by far the largest producer of goods in the world. There was a genuine fear in Washington that the destruction of the European economies and productive capabilities would prevent them from procuring American industrial and agricultural goods. To rectify this, the European economies needed an external injection of stabilizing financial support. Fourth, if Washington failed to intervene and Europe fell to the forces of totalitarianism, it would leave the United States and Canada as the only Atlantic democracies. To protect herself against enemies, the United States would need to become a garrison state, permanently mobilized in an enduring state of military readiness with high taxes to match it. This in turn would undermine the very freedoms of a democratic America. Finally, altruistic traditions and beliefs mandated that Americans not stand by while its wartime allies headed for a political and financial abyss.

All of these factors undoubtedly help explain why the U.S. introduced the ERP. At the same time, these schools of thought are strikingly silent on the role of ideology. The notion that cultural or historical consciousness influenced U.S. foreign policy is almost entirely absent from their debates. This approach is made possible by the seemingly shared consensus that, with the end of the Second World War, the United States reached a new dawn in its history; a new starting point. This conclusion is understandable enough. The global conditions in 1945 were after all unrecognizable from those of a decade earlier. But such temporal decisions have consequences for scholarship. For example, starting analyses of the Marshall Plan in 1945 or 1947 reduces the aid operation and the ideas behind it to a postwar narrative spurred on by the new global situation. The result is that the connection between ideology and long axis beliefs about America's role in the world is largely downplayed or ignored entirely. Notions of an American ideology enter into the debate only in the shape of anti-Communism or in the context of empty rhetoric. When policies are draped in morality, as they often were during the Cold War, scholars fundamentally reject them as a cloak for *realpolitik* ambitions. Language and ideas are considered tactical means to strategic ends—artifacts that U.S. foreign policymakers casually remove from the shelf, dust off, and apply to publicly buttress any policy, only to unproblematically return once they have served their purpose. Ideology is dismissed as peripheral and inconsequential, as a term it is introduced solely as an instrument of disparagement to describe the U.S. policies and attitudes of which scholars disapprove. The notion that publicly expressed ideas about America's role in the world can also be articles of belief or expressions of national self-perception is rarely entertained. The problem with this approach, as historian Joan Hoff-Wilson pithily put it in a different context, is that when scholars remove ideas from the determination of foreign policy-making, they arrive at "the tempting, yet highly questionable assumption, that foreign-policy formulation is a completely rational, calculated process." As another historian Michael Hunt puts it, we lose track of important questions about why American policymakers "deployed the particular language they did and how they came to 'inhabit' it."[21]

The closing of the Cold War epoch provides us with an opportunity to historicize the conflict in a way that was not possible for earlier generations of historians who lived through it. This allows us to understand issues, such as the Marshall Plan, in a broader context, as a reflection of the

American idea about the world, rather than a mere reaction to the Soviet Union and international Communism or to concerns about capitalism. In this process, ideology and its relationship to the national self-perception present us with an immensely helpful prism through which to perceive this era. I define ideology as a set of ideas and beliefs, sometimes only poorly or partially articulated, that both establish and justify general outlines, rather than specific blueprints, of the world's future political, social, and cultural order. This same set of ideas also outline the methods, if not a finite or dogmatic path, necessary to achieve this order. As this definition implies, it is helpful to think of ideology as a faith. Like belief systems, ideology is endemic to the mind; it can be adjusted and tweaked when needed, but it is always present. To Americans, it helps define their thinking about the world and their role in it. This definition, combined with a greater emphasis on how culture helps to provide meaning to policy, holds great promise for shaping our perceptions of how ideology functions politically and societally, and, from there, our perception of it influences foreign policy.[22]

* * *

The academic disregard for American ideology as a reflection of identity and beliefs described above is in many respects a curious one. For two and a half centuries, the idea of America has rested on the conviction that its distinguishable and superior quality endows the United States with the duty and the moral imperative to spread its ideals around the world. This belief maintains that the distinctive nature of their democratic ideas, humane ideals, and the superiority of their freedoms ordains Americans with the capacity, authority, and duty to remake the world in their own image. Sharing an inherently optimistic and progressive interpretation of history with other major ideologies, this American mission is defined by normative values that serve as guides for action, as an analysis of reality, and as a basis for political vindication. This belief leads Americans to identify themselves as the "tutors of mankind in its pilgrimage to perfection," in Reinhold Niebuhr's disparaging remark.[23]

This ideologization of American political thought began with the eighteenth century patriots who challenged the colonial policies of the British Empire. They reconstituted what power and liberty meant for a society, but, as Thomas Paine ferociously argued, their goal was never just to reform the Old World; it was to reform the New World as well. They brought to the world ideas of socio-political modernization, visions of human rights, and a quest to bring an end to tyranny, monarchy, and empire. The enduring myth that the United States was an isolationist power

until the Second World War leads Americans to routinely dismiss the might
and endurance of the Revolution's internationalist ideas in the decades
prior to 1941. In reality, they were never far from public or intellectual
life. They survived through the nineteenth century, to the Great War and
beyond. By the time of the Second World War, they were easily invoked
as Americans took it upon themselves to create an American-inspired "one-
world" order. These ideals became crucial to American plans for the United
Nations and the Bretton Woods system, and to Cold War policies as well.

   None of this is to say that the United States is exceptional or possesses
greater moral clarity than other nations about the world. Nor is there reason
to believe that ideology dictates policy at every twist and bend. There is
no doubt that the United States has real economic and strategic interests
around the world and that these influence foreign policymaking. The
Marshall Plan was clearly an effort to contain Communism and to aid U.S.
businesses by creating markets for American goods, but Americans also
believed that it was part of an agenda that went well beyond that. If we
attempt to relay the narrative of the Marshall Plan separate from what
Americans *believed* their agenda to be and treat ideology as nothing more
than an ancillary in a U.S. quest to dominate the postwar global order, we
back ourselves into an intellectual cul-de-sac. In the process, we leave no
room for the power and influence of ideas, and lose sight of the historical
and cultural factors that inspire American beliefs about their role in global
affairs.

   We do not need to subscribe to this American ideology in order to
analyze it. This book argues that incorporating ideology into our
understanding of the United States' global role will help shed further light
on what drives and inspires the nation. As colonial historian Gordon S. Wood
bluntly puts it, if "we Americans were not leading the world towards liberty
and free government, then what was our history all about?"[24] To a nation
so preoccupied with its sense of destiny, the answer to that question is one
of crucial significance. It is particularly important in terms of the late
nineteen-forties because however flawed, misguided, and reckless U.S. Cold
War diplomacy often was, it also contained a moral dimension. That much
is evident from the fact that major policies often contradicted what might
reasonably have been considered traditional state-interest behavior. After
all, if morality was nothing more than a cloak for security interests, the U.S.
would have accepted outright the division of Europe into spheres of
influence proposed by the Soviet Union and Great Britain. If the goal was
American dominance of Western Europe and the extension of an American
empire, Washington would not have made European unity and democratic
organization a prerequisite for Marshall Plan Aid. As we will see below,
Washington's insistence on European unity predictably created a political

and economic bloc the size of which would rival the U.S. in the world. Furthermore, if ideology had not mattered to their Cold War outlook, why turn the conflict into a battle about ways of life as the Truman Doctrine and the Marshall Plan so plainly did? Finally, if American policymakers considered access to markets and consumers the key motivation behind the Marshall Plan, why sell it to the American public as a quest for democracy? The answers to these questions are, of course, that the American public dutifully accepted the responsibility of America's Cold War because it was a quest for democracy against tyranny. The Marshall Plan may have marked, as Henry Kissinger commented recently, "a historic departure" and a "new design" for American foreign policy.[25] But it was a departure in policymaking, not a shift in ideas or visions. If anything, the ideology behind it tapped beliefs that existed long before the Cold War began and would continue to exist long after that conflict ended.

★   ★   ★

"Our hopes for an enduring peace," James Conant told Ohio University's graduating class of 1947, "rest on the ability of this Nation in the next two decades to be the leading partner in a semi-global development of democracy as we Americans understand the meaning of the word."[26] Delivered only four days after the Harvard President sat in attendance during Marshall's speech at his home institution, Conant was recycling ideas that were already established dogma. The United States was now the most powerful and influential nation in the world and its mission was to extend those values to a world eagerly awaiting American leadership. His speech, like so many others of the day, captured the much deeper American mentality that their own historical development could be replicated around the world.

The Marshall Plan reflected this viewpoint. Far more than a humanitarian gesture, a response to the threat of Communism in Europe, or an effort to strengthen the economic climate upon which American capitalism to a large extent relied, it was also a massive modernization project. It mirrored what intellectuals such as Walt Rostow, Walter Salant, and Max Millikan, would soon imagine on a much grander scale, and it reflected the methods and structures of America's own New Deal. The goal was not merely to revive economies, but to put nations on a path to Americanization. Some, including later Secretary of State John Foster Dulles, saw in it a dream of a Federal States of Europe. In that sense, the Marshall Plan symbolized an already existing image of a world order based on American values and ideals. It was a teleological vision: what the United States is today, the world will be tomorrow.[27]

Far more than a policy initiative, the Marshall Plan was part of a mindset that aimed to bring progress to the world and to create a new international system entirely different from the world envisioned by most Europeans. The creation of this system was the real revolution of the Cold War: the manner in which the United States "over a period of fifty years transformed its main capitalist competitors according to its own image."[28] This process was not always easy and it did not always materialize quite as Washington imagined. Nevertheless, the ease with which it was achieved is impressive. This was not a global ideological revolution inspired by fist-shaking charismatic leaders, undergirded by powerful manifestos, or initiated by bombs or promises of the violent toppling of governments, but it was a revolution all the same.

Given the political, economic, social, and cultural alignment that has since taken place in Europe, including the creation of the European Union and the centralization of power in Brussels, it is easy to overlook the radical impact of American post-World War Two plans and influence. The Marshall Plan's demands for European postwar unity and collaboration were not new, after all. In a 1929 speech to the League of Nations, French statesman Aristide Briand had proposed a more formal European arrangement. Based on geography that connected the nations of Europe, Briand insisted:

> [t]here ought to exist some sort of federal link among them.
> They must have the means among themselves for discussing any
> problems . . . and for establishing the general solidarity of Europe.
> . . . It is that connecting link which I desire to establish . . . the
> most important component of that connecting link would be an
> economic agreement. . . . [B]ut also there should be a political
> and a social link.[29]

Despite this and other similar, if less detailed, calls for European unity, it is worth remembering how fractured nineteenth and twentieth century Europe was prior to the establishment of American postwar institutions such as the United Nations and the Bretton Woods organizations. It was a continent dominated by imperial powers and often dictatorial governments. Diplomatic disputes and wars ravaged Europe as nations, deeply suspicious of one another, engaged in constant imperial battles for advantages in an industrializing world. As the lead-up to both world wars as well as the Great Depression demonstrated, there was no European unity. Nothing in their history implied that the European powers would have been able to unite in response to either crippling economic conditions or the threat of international Communism. The American commitments that came with the Truman Doctrine, the Marshall Plan, and the creation of the North Atlantic Treaty Organization (NATO) instilled confidence among Europeans. The European political leaders still had plenty to do on their own, of course. West German Chancellor Konrad Adenauer, French Foreign Minister Robert Schuman, Belgian Prime Minister and Chairman of the United Nations General Assembly Paul Henri Charles Spaak, and many others stepped up to cement European collaboration. They embraced the choices provided by the Marshall Plan—choices they might not have had otherwise. A new Europe emerged as the ERP's goals "merged into a broader political one: the expansion of human dignity as a universal principle."[30] From this followed not only new democracies, but the establishment of a U.S.-led, organized system of shared ideals and values in which nations across the Atlantic were bound together by socio-economic ties, principles, and security alliances. In short, it created the concept we now simply refer to as "the West."[31]

CHAPTER 1

A New Deal for the World

American Plans for the Post-World War Two Order

The Marshall Plan was never a singular endeavor created solely for the purpose of European Reconstruction. It had its origins in America's recent past and a powerfully shared belief that the United States possessed a responsibility to uplift a world in desperate need of guidance. As one State Department speaker explained it to an incoming class of Foreign Service Officers in the 1920s, even if others did not always appreciate the significance of the American role and contribution, this was only to be expected in a world

> where gratitude is rarely accorded to the teacher, the doctor, or the policeman, and we have been all three. But it may be that in time they will come to see the United States with different eyes, and to have for her something of the respect and affection with which a man regards the instructor of his youth and a child looks upon the parent who has molded his character.[1]

It was in this mindset that the Marshall Plan was conceived, as part of an overall interpretation of global developments. It began not in the spring of 1947 as most scholars insist. Its short-term origins, went back at least to the spring of 1919.

For the first six months of that year, Paris was the center of the world. Here, in the aftermath of the Great War, the leaders of the victorious powers joined to design the new world order. They arrived with very different ambitions in mind. France, Great Britain, and Italy sought reparations from Berlin. They wanted compensation for destroyed territory and lost generations. The French were particularly concerned with the permanent removal of Germany as a continental threat to European peace. American president Woodrow Wilson, in contrast, demanded no reparations and no territory. Treated like a deity upon his arrival in Paris, Wilson wanted to give the world something better: a League of Nations to make the world safe for democracy. The story of Wilson's failure is well documented. Unable to persuade the United States Senate to surrender influence to the Executive branch in foreign affairs and too much of an ideologue to compromise on his ideals, he lost the fight for ratification of the Treaty of Versailles and the League of Nations. Instead of global unity, the result was an uncompromising and fractured new international order marred by economic and political chaos.

In popular memory and much scholarship, Wilson often appears as the lone voice of what we now call Wilsonianism. We identify him with the Treaty of Versailles and the League of Nations, but in actuality, Wilson was a latecomer to the ideals that bear his name. Among American progressives, the call for the United States to remake the world arose instantaneously as war broke out in Europe in 1914. It was Wilson who resisted, imploring his countrymen instead to remain "impartial in thought as well as in deed."[2] The young *New Republic* reporter, Walter Lippmann, was one of many American intellectuals who considered Wilson's approach to the war far too timid. Lippmann was no jingoist; he wrote in the spirit of the progressive movement. It "has been more than a century since Thomas Paine proposed to secure the world's peace forever in a league," Lippmann lamented. Americans were being summoned. The Great War presented an opportunity "to make the interests of America coincident with the interest of mankind," he insisted. When Wilson finally came out in favor of such a league of peace in May of 1916, the *New Republic* considered the President's endorsement a "decisive turning point in the history of the modern world" and a "portent in human history." Americans, Lippmann boasted, would shed their neutrality "not to engage in diplomatic intrigue but to internationalize world politics." The league was only the first step. Its real service, he concluded, "may well be that it will establish the first rallying point of a world citizenship." "Democracy is infectious," he asserted after Wilson finally declared war in April 1917, "[T]he entrance of the Russian and American democracies is sure to be a stimulus to Democracies everywhere." Like Paine after 1789, Lippmann expected that the war would "dissolve into democratic revolution the world over." The editorial board of the *New York Times* concurred, adding that the quest for "freedom and civilization" was being launched "with the full sanction and support of the American people."[3]

Wilson's dismissal of the Europeans' traditions of diplomacy drew progressive intellectuals such as Lippmann's editor, Herbert Croly, and

Columbia University professor John Dewey to the cause.[4] Dewey enthusiastically endorsed the President's new world order, contending that the U.S. must ensure that other nations "accept and are influenced by the American idea." A "world federation, a concert of nations, a supreme tribunal, [and] a league of nations" were, he insisted, "peculiarly American contributions." Lippmann shared this jubilance. "The moral basis for our part in the war is a startling perplexing novelty," he privately told a friend. "We should avoid all the tricky and sinister aspects of what is now called propaganda," he stated, "and should aim to create the impression that here is something new and infinitely hopeful in the affairs of mankind."[5]

Despite the passionate emphasis on American principles, these men were not imperialists. They were not imagining access to foreign markets and they were not worried about American security. In their view, civilization hung in the balance. The Great War, Dewey maintained, presented mankind with the "unique opportunity to reorganize the world into a democratic social order, guaranteeing a future of peace."[6] Consequently, this could not be on behalf of the Europeans. Americans would fight "only for another democracy and another civilization." He decreed that the U.S. had solved problems of nationalism by separating "nationality from citizenship." At the center stood, instead, ideas of "language, literature," and "national culture," which he considered "social rather than political, human rather than national interest. Let this idea fly abroad; it bears healing in its wings."[7]

Many progressives genuinely believed that Americans had a special mission in the world to spread liberty. "Good democrats have always believed that the common interests of men were greater than their special interest, that ruling classes can be enemies, but that nations must be partners," Lippmann declared. He called for a "World Federation," a "union of peoples determined to end forever that intriguing adventurous nationalism which has torn the world for three centuries." Democracies had to lead, he insisted. "[N]o machinery we can suggest, no rule of international law is likely to survive, unless the liberal world represents a sufficient union . . . to make it a shield for human's protection, and a standard to which the people can rally." Upon completion of the armistice in November 1918, Lippmann wrote to Wilson's confidante, Colonel House, that he and the President "more than justified the faith of those who insisted that your leadership was a turning point in modern history."[8]

The 1919 Paris Peace Conference, of course, fulfilled none of this excitement. The ideals and the mission that these intellectuals, journalists, and policymakers so fervently promoted lost their energy as the negotiations at Versailles began. There were many causes of the failure in Paris, but the *New Republic* reserved particular scorn for the nationalists in Great

Britain and France. So, too, did John Maynard Keynes, the British economist and financial negotiator at Versailles who resigned from the Treasury in protest over the agreement. Lippmann deemed the European demands of reparations entirely out of touch with the ideological ends that the war should have been about. Perhaps the European opposition was unavoidable; after all, the Wilsonian world order was unlike any system the imperial Europeans recognized or accepted. According to Henry Kissinger's scornful verdict, the "world Wilson envisaged would be based on principle, not power; on law not interest . . . in other words, a complete reversal of the historical experience and method of operation of the Great Powers."[9] The plan had come a war too soon.

The combination of European obstinacy against the League's Wilsonian principles and the absence of American postwar leadership unsurprisingly ensured that the new organization lived up to none of Wilson's dreams. The later President Harry Truman believed that the failure of U.S. and membership and leadership sowed the seeds for the next world war. In 1942, then a Senator, he lamented the idea that the Second World War could be allowed to simply be the Great War by extension. In 1919, "the victors of that war had the opportunity to compel a peace that would protect us from war. . . . They missed that opportunity."[10] Like many others, Truman would come to see the next chance to remake the world not as an opportunity distinct from Versailles, but as atonement for the American failure in Paris.

★   ★   ★

The dramatically different level of leadership demonstrated by Americans following each of the two world wars has ensured that the interwar period is viewed as the highlight of American isolationism in national memory. Despite persistent efforts and considerable evidence to the contrary, historians have found it difficult to extinguish this myth. Those who promote the isolationist thesis often emphasize how leading intellectuals, such as Harry Elmer Barnes and Charles Beard, called for Americans to turn their back on Europe. Similar evidence is found in the voices of conservatives who became increasingly vociferous as another military conflict loomed in Europe in the 1930s. Epitomized in the Nye Committee hearings over the U.S. entry into the Great War, in Republican rhetoric in opposition to the Roosevelt Administration during the 1930s, and in the forceful voices of men like Charles Lindbergh, isolationism is often described as the sole American perspective on global affairs during this period. Its sentiment can be summed up in the words of Henry Cabot Lodge, Jr.—grandson of the Senator Lodge who had fought Wilson over the League in 1919—who, when campaigning for a Massachusetts Senate seat, insisted that:

> We have been waddling too long in war infested Europe. It began when the international theorists wanted this country to experiment with the League of Nations. . . . Europe wanted us when she needed our manpower to finance her affairs. . . . Oh Europe will welcome us to her World Court, she will welcome us to her League of Nations and to her conferences—because there she knows she can outsmart us. But I say—if Europe must have her hates—let her have them. We want no part of it. If Europe wants her wars—let her have them. We want no part of it. If Europe wants to go broke—that's her business.[11]

The routine insistence that this sentiment captures the national attitude toward the world leads to the questionable conclusion that 1945 was *the* comprehensive turning point in modern American history. While much undoubtedly changed as a result of the war, a great deal remained the same. The ideological beliefs that emerged after the war certainly correlated to the world that preceded it. The American belief that their freedoms were central to the human experience and to humanity's progress was endemic to the national historical and cultural consciousness. The visions of the League of Nations did not vanish after 1919 in the United States. Rather, they survived and thrived in Americans' thinking about the global order. American internationalism, in other words, was not a product of the Second World War, but an idea that was central to their ideology. To insist otherwise is to overlook the continuum of American ideas and how central they were to the post-Second World War planning and, eventually, to how Americans approached the Cold War, including the Marshall Plan.

The evidence is overwhelming that in spite of the failure to make the world safe for democracy in 1919, believers in the global spread of democracy and World Federalism remained vocal and influential. They came from all walks of life. Even Republicans, including Elihu Root, Charles Evan Hughes, Frank Kellogg, and Henry Stimson, pressed for American involvement in the world. In the 1922 inaugural issue of *Foreign Affairs*, Root charted a very Wilsonian vision. Outlining a global American agenda, he insisted that the "control of foreign relations by democracies creates a new and pressing demand for popular education in foreign affairs." By implication, being a mere exemplar was insufficient. Hughes went further in a speech to the American Bar Association. Convinced that Americans stood on the side of international justice, he insisted that the creation of permanent international courts should be "a distinct feature" of U.S. foreign policy. A similar internationalism was evident in policies on arms control, international drug trafficking, health and disease prevention, and in the greater support for global economic responsibility, the latter lasting at least until October 1929.[12]

The belief in an American global role extended well beyond Washington. As historian David Ekbladh powerfully demonstrates, ideas of global economic and socio-political modernization were widespread during the interwar period. Pushing initiatives that would inspire the modernization policies of the 1950s and 1960s, non-governmental organizations (NGOs) often took the lead particularly in famine relief. In China, for example, American observers concluded that "the chronic state of famine in China was not the result of natural disasters." Instead, they believed that the problems were products of "society and culture." They began "to promote a new and extensive agenda of reform activities." Similar to what would occur in Europe during the Marshall Plan, Americans singled out ways to provide "economic improvement, improved agricultural techniques, [and] infrastructural improvements." The Great Depression, unsurprisingly, checked some of this enthusiasm, but not for long. Many came to the conclusion that the New Deal vision transferred quite easily beyond America's shores. If it could be done in the Tennessee Valley, it could be done in China and elsewhere. By the 1930s, the earliest development efforts aimed to provide less advanced nations the ability to develop socially, politically, and economically. These programs drew inspiration from global political developments, including the rise of fascism and Communism. As these dictatorial regimes grew in strength during the Depression, American observers reached the conclusion that, as Ekbladh aptly puts it, "all societies carried a latent bacillus for totalitarianism that was easily made virulent by the forces of modernity." Poor and under-developed nations appeared especially susceptible, further supporting the perceived need for American-led international development.[13] Liberals such as Arthur E. Morgan (Roosevelt's head of the TVA), Eugene Staley (who later became influential in the United Nations Relief and Rehabilitation Administration (UNRRA)), Edgar Snow, and Nelson Rockefeller took on increasingly important roles, particularly in China and Latin America. In China, Snow helped launch the journal *Democracy* in an effort to spread American political ideals. The outbreak of the Sino-Japanese War cut its life short, but it was a prime example of the desire among Americans to influence the far corners of the world. Similarly, in Latin America, the U.S. government launched cultural and economic programs to undermine the perceived threat of foreign ideologies in the western hemisphere. It is beyond the limits of this book to expand on these programs in detail, but it is clear that American citizens and officials believed that the world could and should be remade in the United States' image long before European postwar recovery became official policy in 1947.

★   ★   ★

The rapidity and ease with which Americans embraced the worldview of recovery and reform after the outbreak of the Second World War is a testament to its endurance. The U.S. Department of State established committees to study issues concerning global peace, reconstruction, and the economy within less than four months of Hitler's attack on Poland. The decision to place Assistant Secretary of State Sumner Welles, one of the Roosevelt Administration's foremost thinkers on foreign policy, in charge of this was a clear statement of intent.[14] Walter Lippmann, who by then had emerged as the foremost public intellectual in the nation, had been deeply scarred by the failure of Versailles. Yet even someone who had lost faith in the mission to Americanize the world understood the national attitude: in *Life* magazine, Lippmann declared that making the world "whole again" was "the American destiny."[15]

Many conservatives disagreed. They clung to the neutrality laws passed in the 1930s to keep the United States out of another European war. They operated under the delusion that the oceans were barriers rather than, as Lippmann put it, highways to America. American cultural perceptions about the world as well as national security concerns ensured that the anti-interventionist voices were fighting a losing battle. Even if Americans did not favor deploying U.S. military forces to fight Nazi Germany, it did not take long for the pendulum to swing in the direction of international engagement. Following Germany's attack on the Low Countries in the spring of 1940, support for Roosevelt and the Democrats in the polls rose sharply. By May, 66 percent of Americans anticipated voting for a candidate in the 1940 election who would support aid to Britain and France. Across the country, private interest groups rallied to prepare for war. Hunting clubs began forming Minutemen militia groups while the "National League of Mothers of America declared the formation of the Molly Pitcher Rifle Legion," which would provide rifle instructions once a week to its members.[16] Neutrality was dead.

As support for involvement grew, ideology gave Americans a sense of identity and purpose. National security, an end to tyranny and empires, a liberalized global economic order, the permanent establishment of worldwide human rights, and the spread of American values all came to the forefront of public life. The fall of France in June 1940 only crystalized the credence of these ideals and cemented the belief that a world government was necessary to enforce them. Even Henry Cabot Lodge, Jr. abandoned the idea that Europe's wars were not America's problem as he became a fervent advocate for American global leadership. Nothing, however, symbolized this development better than the astonishing rise of Wendell Willkie on the national political scene. Willkie was a former Democrat turned Republican from Indiana with a background in law and business, rather than politics. Though his personal profile had increased during 1939 after *Time* magazine featured him on the cover, he still only stood at one percent in national polls in April of 1940. It did not work against him. As the Low Countries fell to Hitler, Willkie wrested the Republican presidential nomination from both anti-New Dealer and anti-internationalist Ohio Senator Robert Taft and eventual 1944 and 1948 GOP nominee Thomas Dewey. As a result of scholars' commitment to the concept of conservative isolationism as the dominant national mood, Willkie's popularity and foreign policy agenda—which closely mirrored FDR's—have often been overlooked. But Willkie was a far better barometer for the nation's view of the war than were the Republican establishment. In polls, GOP voters singled out not just Willkie's down-to-earth honesty, but also his view of global affairs.

Although Willkie lost to FDR that November, his rise to prominence is noteworthy nonetheless. It tells us that as early as 1940, Americans were gearing up for a fight. Franklin Roosevelt understood as much, and he soon began steering the American people towards war. In December, the president cautioned the American public that an Axis victory would mean a

> new and terrible era in which the whole world, our hemisphere included, would be run by threats of brute force. And to survive in such a world, we would have to convert ourselves permanently into a militaristic power on the basis of war economy.

In a nod to Wilson, he asserted that this was "democracy's fight against world conquest." It was America's duty to fight for "the defense of our civilization and for the building of a better civilization in the future."[17]

In March 1941, Congress aligned itself with this view as the House and Senate voted to formally abandon neutrality. The Lend-Lease Act authorized the President to "sell, transfer title to, exchange, lease, lend, or otherwise dispose of, to any such government [the President deems vital to the defense of the U.S.] any defense article."[18] Realist scholars often assume that it was the Japanese attack on Pearl Harbor the following December that brought the United States into the war. The manner in which that attack exposed the nation's defenses, they argue, explains U.S.

efforts in the Second World War and in the Cold War. They see American actions as direct responses to national security threats posed by Hitler and later by Stalin. There is no doubt that Pearl Harbor exposed the frailty of national security; in that sense, it was the formal *casus belli*. However, it was the Lend-Lease Act nine months earlier that settled the issue. After March 1941, the only serious question was what America's timetable for war was going to be. Senator Arthur Vandenberg (R-MI), a critic of Lend-Lease, understood as much. His diary entry for March 8, 1941 reads: "I hope I am wholly wrong when I say I fear they will live to regret their votes beyond anything else they ever did. I had the feeling . . . that I was witnessing the suicide of the Republic."[19] On this account Vandenberg was wrong. Lend-Lease did not signal the repudiation of American values, but rather the fulfillment of them.[20]

The conclusion that Americans had drawn was infused with ideology: only in a world that adhered to American ideals and principles could Americans truly be secure. Only in that kind of world could freedom be preserved, and only through an active American role could it be safeguarded.[21] This belief was intuitive to Americans because the idealism that underpinned it already permeated their value system. As early as 1940, Secretary of War Henry Stimson, paraphrasing both Abraham Lincoln and the Bible, insisted that the world could no longer survive "half-slave and half-free." For more than 400 years "Americans' ancestors have been struggling to build up an international civilization based upon law and justice," he claimed. Now they were faced with ultimate struggle between freedom and despotism. Stimson believed there could be no compromise in this struggle.[22] Morally, spiritually and, above all, ideologically, the Second World War became one of destiny.

Media tycoon Henry Luce most famously struck this chord in his essay, "The American Century." Although published in early 1941, Luce's title has become a folkloric reference to American economic and military superiority as well as its later cultural and political influence in the world. But his was more than just a motto. Much like Lippmann in 1916, Luce insisted that the war summoned Americans. It "now becomes our time to be the powerhouse from which the ideals spread throughout the world . . . [and] do their mysterious work of lifting the life of mankind." The American vision for the world

> must be a sharing with all peoples of our Bill of Rights, our Declaration of Independence, our Constitution, our magnificent industrial products, our technical skills. It must be an internationalism of the people, by the people and for the people.

He wanted an American global modernization mission. In the absence of proper guidance, he worried that lesser nations would pursue alternative ideological paths towards modernity, paths antithetical to America's visions. Luce alleged that the wars raging in Europe and Asia were not simply about territory or national security, but about values and ways of life.[23] FDR agreed. As historian Warren Kimball states, just as the Great Depression provided the President "a chance to reform America, so the Second World War offered an opportunity to reform the world, not so as to enrich America, but to preserve the nation and proselytize its values."[24]

William Appleman Williams and the revisionists considered Luce's article "nonsense." The corporatist-leaning Emily Rosenberg saw it much the same—nothing more than an attempt to rationalize an American empire and to justify the expansion of American business interests overseas.[25] It undoubtedly was. Luce believed that global restructuring required the modernization of commerce, monetary policies, and development programs that would largely favor the U.S. financial community and American entrepreneurs. And yet, despite the condescending tone present in much American writing during the war, we should be careful not to blindly equate ideology with propaganda. The attitude that what was good for American businesses was good for the world was pervasive both inside and outside of government. Of equal importance, there was a strong belief that unlike the European imperialists, the United States would develop a global economy anchored in cooperation and non-discrimination.

This connection between ideology and a new economic order became clear when Roosevelt met British Prime Minister Winston Churchill in August 1941 to discuss war goals and plans for the postwar order. The meetings exposed the considerable gap in U.S. and British thinking. While Churchill sought a European order dictated by *realpolitik* and was devoted to preserving the Empire, the President's goals were principled and global.[26] The discussions were the first clear sign of Washington's intent to organize the world once the war ended. As Roosevelt's confidante, Adolf Berle Jr., explained to the President, "on the record of the past twenty years and the present conflict, it hardly seems that the British can make a statement of program; and their highly opportunist policy leaves her with little moral authority outside her own territories."[27] In the absence of that leadership, the Atlantic Charter which FDR and Churchill presented to the world after the conference was a highly American ideological statement of intent. The Charter emphasized sovereign rights and the self-government of all peoples, improved international labor standards and social security, and called for the establishment of "a wider and permanent system of general security" to replace the League of Nations.

In a letter to Roosevelt, the influential President of Columbia University Nicholas Murray Butler hailed the Charter as "another Declaration of Independence, but this time of international independence." The *Washington Post* called it "a momentous document freighted with high hopes and great responsibilities." The *Saturday Evening Post*, always more skeptical about grand designs, accurately concluded that the announcement seemed to confirm FDR's ambition to bring the Four Freedoms to all humankind. "Mr. Roosevelt believes [in this] . . . ardently, thinking of it perhaps, as a New Deal for the whole world," the paper concluded. The reporter Raymond Clapper captured much of the national sentiment that grew from the Atlantic Charter when, echoing Luce, he declared that:

> [as] an American, I should be very proud to end my days believing that in generations to come, schoolchildren all over the globe would read in their books about the United States of America and what it did for the human race. . . I should like to have them read also of America as the nation that liberated the race from the most awful form of bondage that has inflicted it, the bondage of war. I should like to have them read of America as a nation which used [its gifts] not only to build a civilization for its own people but also to benefit all humanity.

U.S. Ambassador to London John G. Winant summed up Clapper's opinion when, shortly after, he announced that "[W]hat many of us now have to come to want is world citizenship." Even the editors of the *Saturday Evening Post* understood this sentiment and the mysterious stranglehold it had on American cultural identity: "The savior complex is the grand and costly American emotion. We cannot expect other people to understand it, since we do not understand it ourselves. . . . It is our business. These zealots for a government of mankind are Americans."[28]

Once we recognize that Pearl Harbor, still three months away as this national mood swept the country, was not the trigger for the American determination to redesign the world, the argument that national security concerns inspired Washington's war and postwar plans appears less convincing. It did not require an attack on the homeland to inspire this American mission. Hirohito and Tojo merely converted the remaining doubters.

> The book of human history has been thrust into our hands. . . .
> We will write there what we believe . . . a thousand years hence a sane and better world will remember us as we remember those from whom we inherit for liberty and justice a greater love than the love of life.

wrote the editors of the *Saturday Evening Post* four months after the attack on Hawaii. Speaking ringside at the highly anticipated Joe Louis v. Max Baer fight, Wendell Willkie agreed. Referencing his election defeat to FDR in 1940, Willkie told millions of radio listeners that,

> a year ago I took on a champion too. I didn't win . . . [but] both my opponent and myself came out of that struggle in the firm resolve that our American democracy shall not alone live but shall rule the world.[29]

The U.S. Office of War Information (OWI) echoed this message in pamphlets and on posters. Revisionist historians have long held that it was pure propaganda when the OWI insisted that America,

> with its ideas of equality . . . against odds . . . has prospered and brought fresh hope to millions and new good to humanity. Even in the thick of war the experiment goes ahead with old values and new forms. . . . [the] earth shrinks in upon itself and we adjust to a world in motion holding fast to truth as we know it.[30]

Such ideas were no doubt intended to inspire popular support. Once again, though, it was a message that Americans overwhelmingly believed in. Just because a message serves propagandistically does not rule out that it also serves as a component in the actual determination of policy and public beliefs. As historian Justin Hart demonstrates in an eminent book on public opinion and foreign policy, Americans willingly participated in projecting the image of the exceptional nation to the world.[31] Coercion or marketing is not needed to persuade the converted. Addressing the Free World Association, Vice President Henry Wallace chipped in with a call for the liberation of the world. He maintained that while the Bible preached social justice, that concept "was not given complete and powerful political expression until our nation was formed as a Federal Union." This, Wallace believed, was America's mission in the war. His message reflected the re-emergence of the historically and culturally powerful conviction that America had itself become a kind of religion.[32]

Reporter James Reston simply considered the war "a national crusade for America and the American Dream." Admonishing Americans for the political and social divisiveness of the interwar period, he contended that in "our conception of that dream, in the strength of our conviction of the new world it can create and in our willingness to make all sacrifices willingly and without reservation for the democratic ideal" lay the American inspiration for war. The *Saturday Evening Post* added:

> The new world that shall be planned—our own new order—will be founded on the Four Freedoms, on the Atlantic Charter and on a New Bill of Rights. The old Bill of Rights was all right, is still all right, so far as it goes. But times have changed.

If times had indeed changed, it was only to make clearer a development that many had long considered inevitable.[33] Luce continued to feel this sense of purpose more intensely than most. A year after the "American Century," he returned to the topic in a less often cited, but equally powerful article. From his perspective, "America alone among the nations of the earth was founded on ideas and ideals which transcend class and caste. . . . America alone provides the pattern for the future." Acknowledging the likelihood of hundreds of thousands of American men "dead and most of our treasure spent," Luce made clear that the sacrifice would be worthwhile:

> We want the kind of world we want. . . . History is on our side—if we are brave enough. For the grand coincidence of this moment is that the kind of world we require is agreeable to the vast majority of mankind.

Unlike the rest of the world, which was largely preoccupied by the war, Americans were, as Luce pointed out, already preoccupied with the peace as well: "Now we shall prove whether or not the great experiment in human liberty on this continent is anything except a trivial episode in the history of mankind." He was adamant that the opportunity is given to America to "win the war and create a family of nations. That family will require an elder brother, strong, brave, and above all generous. America must be the elder brother of the nations in the brotherhood of man."[34]

Role

* * *

Historians are often tempted to dismiss examples such as these as propaganda intended to inspire the American people. It was that too, of course. But these ideas did not merely fester among public intellectuals or journalists. They translated into postwar policy objectives as well. By 1942, State Department officials worked to design a successor organization to the League of Nations based on the principles of the Atlantic Charter. They placed American traditions at its heart. By March, the Draft Constitution for an International Order contained a strongly worded, 16-article long "Bill of Rights" for mankind. What they had in mind was not the largely symbolic Universal Declaration of Human Rights that eventually emerged in 1948 but an actual bill of rights that protected individuals, not mere principles. Early drafts make clear that American postwar planners aimed to outlaw dictatorship and ensure citizens of the world freedom of religion, freedom of speech, property rights, education, procedural rights, and other ideals lifted from America's founding texts. By the summer of 1943, "human rights" was integrated as Article 9 in the first American draft of what was already informally being referred to as the United Nations Charter.[35]

While the State Department Under Secretary of State Cordell Hull and Sumner Welles prepared language on international security and human rights, postwar economic planning shifted to Secretary of the Treasury Henry Morgenthau, Jr. and his right-hand man, Harry Dexter White. To prevent future economic crises, their top priority became the creation of an international financial system to cope with issues like

Cordell Hull

Cordell Hull was a lawyer and Democrat from Tennessee who in 1933 was appointed to be Secretary of State by first-term president Franklin Roosevelt during the 1930s and 1940s. Hull became the principal advocate for international economic liberalism. While his role in the Roosevelt Administration has often been downplayed by scholars who see him as less influential than FDR's other key advisors, the policies that followed Hull's 12-year tenure as Secretary of State had his indelible thumbprint on them. Cordell Hull possessed a powerful belief in free trade and liberalized economic policies. He viewed non-discrimination, equality, currency stabilization, and reciprocity as the keys to global interconnection and as the solution to permanent peace and to international prosperity. In Hull's view, the 1930s had proven to be a period of failed economic policies. While Americans largely viewed tariffs as an acceptable measure to allow home markets to develop and prosper, preferences of the special kind that empires granted their dominions, Hull considered nothing more than aggressive tools which denied economic competitors equal access to raw materials and investments.

It was Hull's belief that free trade would open up countries and make them less likely to pursue or accept totalitarian governments. From this followed a firm belief that connecting nations within a multilateral framework would help secure the world against future wars. Hull also played a key role in the American push for the creation of the United Nations. In 1945, the year after he finally retired as Secretary of State, he was awarded the Nobel Peace Prize for that role. The principles Hull institutionalized as Secretary of State were key to Marshall Planners' thinking in 1947.

hunger, unemployment, displacement, and social chaos. Between 1942 and 1944, these plans included the design of what would become the International Monetary Fund (IMF) and the International Bank for Reconstruction and Development (IBRD), or World Bank, to help stabilize postwar conditions. Accompanying these ambitious initiatives were American demands for a liberalized economic order that in the process would dismantle Great Britain's prewar position and effectively lead to the end of the British Empire.

> **Harry Dexter White**
>
> Harry Dexter White, one of the chief American negotiators at Bretton Woods was later accused of being a Soviet spy and was under FBI surveillance. Debates continue regarding his alleged guilt. He was interviewed by the House Committee on Un-American Activities in 1948 and denied being a Communist. He suffered a heart attack shortly after. He died at age 55.

This U.S. demand for a reformed economic order dated back to the Lend-Lease planning and the Atlantic Charter talks in 1941. In contrast to the inter-Allied war debt which Europeans had been saddled with after the Great War, Washington was now willing to provide aid with no expectation of repayment. They wanted only "consideration" for their support. This "consideration" would come not as London hoped, in the form of goods, bases, or even unused goods. Assistant Secretary of State Dean Acheson labeled such an outcome as "wholly impossible" and of no interest. Settlement would have to come in policy concessions. The traditional image of the Second World War is, of course, of the United States and Great Britain as allies. Echoing that sentiment, Churchill called Lend-Lease a "most unsordid act in the whole of recorded history." As historians have begun to pay greater attention to the economic order and to ideology, the U.S.-Anglo relationship looks increasingly less special. In hindsight, it is difficult to see how, but the Prime Minister's statement implies that he misunderstood both the long-term intention and consequences of America's wartime support. At the heart of Lend-Lease lay Washington's determination that the U.S. dollar should replace sterling as the world's currency. Even as they guaranteed aid, Americans made their support dependent on their ability to police British exports, thereby limiting London's financial independence.[36]

The most demonstrative example of this was Article VII of the Lend-Lease agreement. It forced London, and later Moscow and Paris, to accede to U.S. desires to dismantle trade regulations and exchange controls, issues of particular importance to Great Britain given the balance of payment difficulties London was bound to face after the war. Article VII highlighted that Americans intended both to provide resources and to reform. The issue came to a head during the August 1941 Atlantic Charter meetings. Here, Sumner Welles put the issue in no uncertain terms to his war-weary British counterpart, the Permanent Undersecretary of State for Foreign Affairs, Sir Alexander Cadogan. American aid, Welles explained, was not dependent on the conduct during the war, but on the postwar establishment of "the freest possible economic interchange without discriminations, without exchange controls, without economic preference utilized for political purposes and without all of the manifold barriers which had . . . [been] responsible for the present world collapse." This demand deliberately targeted the 1932 Ottawa Imperial Preference Agreements between London and its dominions. Washington insisted that the Ottawa system, which either excluded non-members or forced them to sell below market price, would have to come to an end. A frustrated Cadogan aptly described Welles' position as "rather impertinent blackmail."[37]

Washington expected similar concessions from the Soviet Union. As Roosevelt told one reporter in 1943, he expected the war to have calmed the revolutionary enthusiasm in the Soviet Union. He now anticipated all major powers participating in a "social as well as international peace, with progress following evolutionary constitutional lines." This implied that not only would the Soviet Union reform, but that there would no longer be a place for planned political and economic systems or discriminatory imperial practices.[38]

The Treasury Department's position became fully evident during the international meeting of the United Nations Monetary and Financial Conference in the summer of 1944 in Bretton Woods, New Hampshire. To Morgenthau and White, the IMF, the IBRD, and the free trade principles targeted the complete reformation of the international financial order. In advance of the conference, officials unleashed a torrent of articles explaining the need for changes to currency and trade policies, and for American leadership.[39] In the Senate, Harry Truman (D-MO), Elbert Thomas (D-UT), and Hartley Kilgore (D-WV) sponsored a resolution arguing that "enduring peace" depended on the "abandonment of political nationalism and economic imperialism and autarchy." The resolution declared America the "nominated nation" and its purpose to be the establishment of a "progressive future for ourselves and for the world 3at large."[40] Americans understood the pressure this put on their allies. As Morgenthau wrote to White, the Bretton Woods talks would disclose whether the Soviet Union was

> going to play ball with the rest of the world on external matters, which she [had] never done before and [if] England [was] going to

play with the United Nations or [if she was] going to play with the Dominions.[41]

The delegates from the 44 countries who convened at Bretton Woods in the summer of 1944 sought agreements on sustainable long-term solutions to the problems plaguing the international economic system. In Roosevelt's conference-opening speech, delivered by the State Department, he summed up the attendees' mission: "[C]ommerce is the lifeblood of a free society. We must see to it that the arteries which carry that blood stream are not clogged again." Even insular one-party states were expected to liberalize and to abandon discriminatory policies of monopolism and monopsony in the realm of international trade. Liberalization and inter-dependence were to replace preferentialism and nationalism as the prime pillars of the international economy.[42]

The administration envisioned that its goals could be achieved through the establishment of institutions that would stimulate cooperation on currency exchange, development, and trade. The chief aim of the proceedings was to ensure that all participants adopted monetary policies with controlled exchange rates in which their currency would be tied to the U.S. dollar, which in turn would be tied to gold. The dollar would take on the role played by gold under the prewar system, in effect making it the principal currency.[43] The IMF would assist countries with loans to cope with short-term balance of payment problems resulting from the war, to restore currency convertibility, and to bring an end to nations' irresponsible practices of currency devaluations. In contrast, the IBRD was to provide continuing aid for reconstruction projects in devastated and less advanced areas to help secure long-term welfare and peace.[44] Global recovery and reconstruction would follow these reforms.

As the war entered its final year, the United States was economically healthier and wealthier than any nation. In 1944, the country produced almost 50 percent of the world's goods. In light of this, it is unsurprising that these new organizations were U.S.-designed and U.S.-led. This financial power allowed Washington to secure for itself practical control of the distribution of finances to countries in need. This did not mean that the U.S. would solitarily govern the appropriation of funds, but rather that it was the only nation with the influence necessary to veto aid or any change to the organizational structures.[45] The Administration may have frequently insisted that these new institutions be "financial institutions run by financial experts" and executed "wholly independent of political connection"—a position advocated by Morgenthau during his Senate Committee testimony on the agreements—but that was a simplified view.[46] The Bretton Woods system had clear financial advantages for

U.S. industry. Elimination of trade barriers would lead to thriving exports, particularly in the immediate postwar era as other nations struggled to rebuild.

In the eyes of historians Joyce and Gabriel Kolko, the key U.S. goal at Bretton Woods was therefore nothing more than a world where *American* business "could trade, operate, and profit without restrictions anywhere." But Bretton Woods was not simply an extension of the Open Door Policy. It was not a path to establish American world hegemony over the flow of money and trade or an attempt to gain unrestricted access to the closed Russian market. The Kolkos' view ignores the heavy emphasis Americans placed on multilateralism. Bretton Woods was not a zero-sum system. It did not target U.S. economic success at the expense of others, but was designed to reinforce the financial strength of all its members. Moreover, the system was neither aimed at socialist economies nor was it the first step in an aggressive Cold War policy.[47] American postwar planners assuredly believed that a way could be found "whereby nations with capitalistic, socialistic, and 'mixed' economies could function together," one key economist at Bretton Woods explained. Negotiators went to great lengths to create a system that *included* the Soviet Union. Americans believed that an "orderly world trading system required the cooperation of the Soviet Union and that all countries would benefit by the establishment of such a system."[48] Moscow's approval of the Bretton Woods structures at the end of the conference implies that Stalin concurred.

★   ★   ★

Nothing reflected the collective American hopes for the postwar world as intuitively as the populist language of Wendell Willkie. In 1943, he published the small book *One World*, a narrative of his 1942 tour of Europe, North Africa, Latin America, Russia, and Asia. In the process he coined a phrase that came to capture what American postwar planning was all about. *One World* presented a passionate account of a world free of imperialism and dependency. Connecting America's history with the world's future path, a *New York Times* reviewer highlighted how Wilkie instilled in his readers the idea of "a world opening up frontiers that are no longer."[49]

He was not calling for U.S. global dominance, but he was mobilizing Americans to lead and better the world in a new developed internationalism. A year later in *An American Program*,

One World

According to the publisher, Willkie's book, when adjusted for population-size, was the best-selling pamphlet in American history since Thomas Paine published *Common Sense* (1776).

Willkie summed up this belief when he announced that we "are fighting a war for freedom; we are fighting a war for men's minds. This means that we must encourage men's just aspirations for freedom not only at home but everywhere in the world." Willkie made his readers feel, as Lord Halifax, the British Ambassador to Washington, cabled home, "that America is rising to the height of its material and spiritual power . . . [and] that a missionary world task is before the United States which the nations are eagerly and desperately expecting it to fulfill."[50]

That task would get its most pronounced lift in the form of the United Nations Organization. In August 1944, Under Secretary of State Edward Stettinius, Jr. led the U.S. delegation at Dumbarton Oaks where representatives from the U.S., Great Britain, the Soviet Union, and China gathered to begin exploratory talks on the League's successor. The conference was the first collective attempt by the Grand Alliance to establish a new postwar security order. Capturing the ideals laid out in public and private over the course of the war thus far, Stettinius' delegation arrived with a highly progressive agenda that targeted new international responsibilities, included strong emphases on social and economic fields, and championed human rights. In contrast, Soviet and British proposals were conservative, seeking only to deal with issues deemed vital to immediate postwar cooperation. No wonder, then that both nations balked at the American proposal to,

> [make it] the duty of each member of the organization to see to it that conditions prevailing within its jurisdiction do not endanger international peace and security and, to this end, to respect the human rights and fundamental freedoms of all its people and to govern in accordance with the principles of humanity and justice. Subject to the performance of this duty, the Organization should refrain from intervention in the internal affairs of any of its members.[51]

Washington wanted an organization in which a member's inability to preserve *internal* tranquility and rights could lead to the organization's intervention. It would undoubtedly have proven difficult to push such a high-minded Charter through the U.S. Senate, but it was nonetheless telling of the spirit that dominated American thinking.

As it were London and Moscow dismissed any connection between global peace, "human rights," and "fundamental freedoms." Europeans had seen too much death and turmoil to merit such unlimited faith in the natural progress of mankind. Both nations preferred to protect what they already controlled rather than risk further uncertainty on another Wilsonian illusion. In light of their imperialistic mindset, both also likely felt that they had much to lose. This Anglo-Soviet obstinacy forced Americans to compromise with a heavily watered down reference to human rights.[52] The inability to push London and Moscow on human rights the way they had on economic issues reflected the war's development. Prior to 1943, the prospect of a Nazi victory in Europe still existed. By the 1944 Dumbarton Oaks talks, the Allied victory was only a matter of time. As that became more apparent, U.S. leverage subsided.

The following February, FDR met Stalin and Churchill at Yalta in Crimea. The agenda included the future of the territories and peoples soon to be liberated from Axis occupation, Soviet support for the war against Japan, and agreements regarding the United Nations, scheduled to be formalized later that year at a conference in San Francisco. To emphasize the Alliance's support for the Atlantic Charter, Roosevelt pressed Stalin to sign The Declaration on Liberated Europe under which the signatories promised support for democracies "through free elections of governments responsive to the will of the people" of all occupied European nations. Moscow initially viewed this with suspicion, but as Molotov later explained, words were cheap; what mattered was the correlation of forces. In Eastern Europe, that correlation favored the Communists.[53]

FDR likely understood these practical limitations; however, having Moscow on record as supporting democratic principles instilled some hope that the Soviets could be held to this later. Upon his return to Washington, the president hailed the Yalta Protocol. In front of a joint session of Congress, he declared that the peace would "be based on the sound principles of the Atlantic Charter." FDR's chief advisor, Harry Hopkins, summarized these feelings, claiming that after Yalta, we

> really believed in our hearts that this was the dawn of a new day we had all been praying for . . . that we had won the first great victory of the peace—and by 'we' I mean *all* of us, the whole civilized human race.

On relations with the Soviets, he believed that they

> had proved that they could be reasonable and far-seeing, and there wasn't any doubt in the mind of the president or any of us that we could . . . get along with them peacefully for as far into the future as any of us could imagine.[54]

The State Department's newly created Division of Public Liaison (DPL) initiated a domestic campaign in support of the Yalta Protocol, the Bretton

Woods organizations, and the United Nations. In a manner that would be copied a few years later when officials sought to ensure public support for the Marshall Plan, U.S. officials worked with private interest groups, including church and labor organizations, to highlight the export of American values.[55] It was a message the American people were ready to hear. If, in December 1941, the Second World War had been a war for vengeance, by 1945 it had also become a war for righteousness.

★　★　★

The San Francisco Conference was to be the crowning achievement in America's emergence as the global leader. Getting ready to deliver the primary address, FDR relocated to the Little White House in Warm Springs, Georgia on March 29, 1945 to prepare. Here, on April 12, 1945, the president suffered a cerebral hemorrhage. He died within the hour.

On April 16, in his first major policy announcement, the new President Harry Truman made clear that he intended to pick up where FDR had left off. In his words, the world was looking "to America for enlightened leadership to peace and progress. Such a leadership requires vision, courage and tolerance. It can be provided only by a nation devoted to the highest ideals."[56] Nine days later, he opened the San Francisco Conference with a radio address in which he reminded the delegates that the awesome responsibility of creating a just and free world rested on their shoulders.[57] The public's hopes were high for the new organization. An elated Stettinius informed Truman of ever increasing public support. An April Gallup poll showed 83 percent of Americans favored U.S. membership and U.S. global leadership.[58] There was nothing remarkable about the public's affection for the new organization. Largely viewed as the apotheosis of Wilsonianism, the U.N.'s principled ideals of justice, rights, and liberty for mankind were custom-made to the predilections of American opinion.

After two months of deliberating and negotiating, the conference concluded on June 25. It had not gone as Americans had hoped. The Human Rights bill for mankind had been postponed though Washington expected it to be taken up as one of the first agenda items once the U.N. was up and running. There were disagreements, too, over veto power and other issues, but the United States had the

Upon FDR's Death

Unaware of the president's death, Truman was called to the White House in the afternoon on April 12. At the First Family's quarters Eleanor Roosevelt told, "Harry, the President is dead." Truman responded, "Is there anything I can do for you?" "Is there anything I can do for you?" Mrs. Roosevelt countered, "for you are the one in trouble now."

organization it wanted. President Truman applauded the delegates and the charter as a "victory against war itself"; it "had given reality to the ideal of that great statesman of a generation ago—Woodrow Wilson." "Let us not," Truman explained, "fail to grasp this supreme chance to establish a world-wide rule of reason—to create an enduring peace under the guidance of God."[59] The world now had "a solid structure upon which we can build a better world." He shared Vandenberg's view of the Charter as "an emancipation proclamation for the world." The *Washington Post* euphorically compared the achievement to the 1787 Constitutional Convention.[60] A week later, in front of the U.S. Senate, Truman added that "improvements will come in the future as the United Nations gain experience." This was only the beginning of a more perfect society of nations. The Senate concurred, ratifying the United Nations Charter 89–2 and the Bretton Woods Agreement 61–19.[61]

These romanticized views would help create inflated and unreal expectations for the United Nations.[62] At the same time, the ambitious agenda was entirely unsurprising. As Wilson's heirs, Roosevelt and Truman sought to reform the world. But whereas Wilson had merely sought to make the world safe for democracy, the post-Second World War plan and the creation of the United Nations signaled the intent to democratize the world even as they believed they were saving it. The Rooseveltian foreign policy that Truman continued was intended as a "New Deal for the world." The institutions and principles intended to promote collective security, stabilize and grow economies, and ensure the protection of individuals through international rules and justice sought to reshape and redesign the international order along American-inspired ideals. Roosevelt was certain that "Americanism . . . was so very sensible, logical, and practical that societies would adopt those values and systems if only given the chance." At times, as in the case of Lend-Lease, slight coercion was required to ensure that this American agenda succeeded, but FDR considered these legitimate means to an end.[63] Such coercion would be needed again in the Marshall Plan negotiations in the years to come but many of the visions survived.

In retrospect, it seems astonishing that although the plans for both Bretton Woods and the United Nations aimed to undermine the British Empire and the Soviet Union's Communist ideology, there were, by and large, no serious discussions or considerations among Americans that their creation led down an irreconcilable path. The U.S. was certainly aware that procedural and technical differences existed between Washington and Moscow, but as Harry Dexter White later expressed it, to the best of his recollection, no "influential person expressed expectation of the fear that international relations would worsen" after the war.[64] In hindsight, the outbreak of the Cold War that soon followed appears a logical outcome of superpower goals and mutually exclusive ideologies, but FDR always expected that others would, by hook or by crook, come around to the American one-world vision. He was both a pragmatist and a global visionary, but he possessed a remarkably limited sense of how to navigate the world beyond the personal relationships he established with other leaders.[65]

Maybe the passionate journalist William Henry Chamberlin captured it best when he charged that the American wartime attitude was simply "a depressing compound of profound factual ignorance, naiveté, wishful thinking, and emotional hysteria." Lord Halifax made the same point— only more articulately—to London. The problem, he argued, was the American permanent tendency to believe in

> declarations and blueprints . . . to cure most of the ills of the world; this naturally leads to a sharp sense of 'let down' whenever events refuse to conform to the aspiration of men of good will and generates amongst them a corresponding tendency to blame the outside world . . . for wantonly putting obstacles in the path of idealistic American statesmen.[66]

Nonetheless, Americans had by 1945 accepted the responsibility for the world's future and certainly for Europe's future. Around the corner lay the burning question of how to bring the nation's values to bear on a region of former allies and enemies that was both traditionally hostile to foreign influence and in dire need of outside assistance.

CHAPTER 2

The World America Made

Towards the Marshall Plan, 1945–1947

Citizens rejoiced in the streets of Europe and the United States as the Second World War came to an end in May of 1945. It was a jubilation only partially matched in official circles. While Germany's surrender was welcome news, the world's future appeared even more uncertain than had been the case after the previous war ended in 1918. Close to 65 million people had died as a result of this anthropogenic disaster, most of them in Europe. The war had wreaked havoc on economies, political circumstances, and social conditions. Everywhere across the continent, despair was evident.

Stories describing these dire conditions began siphoning through to the Truman White House even before the war ended. The Missourian had been president for only two weeks when Assistant Secretary of War John J. McCloy delivered a firsthand account from across the Atlantic. The news was not good. McCloy described the Central European situation as one of "complete economic, social, and political collapse . . . unparalleled in history." While he saw some hope in France and Belgium, he warned that without some "reestablishment of their economic life they too can very well be torn apart by the collapse now in effect all over Middle Europe." A fact-finding mission undertaken by Judge Samuel Rosenman informed Truman in similarly ominous language that, except "in the rural, food-raising areas, a dangerously low level of nutrition generally exists; coal production meets not even minimum requirements; ports have suffered great damage by bombing and demolition. Railroads, canals, and highways have been wholly or partially destroyed."[1] Based on this observation, Truman concluded that, absent a reversal of the situation, there would be no "fertile ground in which stable, democratic and friendly governments can be reared."[2] But the task ahead was not merely one of removing rubble, rebuilding railroad networks, restoring power grids, or reconstructing dwellings. Much of Europe was broken psychologically. Since none of the international organizations intended to handle postwar recovery were yet operational, the immediate task fell largely to the American-funded United Nations Relief and Rehabilitation Administration. But UNRRA's principal expertise was in contributing emergency aid and helping repatriate and assist refugees. It lacked the capacity and the resources for the continent-wide task ahead. As a result, between 1945 and 1947, the responsibility increasingly shifted to the United States. Americans did not shy away from the task of European recovery; circumstances demanded U.S. leadership, and ideology inspired it. The postwar sense of mission described in the previous chapter was well symbolized by James Byrnes, who became Secretary of State in July of 1945. In a telling cartoon published in major newspapers, Byrnes stands holding two doctor's bags, looking at the bruised and beaten globe needing a cane for support. The caption reads, "Doc Byrnes and patient." Attached to the cane is a sign that simply reads "our world." Another cartoon depicts Death casting its gaze across the lands of a charred and wrecked European continent and defines "famine and pestilence" as new foes to conquer. By the end of the year, the *Saturday Evening Post* pithily added that "World Relief is America's Job."[3]

This self-assumed responsibility for the world's well-being notwithstanding, the Truman Administration remained committed to the Rooseveltian "one-world" order. The expectation remained that securing the world's long-term recovery and financial health would be a multilateral effort. Washington anticipated that wartime collaboration would continue and that both Great Britain and the Soviet Union would actively contribute to Europe's postwar recovery. This quickly proved to be unrealistic. For America's allies, VE day symbolized only a pyrrhic victory. The British and the Soviets emerged from the war with the psychology of victors, but the economies of defeated powers. During the war, British imports had been financed by a combination of Lend-Lease aid, loans, and the sale of overseas assets. It was London's hope that aid would continue long enough after the war ended for England to rebuild and reestablish its export industries. The Japanese surrender in August crushed this hope. As per the Lend-Lease agreement and the law, the Truman Administration suspended Lend-Lease on August 19. Britain's immediate outlook was dire. Its considerable trade deficit and massive debts left her with inadequate resources with which to procure essential foodstuffs and vital raw materials. The situation was not helped by the new Labor Government's commitment to a dramatically enlarged welfare state. The chief British economist John Maynard Keynes compared the situation to a financial Dunkirk: an unmitigated disaster, unless help arrived.

In recognition of these circumstances, the Truman Administration agreed to a $3.75 billion loan at a low two percent interest rate to Great Britain and to write off $650 million already owed. The debates over the loan conditions were ugly. As in the case of Lend–Lease, Washington's demands were far in excess of what many in London, including Keynes, hoped for or thought reasonable. Of particular concern was the American insistence on the convertibility of the pound sterling within one year, an issue that would later have great impact as nations with sterling reserves began to draw dollar reserves from Britain. Churchill, now in the opposition and happy to indict Clement Attlee's Labour government for having accepted a raw deal, called the sterling convertibility "too bad to be true." In the House of Lords, Lord Woolton argued that, "to-day we are surrendering what I conceive to be our just rights. We are surrendering them to the power of the dollar, because those responsible for the affairs of this country do not dare to retreat on the economic fastness of the Empire." The problem was that there hardly was an Empire to retreat to. Great Britain was the largest debtor nation in the world. London had no choice but to accept the terms.[4]

The American commitment to the new international order played a key part in the decision to extend loans to Britain. While Britain was hardly the country most in need of aid, or the only one knocking on Washington's door, its importance to the global economy was unparalleled. Moreover, as Keynes implied upon his arrival in the U.S. to discuss loan terms, if the U.S. failed to provide support, Great Britain would likely return to its interwar bilateral trade arrangements. The result would be the revival of economic blocs and the collapse of the Bretton Woods system before it even began. "Economic nationalism with all the fierce rivalries which that means will be unleashed," the columnist Marquis Childs warned.[5] Since the United States had already accepted the role as the principal benefactor of the IMF and the World Bank, as well as the leading part in the United Nations, the burden of reconstruction would have fallen to Washington either way. The pace of international events in the summer of 1945 meant that it now did so in a far more piecemeal manner than had been anticipated. The loan was an emergency measure not only to keep Britain afloat, but also to safeguard the entire global order Washington sought to build.

Other nations faced similarly difficult conditions. While postwar Belgium, Italy, and the Scandinavian countries emerged with some of their industries and agriculture fairly intact, circumstances in these countries were positive by comparison only. Denmark's decision to accept Nazi occupation rather than fight, for example, had protected both its infrastructure and its farm output, but, like others, she suffered from dramatically declining export markets, most notably Germany. Conditions in the Netherlands and France were grimmer. Here, raw materials were scarce, agricultural production dramatically down, and the physical destruction considerable. In Greece, conditions were even worse. Extensive fighting and a heavy-handed occupation had left 3,000 villages destroyed and a quarter of the Greek people homeless. Ten percent of the nation's seven million people perished during the war.[6] It was a situation mirrored in Eastern and Central Europe. At least 20 million died in the Soviet Union as a result of the war. In Poland, some 17 percent of the prewar population succumbed between 1939 and 1945. Nowhere in Europe was the devastation greater than in Germany. The Allied strategic bombing campaigns and the brutality of the ground invasions from east and west had laid waste to the country.

The situation in Germany posed a particular challenge. The wartime demand for unconditional surrender had been accompanied by a pledge to occupy the former enemy at the end of the war. Victory made the Allies responsible for Germany's future. When Truman met Joseph Stalin and the new British Prime Minister Attlee in Potsdam outside of Berlin in the summer of 1945 to discuss the issue of Germany's future, the principal agreement was to de-Nazify and demilitarize the former enemy. Although Germany would remain under occupation status for the foreseeable future, the idea of democratization and independence was clear. The decision to divide Germany into four military occupation zones under U.S., Soviet, British, and French control was a temporary measure intended for administrative purposes. The provisional nature of the division was underlined by the establishment of the Four Power Allied Control Council headquarters in Berlin, deep inside the Soviet zone, and by the decision to divide Berlin into four similar zones as well. The expectation was that once political leaders untainted by the Nazi past were able to undertake the responsible governance of their nation, Germany would be reunified.

The task at hand was formidable. From the beginning, the agendas of the Soviet Union and France conflicted with the joint goal of eventual German recovery. Both Moscow and Paris wanted reparations and the permanent weakening of Germany. French President Charles de Gaulle, who had not been invited to Potsdam, saw little reason to abide by the agreement. The viewpoint of the French government was that Germany ought to be either broken up or that, at the very least, her major industrial resource areas be internationalized. The Soviet Union, for its part, soon began to seize German machinery, railroad tracks, and factories, as well as raw materials, for its own citizens. Moscow also retracted a commitment to provide agricultural products from its zone to the three Western zones in return for the industrial equipment and coal it had already received from them. This Soviet approach mirrored the infamous, but long since scrapped American Morgenthau Plan, which had aimed to keep Germany permanently pastoralized and deindustrialized. The rape of some two million German women by Soviet soldiers served as further evidence that the former enemy's recovery was not on Moscow's agenda.

U.S. Army General Lucius Clay, who ran the American occupation zone, did not view French or Soviet policies kindly, nor was he particularly impressed by his own State Department's lack of a comprehensive strategy for Europe as a whole. While some in Washington insisted that Germany's standard of living should not exceed that of its neighbors, Clay recognized that European recovery hinged upon the revival of Germany both as a producer and consumer of goods. Much to his consternation, however, Washington vacillated through most of 1945 and 1946. The lack of fuel across Europe, for example, led to a decision that Germany would provide fuel for other European areas without compensation. The measure provided some stopgap relief in neighboring countries, but it only doubled the blow in Germany. Here, the situation was further complicated by the zones' inability to handle the greatest forced migration of people in European history. In order to prevent a repeat of ethnic crisis caused by the artificial design of post–First World War borders, in 1945, millions of Germans were forcibly marched back into Germany from their homes in territories east of the Oder-Neisse and from the Sudetenland. Soon, some eight to ten million refugees—lacking food and shelter—arrived in Germany's cities. Of the more than half a million people that passed through Berlin between the summer and fall of 1945, some 40 percent were orphaned children. Overpopulation and a lack of resources pushed living conditions to their limits. By early 1946, the general in charge of the British zone had to cut caloric rations to 1,000 per person, well below starvation levels. In the American zone, the rations hovered between 1,200 and 1,500. It was "barely enough to survive," Clay reported home. Frustrated with Washington and upset with America's occupation partners for their lack of collaboration, he explained to Army Chief of Staff Dwight Eisenhower that "a failure to obtain economic unity" to ensure that goods, people, and services could move freely between the four occupation zones before the next winter would be disastrous. "The suffering of the German people will be a serious charge against democracy," he continued, and it "will develop a sympathy which may well defeat our other objectives in Germany."

In the summer of 1946, Clay urged Washington to take steps to promote "recovery, re-education, responsible self-government under democratic procedures, and the eventual acceptance of Germany into the United Nations on terms of equality." U.S. determination to secure this outcome, he advised, needed to be more transparent to the Germans and to Washington's allies. Clay's push for the merger of the zones reflected both his concern for the deteriorating humanitarian situation as well as a growing fear that the Soviets, working through German Communists, were seeking to take advantage of the poor conditions across the entire country to extend Moscow's influence. If nothing was done to enhance conditions, Americans would bear the principal blame. As he drily observed, "becoming a Communist on 1,500 calories a day and a believer in democracy on 1,000" was not a choice for those who were suffering.

In the summer of 1946, increasingly desperate, Clay reached out directly to Secretary of State Byrnes, then attending a Foreign Ministers' Conference in Paris, to come to Germany to personally and publicly clarify Washington's position.[7] While some Francophile State Department officials opposed Clay's agenda for German recovery, Byrnes was not among them. A former South Carolina Senator and Supreme Court Justice, Byrnes had resigned from the Bench to serve as Roosevelt's Director of Economic Stabilization. In that capacity, he was responsible for the control of domestic wages, rents, and prices. In 1943 he took over as head of the Office of War Mobilization, tasked with procuring, transporting, and distributing goods and services to the U.S. military and to civilians. In these roles, Byrnes learned the importance of aid and support in times of crises. Byrnes shared Lucius Clay's belief that the importance of the former enemy's revival greatly outweighed the concerns among former allies. While visiting Stuttgart in early September, the Secretary of State delivered one of the most powerful speeches ever given by a U.S. official on foreign soil. In front of a joint German–American crowd, Byrnes clarified any misunderstandings regarding his department's position. In powerful language, he committed the United States to the stabilization and democratization of Germany, and to the sanctity of her borders. But Byrnes was not finished. In a dramatic gesture, he made the urgent unification of the four occupation zones American policy and promised the German people sovereignty and eventual independence under international supervision. He assured his audience that, despite the war and the occupation

> we do not want Germany to become the satellite of any power.
> . . . The American people want to return the government of
> Germany to the German people. The American people want to
> help the German people to win their way back to an honorable
> place among the free and peace-loving nations of the world.

As the crowd rose to its feet in applause and the band played the "Star Spangled Banner," Senator Arthur Vandenberg, on stage with Byrnes, told the Secretary that the tune had "never before given me such a chill." He understood that Byrnes' speech sent a forceful message to the other occupying powers that, whatever Paris and Moscow's ambitions might be, Washington's commitment to international order remained firm. More importantly, the speech was, as Clay later relayed, "aimed at the Germans. It was an attempt to give them some hope." It was also aimed at Western Europe, to assure them that the U.S. was dedicated to the continent's political and financial recovery.[8]

Byrnes' assurance was desperately needed. In 1947, some 200 members of Congress visited Europe and Germany. Here they witnessed the destruction firsthand. One group included future Secretary of State Christian Herter (R–MA) and House members Everett Dirksen (R–IL) and Richard Nixon (R–CA). They returned home deeply distressed. In his memoirs, Nixon counted his visit to war-torn Europe to be

> among the most sobering experiences of my life. . . . We found families huddled in the debris of buildings and in bunkers. There was a critical shortage of food, and thin-faced, half-dressed children approached us not to beg, but to sell their fathers' war medals or to trade them for something to eat.[9]

★ ★ ★

Most early narratives of the Marshall Plan claimed that conditions steadily deteriorated not only in Germany, but across Europe between the end of the war and the arrival of Marshall Aid in 1948. Recent scholarship has made clear, however, that while the economies of some countries continued to struggle, most began to recover during 1945 and early 1946. While coal and agricultural output remained low, many industries picked up as governments took active steps to encourage higher employment. In several countries, interest rates were kept artificially low and imports were dramatically increased in order to fulfill citizens' immediate needs. The result was dramatic balance of payment deficits but also vastly improved conditions. According to many economic historians, the financial outlook so improved by 1946 that the principal problem facing most European nations was simply one of paying for dollar imports. In Alan Milward's view, European confidence in the future was high, and the trajectory of improvement implied that, apart from France and Holland, the 14 other eventual Marshall Aid recipients no longer faced a "production crisis," only the problem of making international payments. Since the Marshall Plan did not go on to target that particular issue, but instead sought to further boost productivity, which was already improving, the Milward

[margin note: Good sign]

school of thought insisted that full economic recovery would have occurred without Marshall Aid.[10]

From a strictly macroeconomic perspective, the numbers confirm this. Except for Germany, investment across Western Europe was higher as a ratio of GDP than since the end of the Great War, and production was on the rise. Even if we factor in the overall lull in productivity that followed in 1947, growing inflation, and flourishing black markets, the direct financial impact of U.S. aid in rectifying these conditions has undoubtedly been overstated both in American national memory and in much scholarship. Marshall Aid may have prevented declining growth for a brief period, but it was not the critical marginal quantity that saved Europe. To use the economists' cliché, "all other things being equal," Europe was on the road to recovery long before American assistance arrived.

The problem with this narrow approach is that all things were not "equal" in the tense and chaotic mid-1940s Europe. The psychology of the emerging Cold War and the legacy of the period following the outbreak of the First World War in 1914 ensured that whatever the potential future economic prospects, socio-economic and political uncertainty dominated. Recovery without outside assistance would have required extensive austerity measures, well beyond what was already in place. Rationing, already at critical levels in several countries, would have had to have been increased even further. The Marshall Plan's principal strength would be that as it committed the U.S. to Europe's democratic future, it provided a safety net greater than the sum of its parts.

Polls and individual firsthand observations overwhelmingly corroborate the necessity of that safety net. Gallup surveys from across Great Britain confirm that Britons considered their "most important problems" to be economic: housing, food, and fuel shortages consistently ranked highest. In January 1947, 33 percent placed concerns of inadequate dwellings at the top of the list, 19 percent cited fuel, and 17 percent the continued food rationing. Only two percent considered foreign policy the greatest problem facing Britain. By September 1947, 75 percent considered the economic situation in Britain "serious." In January 1948, 65 percent considered it harder to make ends meet compared to six months prior. By September of that year, a full five months after the U.S. Congress approved the Marshall Plan, 34 percent of Britons believed that the economic situation was still deteriorating and 35 percent thought it held steady, while only 24 percent believed conditions had improved. It was not a view that changed much through most of 1948.[11] Whatever the potential for recovery, British citizens were not experiencing it.

These economic problems created an acute sense of hopelessness. Walter Lippmann believed that Britain had been pushed to the brink because recovery demanded an "extraordinary effort from a people who are tired from the immense strain of war, who have had little rest or recreation from the nerve-wrecking exertions and anxieties" of economic depression and conflict. In his view, the British needed "more help," or economic conditions would be critical. The outcome of greater chaos would be "more drastic government compulsion. . . . For free enterprise is a system which works only when there is security and plenty." In the absence of U.S. support, the British, he concluded, "will have neither." They would be unable to do "anything but resort to the strongest kind of government-directed collectivism."[12]

These difficulties were felt even more harshly on the continent. The combination of a harrowing winter and a worldwide grain shortage in 1947 exacerbated the already unstable situation. In 1947, France produced only half as much wheat as the year before. The government had no choice but to cut bread rations by another 20 percent. French polls shared the same gloomy outlook as the British. In early 1947, 41 percent believed the food situation had deteriorated since 1946. Only eight percent saw improvement. Less than a quarter expected to be able to heat their homes throughout the winter, while a majority expected further price increases. By April, French respondents considered the dismal living conditions in France second only to Greece.[13]

Germany bore the brunt of the continent-wide decline in 1947. Across the Western occupation zones, the daily available calories dropped from 3,000 in 1938 to 1,200–1,400 by 1947 and 1948. In many other countries, the average caloric intake fell to between 60 and 80 percent of the mid-1930s level, when the region was already impacted by the Depression. The industrial productive capacity in Germany stood at 41 percent of the 1937 level, at 79 percent in the Netherlands, and at 40 percent in Austria. Of all the European countries, only Norway was exceeding its 1937 productivity levels in August 1947.[14] Poor harvests across Europe in 1947 made further reductions in living conditions inevitable.

★   ★   ★

These conditions raised the specter of the 1930s. The lesson Washington had drawn from the Depression of the 1930s was that radical ideologies thrived in times of despair. It was the miserable conditions of the inter-war period that had drawn Germans and Italians to the false promises of radicalism. A similar outcome now threatened U.S. postwar plans for stable democratic conditions across Europe. Leftwing forces appeared to be steadily gaining ground everywhere. Inspired and often directed by Moscow, Communist parties in France, Italy, Greece, and, to a lesser degree, Denmark importunately challenged political establishments. This ran counter to U.S. wartime expectations. A joint Office of Strategic Services and State Department assessment concluded in advance of FDR's meetings with Stalin at Yalta in 1945, that Moscow would seek to secure and develop its influence *only within* the frontiers of 1941. While the Soviets might seek extended influence in Eastern Europe for security purposes, few associated this with Communization.[15] Most experts echoed *Time* magazine's assessment that Moscow was no longer an agent of revolution. Stalin's postwar policies would be neither "revolutionary" nor "internationalist."[16] By 1946, such optimism was being proven false. Reinhold Niebuhr was blunt; he called for the U.S. to prevent the conquest of Western Europe by "the unscrupulous Soviet tyranny." *Life* magazine concurred. The global American mission demanded permanent and comprehensive U.S. involvement, Henry Luce's publication insisted, as it reverted to the ideological American mission it had pushed during the Second World War. In the editors' eyes, the situation was clear: "the risks are great, the stakes high, the challenge not to be refused."[17]

As Byrnes delivered his speech in Stuttgart in September of 1946, Communist opposition appeared to be everywhere on the march. In Denmark, the Communist Party claimed above 12 percent of the vote in the country's first postwar election. In Belgium, they became the third largest political party. If the situation in these smaller European countries flew somewhat under Washington's radar, developments elsewhere were viewed with particular concern. When the Italian Communist leader Palmiro Togliatti returned from exile in the Soviet Union in 1944, he boasted of a "groundswell of support for Communism" and "that Moscow's image was far more positive than Washington or London's." This was not empty rhetoric. By 1945, the Italian Communist Party (PCI) membership reached 1.7 million. Dire economic conditions played into its hands. As food shortages intensified, causing people to turn to the black market, membership soon exceeded two million.[18] Divisions among Italian leftwing parties limited the PCI's votes to a still considerable 18.9 percent, making it the third largest party with numerous cabinet positions. In January 1947, the Christian Democratic Prime Minister Alcide De Gaspieri traveled to Washington, where he found Truman's Administration deeply troubled by the growing influence of the political left and very receptive to providing emergency relief aid to Italy.[19]

The situation in France appeared equally concerning. In late October 1946, U.S. Ambassador to Paris Jefferson Caffery explained that the "financial, economic and food crisis . . . has a most depressing effect on French morale." Prices were outpacing wages, and Communist and Socialist popularity was on the rise. "Frenchmen," he reported "are beginning to feel that . . . since democracy in France does not appear to produce results, some form of authoritarian government is needed . . . [either] a dictatorship by the Communist Party or an authoritarian regime under [Charles] de Gaulle"[20]

The November Assembly elections confirmed Caffery's fears. Maurice Thorez' French Communist Party (PCF) claimed 28 percent of the vote, making it the majority party. The result put Thorez in a position to form a coalition government, but since no other party was willing to entertain a Communist-led government, he had to accept a position in a five-party coalition headed by the Socialist Léon Blum. This did not inspire much confidence amongst Americans. After Thorez completed a "clandestine" trip to Moscow, a source informed Caffery that the Communist view was that the

> **Charles de Gaulle**
>
> In January of 1946, Charles de Gaulle abruptly resigned as head of the French government after a furious row about Communist representation in the government. He likely hoped that he would be returned as an even more powerful executive. The move backfired and he would spend the next 12 years outside of government. At age 67, with France embroiled in a war in Algeria, de Gaulle finally returned to power in 1959.

> international situation is favorable to . . . the interests of the Soviet Union [and] while [Moscow] is not prepared for war and its military preparations will not be completed for a number of years . . . the necessity to *gain time* . . . while endeavoring to maintain and consolidate positions already required [is needed]. The policy and tactics of the French Communist Party must follow *closely in line with this perspective* (italics in original).

A month later, U.S. Ambassador to Moscow Walter Bedell Smith informed Washington that he considered the assessment from the Paris Embassy the "most accurate revealing exposé of present Soviet tactics not only in France but throughout the rest of Europe."[21] Available evidence now makes clear the accuracy of Smith's assessment. While they may have appeared independent, the European Communist parties' allegiance was not to their constituencies, but to their master in the Soviet Union. As Europe's malaise grew, Stalin's agents were undermining Washington's agenda for a democratic Europe.

The ballot box was not the only path to power sought by European Communists. The situation in Greece became so dire that it eventually forced Washington's hand in Europe more broadly. In October 1946, Loy

Henderson, the Director of the State Department's Office of Near Eastern and African Affairs, warned that without international aid to support the nationalist regime, Greek Communist insurgents would likely prevail in the civil war that had raged since 1944. Cross-border Communist incursions and support from neighboring Bulgaria, Albania, and Yugoslavia made such an outcome increasingly likely. Although concerned by Henderson's report, the Truman Administration still believed in the international order. Rejecting the request for U.S. unilateral aid to Greece, Under Secretary of State Dean Acheson pushed for a U.N. solution.[22] Under Article 34 of the United Nations Charter, the U.S. insisted in the Security Council that the on-going cross-border shootings in the Balkans were "likely to endanger the maintenance of international peace," and recommended an exploratory investigation of the situation. Moscow vetoed the request because it did not single out Athens as the aggressor. The absence of evidence to support Soviet counter-accusations against Greece caused the interim U.S. Ambassador to the U.N., Herschel Johnson, to publicly condemn this irresponsible politicization of the organization. The lifeblood of the U.N., Johnson insisted, rested on the veto being "the rare exception to the rule."[23] Moscow countered that the Greek regime ignored the wishes of its people.[24] While it was true that the Greek government under Konstantinos Tsaldaris was no model democracy, he was the elected leader, and his government a formal and founding member of the U.N. As a result, while Moscow could block a U.N. investigation, the Soviets could not prevent Tsaldaris from addressing the organization, which he did in November. In a stirring oration reminiscent of Haile Selassie's 1936 speech to the League of Nations—where he deplored the Council's failure to protect Ethiopia from Mussolini—the Greek Prime Minister formally charged the countries of Yugoslavia, Albania, and Bulgaria with "lending their support" to Communist guerillas. Citing over 30 instances of infiltration and interventions against Greek soil, Tsaldaris thundered that the U.N. could not "permit a few dealers in ideology [to] receive assistance from foreign countries for imperialistic ends. . . . For in that event, responsibility would rest upon all the United Nations, and in particular upon the Great Powers."[25]

Great Britain had been the principal guardian of Greece since the Second World War, but as the pressure mounted on the Athens government, a growing number of U.S. citizens called for a greater American role. Sumner Welles, now a private citizen, believed that failure to engage would undermine the entire American global democratic project and, by extension, his country's international legitimacy. Joseph and Stewart Alsop agreed. As two of the nation's most influential reporters, they vocally criticized the Truman Administration's lack of action.

"[K]eeping your fingers crossed" they stated, "cannot be described as having a policy in the field of world relations, . . . however, crossed fingers seem to be the only visibly American response" to Soviet policies. Support in the U.N. for Greece was not enough; the Alsops insisted that the United States needed a program to provide support "on a much larger scale, in all economic and political soft spots."[26]

Encouragement followed on December 19 when, after heated debates in the Security Council and growing international pressure, the Soviet Union refrained from vetoing an American-backed measure to deploy a multinational investigative U.N. mission to the Balkans.[27] Elated American reporters viewed this development as a sign of rediscovered "big power harmony." The *Washington Post* concluded that Moscow was not "prepared to do anything that would cast doubt on her new policy of cooperation with the west." Lippmann optimistically viewed it as a "stabilization of the balance of power" and a clarification of "the limits of the sphere of influence established at the end of the war."[28]

In one of his last acts as Secretary of State, Byrnes in January 1947 appointed the highly respected reporter and former Roosevelt advisor Mark Ethridge as the head U.S. delegate to the United Nations Balkan Committee investigating the Greek matter. Years later, Ethridge bitterly recalled how misplaced his optimism for a U.N.-orchestrated solution had been. Determined to place the sole blame on the Greek government, the Soviets did everything they could to prevent U.N. observers from exploring the situation outside the capital. They were certain, Ethridge reported to the State Department in mid-February, "that Greece is ripe plum ready to fall into their hands in a few weeks." Awaiting the inevitable Communist takeover, the Soviet delegation was simply stalling for time.[29]

This conclusion fast-tracked a debate over what the Alsops considered the "greatest unresolved problem of American foreign policy: The relationship between political foreign policy and economic foreign policy."[30] The responsibility for finding a solution fell to George C. Marshall who, in January 1947, replaced Byrnes in the State Department

Truman could hardly have picked a more competent man for the job. Marshall was not only a brilliant general, he was also an outstanding administrator. He knew how to get results.

During the First World War he had worked under General John J. Pershing, the commander of the American Expeditionary

Marshall's Confirmation

The U.S. Senate unanimously confirmed Marshall as Secretary of State though many in Congress actually worried that making a military man the nation's chief diplomat would undermine the constitutional process.

Figure 2.1 January, 1947: James Byrnes (right) congratulates George Marshall
(left) upon his swearing in as Secretary of State. President Harry S.
Truman stands between them

Force in Europe. Recognizing Marshall's talent, Franklin Roosevelt in
1939 made him Chief of Staff of the U.S. Army. He served with distinction
and loyalty though his wartime role, in the eyes of many, was less apparent
than such battlefield commanders as Dwight Eisenhower and Douglas
MacArthur. Conscious of Marshall's talents, Truman in 1946 deployed
Marshall to help mediate a solution to the Chinese Civil War. It was a
thankless and unsuccessful task but the failure in China did not deter
Truman. "The more I see and talk to him the more certain I am he's the
great one of the age," Truman observed.[31]

The complexity of the global situation facing Marshall when he took
over at Foggy Bottom would have been unimaginable to any of his
predecessors except Byrnes. Used to the streamlined hierarchy and
straightforward nature of the military, Marshall believed that the many
different postwar institutional structures to which Americans remained
committed clouded the capacity of the U.S. to execute. The U.N., the
IMF, and the World Bank were all good long-term vehicles for recovery
and development, but none of them performed to the standards needed

in early 1947. Growing Communist pressure on the democratic process in Europe made it clear that Washington could no longer just keep its fingers crossed. UNRRA had also come up short. Marshall fundamentally shared the view of the Greek Director General of Housing and Reconstruction, Constantinos Doxiadis, that UNRRA was "a first aid program and nothing else." From this perspective, UNRRA could

> provide food and supplies, but it could not ensure Greece's recovery from the triple blow of war, occupation, and civil strife. To prevent a political collapse, Greece needed funds for importation of goods, rebuilding of industry, direct military assistance, food, the provision of administrators, technicians, [and] economists.[32]

Labeling Greece an "old-fashioned economy . . . [with] no special aptitude for either politics or rebuilding," *Life* magazine tersely pronounced that only the U.S. could rescue the last non-Communist holdout in the Balkans.[33]

In late February 1947, Marshall delivered a powerful speech at Princeton University that effortlessly captured the need for a greater American ideological commitment in the world. Recalling how no force had come to rescue Athenian democracy during the Peloponnesian Wars, Marshall urged the university students to recognize the significance of history's lessons and the duty these lessons placed upon their own generation. Summoning the American people to prevent threats to democracy from once again overwhelming the forces of freedom, he asked his audience to "fully understand the special position that the United States now occupies in the world." Quoting Oliver Wendell Holmes, he insisted that, "[M]an is born to act. To act is to affirm the worth of an end, and to affirm the worth of an end is to create an ideal." Commenting on the speech, even Lippmann conceded that there was no "escape from that responsibility. . . . It is impossible to evade the consequences of history." He continued, saying,

> there is no way in which the United States can stand safely aside and mind its own internal business . . . while all about it the world sinks into disorder and squalor, and the violence of a desperate struggle for mere existence.[34]

Marshall's Princeton speech became an echo for the situation in Greece. The day before he took the podium, the British Embassy in Washington informed the State Department that London would "be obliged to discontinue the financial, economic, and advisory assistance" they had been providing to Greece and Turkey, and pressed the U.S. to assume its role.

Working in utmost secrecy, the State Department's Dean Acheson and Loy Henderson began working on an American response that would bring an end to the "keeping the fingers crossed" policy.[35] As they relayed the situation to Marshall, only U.S. aid could avert "the capitulation of Greece to Soviet domination [which] might eventually result in the loss of the whole Near and Middle East and northern Africa." Such an outcome "would consolidate the position of Communist minorities in many other countries where their aggressive tactics [were] seriously hampering the development of middle-of-the-road governments."[36] On February 27, President Truman, Marshall, and Acheson met with high-ranking Congressmen from both parties to argue the necessity of taking up Britain's mantle in the Near East. As he had made clear at Princeton, Marshall believed the world had "arrived at a point in history" unparalleled "since ancient times."[37] Congress, the press, and the public needed to understand that far more than Greece, Turkey, or the Middle East was at stake, as Truman's Press Secretary Eben Ayers explained in his diary.[38] The State Depatment's Joseph Jones suggested that any public message downplay the financial aid issue in the Mediterranean crisis and instead emphasize "the necessity for bolstering democracy around the world." The decision to take over Britain's role was, as he explained it, not purely a financial contribution, nor was it an attempt to pull "British chestnuts out of the fire." It had to be presented in terms of the mortal danger the spread of Communism posed to "democracies throughout the world." In Acheson's words, the "public presentation" should not specifically target the Soviet Union; instead, it should stress "individual liberty . . . the protection of democracies everywhere." It was not "a matter of vague do-goodism," but rather "a matter of protecting our whole way of life and of protecting the nation itself."[39]

Cold War revisionists dismiss this attempt to define the Greek affair as a battle for democracy. They see it as nothing more than exaggerated rhetoric. However, this interpretation too casually overlooks conversations between the President's advisors and their belief in the United States' ability to reshape the global order. Under Secretary of State for Economic Affairs Will Clayton—one of the period's most astute thinkers on U.S.-European affairs—summed up the shared view of the situation when he wrote to Marshall that the "United States must take up world leadership and quickly to avert world disaster." Elaborating, he argued that the American public needed to understand what was at stake. Far from conjuring up an exaggerated threat, however, Clayton insisted that to "shock them, it is only necessary for the President and the Secretary of State to tell the truth and the whole truth." In his opinion, freedom was under threat, and the situation demanded American world leadership.[40]

This kind of ideological rhetoric did not sit well with George Kennan. He opposed sending signals that would exacerbate the relationship with Moscow, and instead recommended a simple public statement "confined largely to the needs of the Greek people."[41] As he had explained in an address to the Council on Foreign Relations in January, it was "perfectly possible for the U.S. . . . to contain Russian power if it is . . . done courteously and in a non-provocative way." If the U.S. held the line, internal changes in Russia would occur organically.[42] Kennan was his generation's most perceptive observer of Soviet affairs, but he was out of touch with the ideals that made Americans tick. As Truman's 1947 State of the Union Address two months earlier made obvious, the President believed that "stability can be destroyed when nations with great responsibilities neglect to maintain the means of discharging those responsibilities. . . . We have a higher duty and a greater responsibility than the attainment of our own national security." No matter what Kennan may have believed, Americans found such a message far easier to embrace than one of calculated compromise. As *Life* put it, the Soviet Union was "an idea as well as a country . . . we must win the billion-odd people in the grandstand to our side by a demonstration that ours is the better idea, the better system."[43]

On March 12, Truman took that message to a joint session of Congress. Ignoring Kennan's call for caution, the President expanded the United States obligation from aiding Greece to protecting the entire world from tyranny. Asking Congress for $400 million in aid to ensure Greece's and Turkey's survival as free nations, Truman asserted that among America's primary objectives in the world was the "creation of conditions in which we and other nations will be able to work out a way of life free from coercion. This was a fundamental issue in the war with Germany and Japan." The President stressed that, "Our victory was won over countries which sought to impose their will, and their way of life, upon other nations." As such, Americans needed to remain committed "to help free peoples to maintain their free institutions and their national integrity against aggressive movements that seek to impose upon them totalitarian regimes." As Truman interpreted it,

> nearly every nation must choose between alternative ways of life.
> The choice is too often not a free one. One way of life is based
> upon the will of the majority, and is distinguished by free
> institutions, representative government, free elections, guarantees
> of individual liberty, freedom of speech and religion, and freedom

> from political oppression. The second way of life is based upon
> the will of a minority forcibly imposed upon the majority. It relies
> upon terror and oppression, a controlled press and radio; fixed
> elections, and the suppression of personal freedoms. I believe
> that it must be the policy of the United States to support free
> peoples who are resisting attempted subjugation by armed
> minorities or by outside pressures.[44]

Thus, Truman's Doctrine made the protection of global liberty America's
cross to bear.

★ ★ ★

George Marshall was not in the audience during Truman's speech. He
was attending a Foreign Minister's Conference to discuss Europe's future
with Joseph Stalin and his British and French counterparts, Ernest Bevin,
and Georges Bidault. En route to Moscow, he consulted with Caffery and
Clay, and he witnessed firsthand the socio-economic and political
conditions in France and Germany. The newly appointed Secretary of
State expected a tense encounter in Moscow. The good relationship that
the U.S. had hoped to establish with the Russians at the end of the war
had by then deteriorated steadily. In some respects, this was to be expected.
Even in a world of relative global harmony, great powers always possess
different interests and ambitions. From the Truman Administration's
perspective, however, Stalin had abandoned all but the faintest pretensions
of collaboration and appeared set on withdrawing from other international
commitments. Prior to Moscow's attempt to block U.N. efforts in Greece
and to undermine efforts in Germany, the Soviets had, in early 1946,
informed Washington that they would not ratify the IMF and World Bank
accords after all. In light of the destruction caused by the Second World
War in the Soviet Union, Stalin's regime would have been a prime
candidate for Bretton Woods' financial support. Any ordinary regime
would have wanted to exaggerate that destruction to further increase aid,
but the Soviet Union was no normal power. "I like Stalin," Truman wrote
in a letter to his wife from the Potsdam conference in 1945. He "is
straightforward. Knows what he wants and will compromise when he can't
get it."[45] Harry Truman and Franklin Roosevelt's grave error was their
belief that the Soviet Union had abandoned its revolutionary spirit, and
that Stalin was a man with whom you could do business. He may have
been a pragmatic politician at times, but Stalin was also a convinced
Communist, and his entire system of governance was driven by a paranoid
fear of the outside world's intentions. Fearful of exposing the Soviet

Union's socio-economic conditions as required under Bretton Woods, and likely concerned about the leverage participation would give Washington over him, Stalin increasingly withdrew from the new Americanized world order.[46]

Marshall thus had little reason for optimism before arriving in Moscow on March 9. As he confided to the French Foreign Minister Bidault after the first day of meetings, the U.S. wanted the U.N. to take the lead, but it remained "a very young child, without tradition, [and] without experience." For now, the U.S. remained committed to the Four Power solution in Germany and to a democratic Germany but strongly opposed the Soviet Union's ultimatum that reparations beyond those already agreed upon at Potsdam were "an absolute condition . . . [for] economic unity" and a zonal merger in Germany.[47] Throughout the five weeks of meetings, Marshall met little but inflexibility from Soviet Foreign Minister Molotov. On April 15, the Secretary of State met privately with Stalin. It was another fruitless conversation. It reflected two radically different views of Europe's future. The United States considered Germany's recovery vital to Europe's future, while the Soviet leader remained interested only in reparations. There was no middle ground.[48] The British were equally frustrated with Stalin's unwillingness to compromise. To Prime Minister Clement Attlee, Bevin wrote home on April 16: "a bridge could have been build and the antagonism growing so fast in the U.S.A. would have been checked. . . . Russia has made a bad mistake, as bad as when she linked up with Hitler in 1939."[49]

On April 24, a fatigued and discouraged Marshall returned to Washington after six weeks. He had been one of the most effective organizers in the history of the U.S. military but the obstinacy of high-stakes diplomacy frustrated him, and the meetings with the Soviets left him uneasy about Europe's future. The European downward spiral gave Moscow a clear advantage. Marshall recognized, perhaps for the first time, that the need for immediate American action extended well beyond Greece. Back in Washington, the Secretary of State tasked George Kennan with heading the State Department's newly designed Policy Planning Staff (PPS) and instructed him to design him a plan to fix the mess Europe was in. Perhaps exasperated by the slow-moving process at the Foreign Ministers' Conference and likely aware of Kennan's tendency to at times engage in longwinded rhetorical prose, Marshall presented him with only one demand: "avoid trivia."[50]

While Kennan went to work on a new American policy, Marshall took to the airwaves. On April 28, the Secretary delivered an extensive radio broadcast to the American people in which he relayed his recent experience in Moscow. Broadcast across the networks, the speech reiterated the warnings Marshall had made at Princeton against the danger of public complacency. He considered the situation in 1947 equally, if not more, serious than the war. Marshall explained to radio listeners that the "future of our civilization" was at stake on the European continent. The Soviet Union's demands for extended reparations drawn from the other zones and her opposition to economic unity, and, consequently, German recovery, undermined Europe's hope for a stable and democratic future. We "cannot ignore the factor of time involved," Marshall insisted. "The recovery of Europe has been far slower than had been expected. Disintegrating forces are becoming evident. The patient is sinking while the doctors deliberate." The metaphor echoed Ethridge's "ripe plum" metaphor concerning the Greek situation two months earlier. Apparently, believing that time favored their cause, the Soviets appeared willing to let the situation play out.[51] The Americans were not.

During Marshall's European travels, the State Department had publicly pushed a similar message, though much of it had centered on the Near East. Assistant Secretary of State Will Clayton explained to Congress in March that, while UNRRA "succeeded in preventing actual starvation, [it] has been far from sufficient to restore Greece to a position where she could become self-supporting. . . . Such assistance can only come from the United States in the time and in the amount required."[52] This push for a unilateral American role was not received equally well across the political spectrum. Former Vice President Henry Wallace believed that the Administration's initiatives undermined the U.N., and he prophetically warned that the strong ideological message meant that in the future, "every reactionary government and every strutting dictator will be able to hoist the skull and bones and demand that the American people rush to his aid."

Henry Wallace

Wallace's career was one of twists and turns. He could have become president had FDR not put Truman on the ticket in 1944 when many in the Democratic Party deemed Wallace too much of a leftist. In 1946, working as Truman's Secretary of Commerce, Wallace was fired by the President for his open criticism of U.S. foreign policy. In 1948, he ran an unsuccessful bid for the presidency as a third party candidate.

From the opposite political wing, the ultra-conservative Robert Taft agreed. Regarding the Truman Doctrine as a "complete departure from previous American policy," he feared that it would provide carte blanche for unprecedented global commitments.[53] Opponents in the Taft mold were limited in number, but, given the status that the Ohio Senator enjoyed in the GOP leadership, it nonetheless forced a showdown in the Party. Vandenberg, now Chairman of the Senate Foreign

Relations Committee and a likely challenger against Taft for the 1948 Republican presidential nomination, particularly wrestled with the implications of the Truman Doctrine. Unlike Taft, who fundamentally disagreed with any expanded American global role, Vandenberg wondered what the future would hold for America in the world. "If we falter in our leadership, what happens? It may endanger the peace of the world," began the Michigan senator during a Senate Foreign Relations Committee meeting. The development left him pondering, however, for,

> if the peace of the world is not the jurisdiction of the
> United Nations fundamentally, and if our obligations to the United
> Nations do not cover the peace of world, I do not know what the
> hell they do cover, and I do not know why there should be a
> United Nations nor why we should be in it.[54]

Vandenberg's close friend, Henry Cabot Lodge, Jr., disagreed. He had, by now, become a committed internationalist, certain that the world needed an activist United States. Lodge considered Taft's position archaic and a threat to both America's global role and to the GOP. In later years, Lodge would launch a campaign to overthrow Taft's power and move the GOP firmly toward Truman's position on foreign policy.

For now and in response to Vandenberg's query, Lodge insisted that globally, Americans were "deeply involved from a material, spiritual, and an ideological standpoint." "Now we have a choice . . . whether we are going to repudiate the president and throw the flag on the ground and stamp on it or whether we are not," he said at the Foreign Relations Committee, and "it seems to me those are the horns of the dilemma we are on, and to me it is not a hard decision to make." Lodge was going to stand with the president, Democrat or not. Influential Republican foreign policy expert, John Foster Dulles, agreed. He "called out again and again for more intellectual and moral vigor in the world leadership which history has thrust upon the U.S." Even before the Truman Administration came around to this view, Dulles prophetically announced that once

> the full implications of the Soviet system come to be better
> understood by the American people . . . it will revive in them the
> spirit which led their forebears to pledge their lives, their fortunes,
> and their sacred honor to secure their personal freedoms.

Over Taft's opposition, the Republican-controlled House of Representatives voted 287–107 in favor of Truman's aid package to Greece and Turkey. The Senate followed suit, voting 63–23.[55]

Crisis in the Grand Old Party

Between the 1932 elections and the end of the Second World War, the Republican Party found itself in a political wilderness. For well over a decade, the party leadership proved unable to effectively challenge Franklin Roosevelt's stranglehold on the White House or to stem the progressive direction in which the country was heading under FDR's New Deal. On foreign policy, the GOP was further isolated by its unwillingness to support a more interventionist role in response to the growing threat of fascism. The shift from FDR to the less experienced Harry Truman provided the Republican Party an opening, and during the 1946 midterm elections, the pendulum swung the GOP's way. The party picked up 55 seats in the House of Representatives and 12 in the Senate to gain control of Congress. Fairly or unfairly, the Democratic establishment blamed President Truman—whom they believed had not earned the right to be president—for the defeat. There were even calls from prominent Democrats for Truman to appoint a Republican Secretary of State, resign, and thus, under the Presidential Succession Act then still in existence, hand the White House to the GOP.

As weak as Truman appeared to be in 1946, the Republican victory was a mirage. Shortly after the November election, Massachusetts Senator Henry Cabot Lodge, Jr., a rising GOP star who had just returned from Second World War duty to reclaim a Senate seat, warned the party of the need to modernize. Lodge did not consider the election a vote for the Republicans as much as one against the Democrats. He wanted the Party to recognize that the 1930s and the first half of the 1940s had fundamentally changed the country. The U.S., he insisted, had become a progressive nation at home and in the world. The idea of an enlarged Federal government with extensive responsibilities should no longer be anathema.

The traditional conservative leadership, which coalesced around Ohio Senator Robert A. Taft, did not heed Lodge's warning. Convinced that their non-internationalist policies still held sway, they criticized Truman's foreign policies, including the Truman Doctrine, the Marshall Plan, and later the creation of NATO. They also helped gut the President's domestic programs on civil rights, health care, and economic equality. As they did, these conservative Senate and House members failed to recognize how dramatically the ground was shifting underneath the establishment. As the Cold War captivated American society, the old guard lost momentum. During the 1948 presidential campaign, they at first presented a moderate and progressive party platform, which Lodge had had a major hand in authoring. When President Truman called Congress in for an emergency session and asked the GOP to make good on its own publicized agenda, the leadership recoiled. Truman branded them as hypocrites. In 1948, against all odds, the public overwhelmingly stood with President Truman against Republican Thomas Dewey, electing him for another term as president. Nothing had exposed the lack of leadership and the extent to which the Republican Party was out of touch with the direction of the United States than its opposition to the Marshall Plan and the growing American global role in the postwar world. In early January 1949, the *New York Times* captured the widely shared view among Republicans: "Wanted by the GOP: A Program and a Leader." By 1952, Henry Cabot Lodge found that leader in the form of war hero Dwight Eisenhower. Ike's landslide victory on his way first to the presidential nomination and then in the general election purged the party of its old conservative ideals. The result was a far more progressive and more centrist GOP as well as the dismantlement of opposition to internationalism.

Marshall later rejected the view that the Truman Doctrine and the eventual Marshall Plan were two halves of the same walnut, but there is no doubt that the two were closely connected. Between March and May, the Doctrine's principled ideas converged with the need for intricate policy planning for Europe's future. On May 23, Kennan's PPS completed its proposal for a solution to the European crisis. Echoing his opposition to what he considered the Truman Doctrine's excessive moralism, Kennan proposed an agenda that extended U.S. aid to Europe without antagonizing Moscow unnecessarily. The report concluded that, "the present crisis results in large part from the disruptive effect of the war on the economic, political, and social structure of Europe." In the author's view,

> further communist successes would create serious danger to American security . . . [nonetheless] the American effort in aid to Europe should be directed not to the combatting of communism as such but to the restoration of the economic health and vigor of European society. It should aim . . . [at] the economic maladjustment which makes European society vulnerable to exploitation by any and all totalitarian movements and which Russian communism is now exploiting.[56]

While Kennan attempted to define a new European policy, Clayton toured the continent. What he experienced shocked him much in the same way it had previous American observers. Clayton was already committed to the U.S.-designed model for the world, including free trade and support for stable currencies. Upon his return, however, he called for an even more "bold, far-reaching, generous and practical vision for reviving Europe . . . along free-market lines."[57] On May 27, he explained to Acheson that the U.S. had "grossly underestimated the destruction" of European societies. In his view, the situation was "steadily deteriorating. . . . Millions of people in the cities are slowly starving" across the continent. Agricultural production was running far below prewar levels, and standard of living had dropped alarmingly. "If it should be lowered [further], there will be a revolution," Clayton warned. As in the build-up to the Truman Doctrine, Clayton believed that "if the American people are taken in to the complete confidence of the administration and told all the facts and only if a sound and workable plan is presented," they would support the endeavor. He called for a three-year grant of $6–7 billion a year, "based on a European plan, which the principal European nations . . . should work out. Such a plan should be based on a European economic federation on the order of the Belgium-Netherlands-Luxemburg Customs Union" from 1944, where services, goods, and money flowed freely between the members. In spite of his insistence that this be a European-inspired organization, Clayton was adamant that "we must avoid getting into another UNRRA. *The United States must run this show*." Nobody else was capable.

Clayton's urgency set the tone for George Marshall's speech at Harvard ten days later. Having presented a picture of the grave situation facing the European continent, the Secretary of State told his audience that it

> is logical that the United States should do whatever it is able to do to assist in the return of normal economic health in the world, without which there can be no political stability and no assured peace. Our policy is directed not against any country or doctrine but against hunger, poverty, desperation and chaos. Its purpose should be the revival of a working economy in the world so as to permit the emergence of political and social conditions in which free institutions can exist.

The United States stood ready to assist, but only if Europe united and took the initiative. According to Marshall, "The initiative, I think, must come from Europe. The role of this country should consist of friendly aid in the drafting of a European program and of later support of such a program."[58]

Given the reverence the speech now enjoys, the lack of fanfare surrounding it is surprising. Nothing was done to promote it as a major policy address. According to *Harvard Magazine*, the *New York Herald Tribune's* Stephen White was the only out-of-town reporter to cover the speech, and he came to see the physicist J. Robert Oppenheimer, who also received an honorary degree that day. Few people in the audience grasped the significance of Marshall's 1,442-word talk. Nothing about its tone and style immediately turned heads. The first two paragraphs of the Associated Press' story of the Harvard commencement, for example, recounted President Conant's announcement of a new funding drive.

Only the third paragraph reported that, "General George C. Marshall also spoke, among others."[59] To most, it appeared simply to be an objectively delivered statement of one continent's needs, and one nation's obligation to help. In reality, it was an invitation to the Europeans to act, and it was left to the Europeans to work out how to respond to this offer.

CHAPTER 3

Creating the European Recovery Program, 1947–1948

If Marshall's speech at first generated a rather subdued response in the United States, its impact across the Atlantic was immediate. Dean Acheson provided advance notice of the speech's significance to British diplomats in Washington, but Foreign Secretary Ernest Bevin first learned of Marshall's address from Leonard Miall's BBC broadcast "American Commentary" on the evening of June 5. On the show, Miall described the Harvard address as a "totally new continental approach to the problem of Europe's economic crisis, an approach which for some, recalls the grandeur of the original concept of Lend-Lease." Bevin understood instantly that Marshall had not offered aid, but rather implied circumstances under which the Europeans might request aid. "It was a looped forward pass," one of the key Marshall Plan implementers later recalled, which "Bevin picked out of the air."[1] The Foreign Secretary believed that the American offer might provide Britain a path forward in which it could scale back its international obligations and help pay for the Labour government's ambitious domestic welfare state.

Ernest Bevin was a veteran politician of Britain's center-left with deep interwar trade-unionist roots. In his childhood he witnessed the poverty and despair of Bristol's working class. It was an experience that instilled in him a determination to promote social improvements for those who had little. As Minister of Labour in

Marshall's Speech

When Bevin heard the BBC speak of Marshall's speech he at first thought it was being broadcast live. Surprisingly enough, the British Embassy in Washington had not deemed the speech important enough to deliver over the wire but had instead sent it by diplomatic pouch.

Churchill's wartime coalition government, Bevin was granted considerable leverage by emergency laws to increase production and he conscripted close to 50,000 men to work in Britain's coal mines to ensure energy supplies during the war. Even as he did, Bevin helped secure wage increases and improved conditions for the working class. Upon becoming Prime Minister in the summer of 1945, Clement Attlee chose Bevin as Britain's chief diplomat. It was, in some respects, a strange choice. As Dean Acheson later recalled, Bevin was hardly diplomatic. He had a "quick temper" that could "flash without warning and seemingly by accident." But as Foreign Secretary he worked hard and he brought with him into office a passionate dislike for totalitarianism in all its forms. Bevin was not an intuitive negotiator or politician in the mold of Churchill or James Byrnes and he did not have the lawyer's skills of an Acheson but he still proved highly effective. His prescience on the Marshall Plan is a sign of that. When Sir William Strang, the Permanent Under Secretary of State for Foreign Affairs suggested that perhaps the British Embassy in Washington should inquire with Marshall's office as to what the General's speech meant, Bevin's reply was crisp and insightful: "we know what he said. If you ask questions, you'll get answers you don't want. Our problem is what we do, not what he meant."[2] Bevin understood that the ball was in the Europeans' court. They had to take the initiative. On June 17, he met his French counterpart, Georges Bidault, in Paris to discuss how to proceed. The only stipulation affixed to Marshall's offer was that Europe would have to devise a collective request for reconstruction requirements. As a result, after initial Anglo-French consultations, Bevin and Bidault extended invitations to nations from both sides of the Iron Curtain to attend further talks in Paris over the coming weeks.

The issue of Communist participation in the Marshall Plan had come up early in American considerations. When Kennan's Policy Planning Staff suggested that the Soviet Union be included in the aid proposal, Marshall initially bristled. He shared Secretary of Defense James Forrestal's concern that there was no chance of Russia *not* joining the Marshall Plan. There were fears that if the Soviets participated, they might try to undermine the program's structures or aim to attain the lion's share of the aid package. Marshall's two key Soviet advisors, George Kennan and Charles Bohlen, knew better. They recognized that the conditions for participation largely mirrored those which had caused Moscow to reject the Bretton Woods system 18 months earlier. There was little reason to believe anything had changed. In fact, if the Kremlin's attitude had changed, Americans should play it straight Kennan believed. As he later recalled in his memoirs, if Moscow responded favorably to the aid program, "we would test their good faith by insisting that they contribute constructively to the program as well as profiting from it. If they were unwilling to do this, we would simply let them exclude themselves." As for the Eastern European Communist countries, Will Clayton observed that, even before Marshall's speech, their participation too was conditioned upon their willingness to abandon the "near exclusive Soviet orientation of their economies."[3]

The unanticipated offer of aid caused anxiety among European Communists in Eastern and Western Europe. A year earlier, they had been riding high, lifted by the popularity of the Western Communist parties and the apparent inability of the non-Communist governments to reignite their economies. By mid-1947, however, they were experiencing growing apprehensions. The Truman Doctrine in March had been followed by the ouster of French and Italian Communists from their respective coalition governments in May. Combined with Marshall's offer of assistance to Europe and his apparent determination to revive the German economy, the balance of influence appeared to be shifting away from Moscow.

Stalin had often proven a master of *realpolitik,* but he was never able to divorce himself entirely from the powerful weight of Communist ideology. Constrained by doctrine, Soviet economists informed the Kremlin that Marshall's offer was "supposed to serve as a weapon for mitigating the imminent economic crisis" sure to strike the United States in the coming years.[4] Stalin appears to have accepted this logic. Why else would the Americans so open up their coffers to the outside world? Working from this theory, Stalin dispatched Foreign Minister Vyacheslav Molotov and a large entourage of advisors to the Paris talks with the other European nations. From London, *The Times* optimistically concluded that the "whole atmosphere of international debate had changed to a healthier and hopefully more helpful mood."[5] This proved to be a miscalculation. While Stalin likely would have accepted aid from the Americans, he would do so only on his own terms. When Molotov arrived in Paris on June 27, it soon became apparent that Moscow was being offered nothing of the sort. Bevin and Bidault explained that they agreed to American demands that all of Europe, including Germany, be treated as a single economic unit, and that each recipient nation would have to disclose its economic conditions to Washington and open its market to American trade. They dismissed out of hand Molotov's counter-offer that individual nations should make their own assessments of economic needs and that these analyses should determine the amount of total credit required under Marshall's program. From Washington, the Soviet Ambassador Nikolai Novikov had already warned Molotov that "a careful analysis of the Marshall Plan shows that ultimately it comes down to forming a West European bloc as a tool of U.S. policy." In Novikov's judgement, American rhetoric of benevolence was simply "demagogic propaganda serving as a smokescreen." Molotov's response to his French and British colleagues reflected this mindset. He considered the American conditions for assistance nothing shy of "a bid to interfere in the internal affairs of European countries" and an attempt to make their economies "dependent on U.S. interests."[6]

The Kremlin's distress was understandable. The offer was, in effect, an ultimatum to the Soviet Union: participate in the American-designed world order on an equal basis with the other European powers, or face the responsibility of formally dividing the continent into an east and west. Critics of U.S. foreign policy, including Russian historians, have long maintained that Washington had coordinated everything in advance, and that Marshall's offer was designed to be rejected by Moscow. That, however, is being too clever by half. First, there was no plan when Marshall gave his speech. Even the Americans did not yet know how it would play out. For reasons of secrecy so few people had been involved in the writing of the speech that no formal proposal for the European Recovery Program's cost, duration, or organization even existed. Second, Marshall's proposal was not a cunning ploy. It followed a vision for the recovery of a democratic Europe that was entirely in line with the U.S. Second World War expectations for extended influence and liberalized economic and political conditions. In light of that, Moscow should hardly have been surprised by Washington's determination, but to Stalin it appeared as a sinister scheme aimed at undermining his own designs on Europe.[7] Moscow's dilemma was that acceptance of the American offer would shatter the Communist sphere of influence and bring Eastern Europe into the "one world" order Americans sought. This would wreck both the buffer Stalin deemed necessary for reasons of national security and the ideological ambitions to extend Communist influence on the continent. Rejecting the offer, on the other hand, would ensure Soviet dominance in Eastern Europe, but place the sole responsibility of organizing, protecting, and supporting that region upon Moscow. It was an unpalatable situation for the Soviet dictator. Stalin loathed weakness and likely also feared conceding to the world that, after the Soviet Union's enormous wartime sacrifice in blood and treasure, his nation needed help. The Soviet leadership viewed global politics as a zero-sum game. If the U.S. gained prestige, the Soviets would have to lose prestige. Participation in a European order made and organized in the U.S.A., Stalin concluded, would put the Soviet Union's wartime and postwar gains at risk. If he had been willing to surrender the ideological vision of Communist influence in Europe and had been able to shed the insecurity that naturally marred his nation after two German attacks in a generation, the Cold War could have ended here. A combination of ideology, interest, and Stalin's personality prevented such an outcome.

In early July, the Soviet delegation walked out of the Paris conference. Stalin had chosen his political and ideological agenda over the welfare of his people. Entirely in line with Kennan's thinking, the reporter Bernard Nover concluded that with this decision the Soviets "transformed into a grim reality what many have hitherto regarded as merely a temporary phase of the postwar situation in Europe, namely, the division of Europe into opposing blocs."[8] As Charles Maier argues, this was, in some respects, a logical result of the previous year's developments. Although neither the Soviets nor the Americans desired a divided Europe, by the summer of 1947, both powers had come to see such an outcome as the lesser evil. From the Americans' perspective, Communist actions in Greece, Clay's observations from Germany, and Marshall's April visit to Moscow proved that the Soviets were simply waiting for Western Europe's socio-economic collapse. European recovery was apparently not in Stalin's interest. In contrast, from the Soviet standpoint, the changing fortunes of Western Communist parties and the fear of a unified and Westernized Germany implied that Moscow's influence would likely be limited to the east. From Stalin's perspective, the risk of participation must have outweighed the potential gains from partaking in the ERP. In the Soviet Union's absence, the British and the French dispatched invitations to 22 nations, including all the nations of Eastern Europe, to join them in Paris for further talks to prepare a united European response to Marshall's offer.

At first, Stalin allowed Eastern European delegations to participate with the instruction to effectively undermine the ERP sessions and hopefully break up the conference. Stalin and Molotov soon had a change of heart, however, and on July 7, the Kremlin ordered all Eastern European governments to renege on their involvement in the talks. What followed was a telling display of the fate that awaited Eastern Europe for the next several decades and would surely have awaited Western Europe had fortune favored Moscow and the Communists on a continental-wide scale after the war. By the summer of 1947, the Soviet Union dominated and dictated policy in nearly all the Eastern European nations. The leadership in these countries understood the need to follow the Kremlin's line. In Czechoslovakia and Poland, however, the situation was different. Here local Communists shared power with other parties and this presence of coalition governments gave Prague and Warsaw the impression that they were free to pursue a more independent "path to socialism." When the Czechoslovakian Communist Prime Minister Klement Gottwald informed Stalin that his coalition government intended to pursue the American aid offer, Stalin "ordered them to Moscow at once." That a delegation that included Prime Minister Gottwald, Foreign Minister Jan Masaryk, and

Minister of Justice Prokop Drtina could so easily be summoned to the court of a foreign state only underlines the Kremlin's power. So did the outcome of the meetings. The "extraordinary conversations" as historian Robert Gellately appropriately refers to them, made clear to Prague the limits of its political maneuverability. Although the impact on Czechoslovakia's standard of living would be powerfully affected by abstaining from the Marshall Plan—some 60 percent of its trade was with the Western world—Stalin was unimpressed. The aim of the Marshall Plan, he lectured the delegation, was "to create a Western bloc and isolate the Soviet Union." Participation by any nation would be considered an act "against the Soviet Union."[9]

Revisionists often imply that Stalin "requested" that the Prague government withdraw from participation and see the Kremlin's decision shortly after to increase trade between the Soviet Union and Czechoslovakia as quite magnanimous.[10] It was, of course, not a request; Stalin did not make requests. He issued orders. "I went to Moscow as the Foreign Minister of an independent sovereign state. I returned as a lackey of the Soviet Government," Foreign Minister Jan Masaryk lamented. The limits of a national Czechoslovakian socialism had been laid entirely bare. "They might have thought they were linked to Soviet Communism by comradeship and shared ideas, but after their appearance as supplicants in Stalin's court, they could hardly doubt that theirs was a master-slave relationship," Gellately succinctly concludes.[11] While the evidence is more limited, the Poles appear to have gotten much the same message. After having first announced Poland's intention to explore the aid proposal, the Polish President informed Stanton Griffis, the U.S. Ambassador to Warsaw that the Poles would not pursue its interest any further. They had been "overruled by a higher authority," he explained. That authority undoubtedly resided in the Kremlin.[12]

Carolyn Eisenberg, Michael Cox, Caroline Kennedy-Pipe, and other revisionist historians, view Stalin's decision as entirely natural. It was the ERP and Washington's actions, they conclude, that precipitated the hardening of the Iron Curtain dividing Europe. In Eisenberg's view, Moscow was largely innocent. All of "the formal steps that led to the partition of Germany [and thus of Europe] were initiated by the United States and Britain in violation of the quadripartite framework established at Yalta and Potsdam," she deduces. From her perspective, American aggression caused the Cold War. If the Cold War began in June of 1947, Eisenberg might have a point. However, as Maier points out, the earlier "suppression of freedom in the East" paired with Moscow's willingness to let Western Europe disintegrate, made the Marshall Plan "a natural reaction" from Washington.[13] Eisenberg's point is only further undermined by the fact that the Soviets were the ones who defaulted on the Yalta-promise of a free Eastern Europe.

From Moscow, the U.S. Ambassador Walter Bedell Smith explained the developments to Marshall like this:

> The lines are drawn. Our response is awaited. I do not need to point out to the Dept. the repercussions of a failure to meet the Soviet challenge in terms of control of Europe, but of the impact which such a failure would have in the Middle and Far East and throughout the colonial world.

The Soviets seemed to believe that if they prevented the West from accessing the breadbasket of Central and Eastern Europe, the U.S. would never be able to fund a sustainable aid package. Smith considered Moscow's step "nothing less than a declaration of war . . . on the immediate issue of the control of Europe."[14]

★ ★ ★

The Soviet rejection of Marshall's proposal opened the door for the creation of a Western bloc. It also intensified the American sense of an ideological mission. "The United States is confronted with a condition in the world which is at direct variance with the assumptions upon which, during and directly after the war, major United States policies were predicated," Charles Bohlen explained in a meeting with high-ranking civilian and military officials on August 30. He continued, saying,

> Instead of unity among the great powers on the major issues of world reconstruction—both political and economic—after the war, there is complete disunity between the Soviet Union and the satellites on one side and the rest of the world on the other. There are, in short, two worlds instead of one.[15]

In that final sentence, Bohlen captured the frustration of the death of the global Rooseveltian vision.

The ambitious postwar project to alleviate Europe would now center on the Western half alone.

The pace at which the European nations responded to this new reality and the American offer of aid that came with it was as remarkable as the audacity of their request. On July 12, Western European representatives—the number of which would eventually grow to 16—convened to create

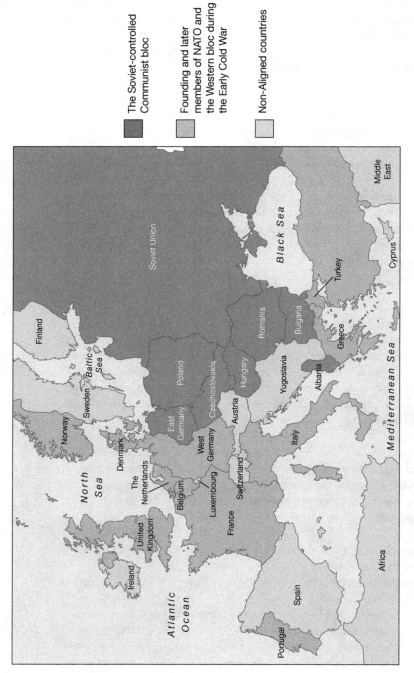

Figure 3.1 Europe in the Early Cold War era

Between 1947 and 1948, the division of Europe along the lines of the Iron Curtain was completed. With the battle lines drawn, the United States began to support the non-Communist world. Marshall Aid would eventually flow to all Washington's Western allies as well as several neutral powers including Sweden, Ireland, Switzerland, and Austria.

the Committee of European Economic Corporation (CEEC) and to prepare a collective aid request to Washington. This was no easy process. While these nations yearned for aid, each had its own reason to worry about what was being offered. Countries with a tradition of neutrality feared being dragged into a war between ideological blocs on the continent; some were concerned that Washington sought to influence their economic and monetary policies too heavily, and others feared the political consequences of collaboration. All European recipients worried about a loss of national sovereignty. Always the odd man out in European continental affairs, Great Britain hoped that in spite of American demands for a unified response, Bevin could carve out an English position as a bridgehead between Washington and the continent or perhaps as an aid recipient apart from a continental-wide solution. Britain's imperial past inflated London's sense of self-importance. Sir Henry Tizard, the chair of the British Defence Research Policy Committee, summed up the reality that Clement Attlee's government only reluctantly came to accept: "[W]e persist in regarding ourselves a Great Power capable of everything and only temporarily handicapped by economic difficulties. We are not a Great Power and never will be again."[16] Britain may still have been the strongest power in Europe, but none of the ERP participants were in a position to make any substantive demands to Washington. For now, they had to shelve their concerns about undue American influence. Confronted with deteriorating conditions, it was clear that the Europeans did not have the luxury of principles.

The situation on the ground made that fact clear. The combination of the harsh winter and the dry summer forced Europeans to increase imports of vital foodstuffs. This forced prices up and further drained their increasingly slim dollar and gold reserves. Several governments introduced tough austerity measures reducing rations and capping all but essential imports. Joseph Alsop described the Parisian mood to the American public:

> Here . . . even the horse meat butcher . . . has no customers
> because his prices are too high . . . at the other end of the scale,
> a minister hurriedly breaks an appointment to hasten to an
> emergency committee so save the franc. These signs unhappily
> disclose the inner reality. Because of insecurity and despair the
> people of France are being driven to the political extremes which
> are always the resort of men losing hope.

The French Communists understood this well. Already expelled from the government, they encouraged strikes and protests. Conditions in Italy resembled the situation in France. Nonetheless, Alsop insisted that the "only danger in Italy and France is inaction in the face of need."[17]

As the Marshall Plan appeared to go ahead, the Soviets stepped up their own pressure on both the West and their satellites. At the U.N. General Assembly, the Soviet Deputy Foreign Minister Andrei Vyshinsky denounced the Truman Doctrine and the Marshall Plan as glaring violations of the U.N.'s principles and as

> an attempt to split Europe into two camps and, with the help of the United Kingdom and France, to complete the formation of a bloc of several European countries hostile to the interests of the democratic countries of Eastern Europe and most particularly to the interests of the Soviet Union.

Shortly after several Western Communist Parties showed their true colors when they joined a Soviet organized meeting in Poland. Here, Stalin's "cultural boss," Andrei Zhdanov, denounced the U.S. for seeking to enslave Europe and blamed American and British imperialism for dividing the continent. He then announced the formation of the Cominform, an initiative that effectively dispelled any lingering myths that an alternative to a Kremlin-directed path to Communism existed in Europe.[18] Across Eastern Europe, the few remaining non-Communist political factions soon vanished. In Poland, the Social Democrats were forced to merge with the Polish Communist Party. Similar developments followed in Hungary and elsewhere as the Soviets cemented their control. In Bulgaria, the Soviets dissolved the non-Communist parties and on September 23, they hanged the only real political challenger, Nikola Petkov.[19]

The Western Communist parties were not in a strong enough position to negotiate with Zhdanov, and there is insufficient evidence in the Cominform documents to indicate that they aspired to do so. Even though Zhdanov ridiculed the French and the Italian Communists for their failure to seize power despite their strong election showings in 1945 and 1946, both now declared themselves ready to push for influence through covert means. The French Communist delegate Jacques Duclos declared that his party was "developing forms of struggle that are not parliamentary." He aimed to "mobilize the people for the fight against American imperialism." The Italians promised waves of "demonstrations, land seizures, economic and political strikes . . . to overthrow the De Gasperi government." These comments make clear that the Cominform was not simply intended to be a Soviet attempt to display unity among the Communist parties. It was, in effect, a successor to Lenin's old Comintern, the intelligence organization created in the early years of the Soviet era to help strengthen Communist parties and to create favorable conditions for revolutions abroad.[20]

The Cominform never proved particularly effective. Its key attribute was the public manner in which it forced the other Communists to fall in line with Moscow's centralized directives.[21] Walter Lippmann saw the organization and the subsequent "decision to crush all opposition in their own orbit" as a sign that the Soviets knew they had lost the fight for Europe. As a result, he believed, the U.S. policy should "push toward a settlement which permits the recovery of Europe and the world." He did not believe that the French Communists were influential enough to challenge for power and events soon proved him right. As the French Communists followed the Cominform line of opposition to the Marshall Plan, they became increasingly isolated. This, combined with Robert Schuman replacing Paul Ramadier as head of the government in Paris and the promises of arriving American aid, undermined Maurice Thorez's PCF permanently.[22] While they would remain a nuisance for the rest of the decade, the French Communists never again threatened a political takeover. In Italy, the PCI pursued similar methods, but unlike in France, many still believed that the Italian Communists posed a threat at the ballot box in the upcoming spring elections. Walter Lippmann was not among them, though. He saw the strikes and protests across Europe as nothing more than "a desperate attempt to disorganize and discredit legitimate representative governments before the European recovery program can begin to work."[23]

In response to the situation in Western Europe, and conscious of the prolonged negotiations with Congress and the Europeans over the nature of the ERP, the Truman Administration pushed through over $500 million in interim aid in November. Over the coming six months, this stop-gap measure provided the first comprehensive aid deliveries of food and fuel to France, Italy, and Austria. The Western zones of Germany, too, continued to receive American assistance through the so-called Government and Relief in Occupied Areas program. The Export-Import Bank played a key role, while more creative measures, such as the assumption of vast parts of Britain's financial responsibilities in Germany, followed as well. Unlike the later Marshall Plan, however, this was nothing more than a patchwork effort.[24]

These interim measures were necessary because finalizing the Marshall Plan's details and administrative structures proved more complex than many of the instigators originally presumed. Its scope and operational demands were unlike anything that had ever been undertaken. There was a need for exhaustive fact-finding and exploration of arguments concerning the cost of the program, European wants, how much America could afford to spend, and how it should be spent. The State Department devised a series of demands for acceptance of a European proposal: recipients of Marshall Aid would have to make commitments to production targets, seek reductions of trade barriers, pursue monetary stability, and establish common objectives and regional organization to pursue these objectives. All of this required conversations, negotiations, and compromises.

Even after Bevin and Bidault's positive response and the creation of the CEEC, plenty of U.S. domestic political concerns still remained. Stalin had solved the first of these when he unilaterally withdrew the Communist nations from the program but further uncertainty arose when, following their first consultations in June and July 1947, the Europeans suggested that they might need some $29 billion—later scaled down to $22 billion—over four years to boost production, generate financial stability, advance economic cooperation, and reduce the dollar gap. The amount, some worried, was likely in excess of what Congress would approve. Other early American concerns involved which kind of conditions could or should be placed upon participating nations and even who would supervise the program on the American end.

To help answer these questions, Truman, during bipartisan meetings with Congressional leaders, supported the creation of a series of independent committees to investigate Europe's needs, the available U.S. resources that could be committed, and the effect the aid program would have on domestic production, prices, inflation, taxes, and other issues. Named after their committee heads—Secretary of Commerce Averell Harriman, Secretary of the Interior Julius A. Krug, and Chairman of the Council of Economic Advisers Edwin G. Nourse—these committees drew on the expertise of government officials and a plethora of consultants from private industry, labor, and agriculture. The House of Representatives also created its own Committee on Foreign Aid, led by Republican Massachusetts Congressman Christian A. Herter. In spite of this careful preparation, the Truman Administration faced the dual task of creating and selling the program to the public and to a Republican-controlled Congress with little respect for the President. A decade earlier, President Franklin Roosevelt had been the chief spokesman for the New Deal and the problems he was trying to fix had been there for all Americans to see. The American people lived the Depression and they rallied to FDR. This time there was no FDR and, even if Truman had wanted to replicate the performance, he possessed none of the communication skills displayed by FDR during his Fireside Chats. Americans were also more removed from the European 1947 crisis. Not everybody believed that solving Europe's woes was their cross to bear. ERP planners were conscious of this. The memory of opposition to ventures overseas that had so marred the interwar period lingered among planners from the beginning.

As a result, State Department officials actively promoted the plan during public appearances. Marshall delivered a series of radio addresses and speeches; he later recalled that he "traveled so widely it almost seemed as though I were running for office."[25] The ERP also received plenty of public support from private citizens and citizens' groups. The most influential of these was the Committee for the Marshall Plan (CMP), which counted among its members numerous former government officials as well as influential members of the business and labor communities. The CMP published advertisements in major newspapers. These included extensive messages about the crucial nature of the Marshall Plan, as well as long lists of prominent supporters and a call for "a million signatures" from citizens who shared the Committee's belief "in common ideals and human dignity." Among the listed supporters was Dean Acheson, who had left the government earlier in the summer to return to private law practice, New York Governor and former head of UNRRA Herbert Lehman, Minneapolis Mayor Hubert Humphrey, Reinhold Niebuhr, former Secretary of War Robert Patterson, Herbert Feis, and numerous religious leaders, university presidents, academics, and lawyers. In a speech at Bard College, Lehman touted democracy as the answer to European and even global international problems. For those who criticized the American role as self-serving, he had nothing but scorn. It "seems monstrous to me," he observed,

> that anyone should attribute sinister motives to the United States in its efforts to bring economic assistance to war-ravaged countries of Europe. . . . No great country . . . has ever been less imperialistic in its outlook or in its purposes, or more deeply consecrated to the cause of world peace.[26]

Lehman was undoubtedly being overly kind to America's historical record but it was a message that resonated with the public. Acheson echoed similar sentiments during an intense North American speaking tour in 1947. Given the nature of his activities, it was no wonder that he later referred to his departure from official duties as having resulted in only a "semiprivate" life.[27] The CMP also published leaflets and brochures that found their way into the hands of Congressmen, newspaper editors, and citizens. This included extended excerpts from "A Challenge to Americans," a *Foreign Affairs* article by the highly respected former Secretary of War Henry Stimson published in the autumn of 1947. In it, Stimson charged that only if Americans were willing to "desert every principle by which" they lived, could they reject Marshall's plan. Failure to do so, he believed, would be "the most tragic mistake in our history."[28]

Not everyone shared this view. After taking control of Congress in the 1946 midterm elections, the Republican legislative agenda had centered on cutting spending and balancing the budget. Following a hardline approach, they rejected Truman's attempts to cement and expand New Deal-style programs at home and sought to curb military costs and American commitments overseas. Many, including Robert Taft, dismissed the Marshall Plan as a tax relief to Europeans and a taxation of Americans. Harold Knutson (R-MN) had only contempt for the visions of "one-worlders, do-gooders, and the internationalists" who favored initiatives like the Marshall Plan. Over the course of the autumn of 1947 and the spring of 1948, others such as Homer Capehart (R-IN) denounced the ERP as "state socialism" while Frederick Smith (R-OH) called it "outright communism." Dismissive of the entire ERP venture, Senator Alexander Wiley (R-WI) insisted pithily that the U.S. was "through being 'Uncle Sap.'"[29]

Republicans had political motivations as well. President Truman was weak. Between 1946 and 1947, his approval ratings, once in the high 80s, slipped into the low 40s and 30s. The GOP leadership expected to reclaim the White House the following year and saw no reason to grant Truman political victories. Conservatives' animosity toward the President only intensified when he vetoed a tax cut in the summer of 1947. Nobody experienced this deeper than Taft. As the most powerful Republican in the Senate and one of the early frontrunners for the 1948 GOP presidential nomination, Taft strongly disapproved of the White House's Cold War commitments. In hindsight, it is easy to dismiss Taft and his fellow anti-internationalists as shortsighted and out of the touch with global affairs, and the role that only the United States could play on behalf of the western democracies. But Taft was an honorable man. He believed in tradition and thought Truman's expansive policies violated the entire spirit of America. His opposition to the Truman Doctrine in March of 1947 had not stemmed from a desire to see Communism succeed in Greece, but from the fair-minded belief that granting the President a blank check to intervene whenever democracy appeared to be under threat would put America on a slippery slope. His opposition to the Marshall Plan evolved along the same lines. As he insisted during the later debates over the ERP, if he were ever to vote for a bill approving the aid program it would only "be with the understanding that there is no . . . obligation, that there is no contract with recipient countries, that they are not our partners."[30]

The combination of the difficulties ironing out the details of the ERP, the propaganda effort on behalf of the program, and the aggressive rhetoric conservative opponents directed at the administration and the Marshall Plan lead many scholars to accept without inquiry the idea that Truman faced stern opposition to the program. In reality, the Marshall Plan was never in danger of not making its way through Congress. Just like the Truman Doctrine before it, and the later Senate ratification of NATO membership, it had overwhelmingly popular support, as was evident by the wide margins with which all three major initiatives eventually sailed through the Congress.

The loud and aggressive accusations that conservatives leveled at the ERP made for good political theater, but they disguised the political and intellectual transformation which the Republican Party was undergoing. The old guard and the Party leadership was, as the Alsop brothers so eloquently summed it up, "endowed with matchless ignorance of foreign affairs."[31] There was a revolution underway inside the party that the leadership appeared to be largely ignorant of. The extent of this internal crisis on both domestic and foreign policy issues would only become clear in the 1948 presidential elections, but chinks were already widespread in the conservative armor in 1947. The best example of this was the number of moderate Republicans who crossed the aisle to support President Truman and the Marshall Plan. Chief among them was, once again, Henry Cabot Lodge, Jr.

Along with fellow Republican Arthur Vandenberg and Democratic Senators such as Georgia's Walter George and Texas' Tom Connally, Lodge launched a ferocious campaign on behalf of the ERP. In speeches, town hall meetings, in articles, and on the Senate floor, he not only promoted the program, but also castigated his fellow Republicans for their shortsightedness. As early as 1946, before even the Truman Administration began promoting forceful Cold War initiatives, Lodge stated in a speech to the Foreign Policy Association in Minnesota that:

> The ideal of a provincial nation of simple, humble people, far from the beaten track . . . has given way to the realization that we have become the world's greatest power. . . . The United Nations Organization is our best hope . . . [it needs] the best that is in us of intelligence, forbearance, farsightedness, and faith . . . so that its muscles will grow strong by experience. . . . Common humanity demands that we help. The question of economic loans should be decided on a broad and farsighted basis. . . . Such loans, even though they may appear to some to be unusually liberal, can in the end be helpful not only to the country that receives them but to the U.S. as well.[32]

This kind of ideological commitment to America's global role followed him through his 1946 Senate election victory and was, as demonstrated in Chapter 2, evident in his position on the Truman Doctrine as well. As a public figure, Lodge echoed the Administration's consistent claim that a Western world united around principles would be beneficial for peace, trade, and international stability. However, he made no secret of the fact that he considered the Cold War an ideological fight or that the Marshall Plan was at the heart of it. As a Second World War veteran, he had spent time in Europe during the final six months of 1945. He was deeply moved by the destruction he witnessed. "Europe's chronic ills—overpopulation, maldistribution of goods and wealth, the failure . . . of leadership," Lodge deduced, "are the facts that create communists." "Above all," he maintained, in this

> war of ideas diplomatic relations have in most respects become public relations—indeed they are the armor in which strategy and economics are clothed. Let us hold aloft a torch which will not only rival but easily surpass Communism as a brightly shining attraction to all the weary people in Europe, old and young, who are looking for a way out of their misery.

While Lodge was adamant that the European Recovery Program could be the cure, he asserted that if the U.S. did not back it up with a comprehensive political and potentially military commitment to the strengthening of Europe, they would lose the Cold War.[33]

★ ★ ★

Marshall shared Lodge's concerns. In December, he returned from yet another dejecting Foreign Minister Conference, this time in London. Once again, the Soviets' continued demands for reparations and apparent disregard for Germany's future clashed with the West's vision for Europe. Molotov's unwillingness to entertain any idea of continent-wide recovery opened the door for the creation of the Tri-zone, the unification of the French zone with the British-American Bi-zone created the year before in Germany. *Life* summed up the reality as it now stood: "Russia and the West Cut German Nation in Half."[34]

Marshall was not an ideologue by nature. He was soft-spoken and meticulous, not a firebrand. Even his Harvard speech contained no word of the Soviet Union, and the Marshall Plan as he proposed it in June— to the extent that there even was a plan at that early stage—never targeted the Soviet Union. Even so, Marshall understood that while he did not seek a Cold War, the defiant Soviet rejection of the one-world order meant that a Cold War was upon Americans, whether they wanted it or not.

Critics commonly draw a distinction between the Marshall Plan and the Truman Doctrine, insisting that Marshall agreed with Truman's overall message and the need for commitment, but found the President's tone too divisive and aggressive. Even so, Marshall also understood the American mind. He recognized that the public identified with the idea of the United States in the vanguard of civilization and the Cold War as an age-old battle for ways of life. "The Soviet Union has recognized the situation in its frank declaration of hostility and opposition to the European Recovery Program," Marshall told the American public upon his return from London. He continued, saying that:

> The success of such a program would necessarily mean the establishment of a balance in which the sixteen western nations, who have bound their hopes and efforts together, would be rehabilitated, strong in forms of government which guarantee true freedom, opportunity to the individual, and protection against the terror of governmental tyranny. The issue is really clear-cut and I fear there can be no settlement until the coming months demonstrate whether or not the civilization of Western Europe will prove vigorous enough to rise above the destructive effects of the war and restore a healthy society. Officials of the Soviet Union and leaders of the Communist Parties openly predict that this restoration will not take place. We on the other hand are confident in the rehabilitation of western European civilization with its freedoms.[35]

Lodge seamlessly picked up that message. In yet another town hall meeting in December, the Republican Senator took aim at those in his own party who insisted the proposed aid amount could be drastically reduced. Anything short of a complete national dedication to the European Recovery Program, Lodge thundered, would result in a "Marshall Plan in reverse . . . with the Americans the money-spenders and the Communists the vote-getters." Europeans would only come together, he believed, if America took the lead:

> We should use our influence to achieve a voluntary integration and unity in Europe in which tariff barriers are removed, financial stability and a solid currency are assured. . . . This is the best hope for avoiding the recurrence of a future European war.

This "cannot, as two modern dictators have found out, be achieved by force, but it can be achieved by inspiration and example. Lafayette brought us a message of freedom 175 ago. Today we can bring the equivalent message to Europe."[36]

On December 19, Truman formally presented Congress with the State Department's findings regarding Western Europe's needs and requested that the legislature pass the aid bill. He proclaimed that

> America's deepest concern with European recovery . . . is that it is essential to the maintenance of the civilization in which the American way of life is rooted. It is the only assurance of the continued independence and integrity of a group of nations who constitute a bulwark for the principles of freedom, justice and the dignity of the individual.[37]

For the next four and a quarter years, the President explained, Western Europe would have to rely on the United States.

The *Washington Post's* editorial board intuitively captured the President's ideological tone. It regarded the Marshall Plan

> as Operation Survival for our free world. It is an investment in our security and our liberties and should persuade Congress to err on the side of generosity rather than economy. . . . The plan gives a purposive direction to our foreign policy to make the world safe for us to live in.

The one-world ideal may have been shrinking geographically, but its message remained alive and well. The *New York Times* concurred. Quoting George Washington and referencing the 1787 Constitutional Convention, its editors insisted that what was at stake was whether the "democratic movement . . . [would] go forward or retreat. This and not a few dollars or a few articles in limited supply, is the issue." The Marshall Plan was well worth it "to light the lamp of democracy." Unsurprisingly, Europeans hailed the message, too. A British Foreign Office spokesman called Truman's address "a world of welcome" and a "tremendous event in the history of postwar Europe." The London *Times* predicted "a grand design to breathe life into the old world by help of the new." The fact that European Communist papers such as the *Communist Daily Worker* in England vehemently disapproved of Truman's speech only added value to the President's message in Europe and at home.[38]

The United States Representative to the United Nations Commission on Human Rights, Eleanor Roosevelt, was not slow to commend Truman for his speech or his actions either. The President and the former First Lady enjoyed a strong connection, evidenced by their extensive and honest correspondence after FDR's death. Mrs. Roosevelt was one of the most perceptive observers of American politics and global affairs in the 1940s and she had front row seats to the problems in Europe. Just before Christmas she wrote to Truman:

> I wanted to tell you how very courageous I thought your message was on the Marshall Plan. . . . The Republicans are playing right into your hands . . . [if] they do a lot of arguing over the Marshall Plan I think they will find themselves in hot water there.[39]

Eleanor Roosevelt's instincts proved prophetic as Truman's clarion call on behalf of a united and democratic West took center-stage during a heavily publicized Senate Foreign Relations Committee meetings in early January. Although the committees created in June shortly after Marshall's speech had independently concluded that the cost of the Marshall Plan would inflict no strain on American economic capabilities, Vandenberg and Lodge both believed that hearings were necessary to disarm opponents in their own party. There was a need for a forum in which challengers could voice their concerns and the program could get a fair hearing where nothing was swept under the rug. A secondary and more sinister purpose to the open forum was Lodge's belief that such a public spectacle would expose those GOP members who, in his opinion, held antiquated foreign policy views. Forcing a debate, he likely recognized, would give the old guard just enough rope with which to hang itself.

Between January 8 and February 5, more than 90 witnesses, including George Marshall, testified in the Senate caucus room. Cabinet members, ambassadors, leaders from industry and agriculture, civic groups and respected citizens, scholars, and reporters were given a chance to present their views. Conservatives like Herbert Hoover called for a smaller program, more limited in duration and cost. He continued to long for a return to the foreign policies of the interwar period. Others, such as John Foster Dulles, promoted the program heavily, but insisted that Europe would have to do its share by forming "a customs union and regional defense pact . . . [establish] production goals for themselves and works towards them." According to Dulles, the U.S., for its part, should stipulate that aid "depends upon the nations' cooperation in attaining these goal . . . [and] include western Germany." The necessity of including Germany had become especially apparent after hundreds of thousands of workers in January left work "for 24 hours to protest food shortages and black-market profiteering"[40] In his Senate statement and subsequent testimony, Marshall pushed the same message he had all through the fall. A veteran in front of Congress and not a man who was easily rattled, he did not waver under criticism. He avowed that Europe would emerge stronger, united and democratic. "The commitments each made to the other, if faithfully observed, will produce in Western Europe a far more integrated economic system than any in previous history."[41]

The vast majority of Marshall Plan narratives, as well as books and articles on the Cold War more generally, insist that the ERP was in serious trouble at this stage. Greg Behrman, for example, gives the impression that conservative opposition could have derailed the program during the hearings, or at least gutted it to the point of ineffectiveness. To imply as much, however, is to confuse rhetoric for power. Despite the accusatory charges that the ERP equaled Communism, was nothing more than a Tennessee Valley Authority for Europe, or was a "giveaway program," the ground, as Lodge predicted, was shifting beneath the GOP leadership.[42] If anything, the public display served to isolate opponents even further. So did a suggestion from Vandenberg to Marshall that rather than request the full $17 billion in one bill, a general continuing authorization expanded over several years would align more with Congressional procedure and would have the added benefit of lowering the appearance of the cost if not the actual amount that would be provided.[43]

Criticism of the European Recovery Program often centered on cost and raised the specter of higher taxes. In their testimonies, Marshall, Acheson, and Secretary of Defense James Forrestal switched the argument. They insisted that the ERP was an investment, not a handout. The cost of not acting, they claimed, far exceeded the amount currently debated. On February 13, the Senate Foreign Relations Committee unanimously approved the program, allowing it to move to the Senate floor for debate.

At this stage, the political threat to the ERP was largely over. While the three-week Senate debate that followed was intense and often aggressive, the opposition was largely reduced to an ever-decreasing number of cantankerous hardline conservatives. Nonetheless, they were able to put up a fight and stall the process, and they did so at every turn. Lodge and Vandenberg led the fight on behalf of the Senate Foreign Relations Committee and, in effect, the Democratic Administration. Defying his own party's leaders, Lodge took the Senate floor over 300 times in defense of the Marshall Pan between January and March 1948. As he did, he faced fusillades of criticism. The fiercest opposition came from William Jenner, James Kem (R-MO), and Kenneth Wherry (R-NE). Collectively, they indicted the ERP as wasteful, unnecessary, and a plain handout to socialist governments in Western Europe. In an extensive tirade, Jenner accused President Truman of misrepresenting the European problem and of wanting to "buy off the dangers of Communism by giving large cash donations from the American taxpayer's pocket." Even worse, in Jenner's view, most of the recipients of the President's largesse were "only a degree or two removed in color from the [Communist] menace from which we are supposed to be protecting them." Conservatives saw little difference between Clement Attlee's Labour government and those on the other side of the Iron Curtain. Kem made clear that he did not consider it "sound policy" to aid England's socialist government, while Republican presidential contender Harold Staasen demanded that no aid be granted to countries that possessed nationalization programs.[44] They also raised the specter of the garrison state, the fear that aid would exhaust the American treasury forcing higher taxes and the expansion of the government's control over the citizenry. In Jenner's view, Truman was plotting to press "our Nation inexorably down the path of state socialism." As Michael Hogan puts it, conservatives worried that the ERP "might actually foster the very kind of totalitarianism it was intended to prevent."[45]

The Truman Administration and its political allies countered that one of the Marshall Plan's virtues was its ability to grease the wheels of European economies, thereby limiting local government control and thus minimizing the risk of local radical political leaders emerging from either the left or the right. Lodge dismantled the so-called "anti-socialist" argument. He shot back that utilities, services, railroad, and other similar services had always been government-run in Europe. "The fact that the European and American do not agree on . . . whether a government should operate the telephone industry does mean that we cannot agree in opposing Communism."[46] The editors at *Life* magazine concurred: "If Congress were to write antisocialist conditions into the ERP bill . . . many a self-respecting socialist government in Europe would probably have to refuse the money and so govern more socialistically than ever." In their view, the test for continuing aid to Europe would be anti-inflationary measures and increased "production and unification. This will work against the inefficiencies of socialism, but it will be a delicate diplomatic step to press it as an argument for capitalism, and Congress had better leave that step to the professionals."[47]

After Lodge, aided by Tom Connally, had countered the exasperating questioning, Taft, who had left the floor attack to his conservative lieutenants, introduced a $1.3 billion cut from the first year's appropriations. The amount mirrored Britain's expected needs. It highlighted the dislike many conservative Senators had for the British, whom they felt had been aided more than enough. It also reflected Taft's belief that assistance should be limited to allocations "to specific countries for specific purposes." Taft wanted an ad hoc approach to European policy. He wanted Washington, particularly Congress, to be able to cherry-pick when to support and when to have the authority to abstain. This insistence illustrated how little he understood the Europeans' position or the importance they placed on a firm American guarantee. It was not enough for Paris, London, Copenhagen, or Rome to hope that the U.S. *would* come to their aid in times of . need. In light of the Communist threat on the continent, they needed a firm American commitment. Lodge rallied Republicans and Democrats to vote down Taft's proposal by a comfortable margin.[48] On March 14, the Senate voted 67–17 to approve the Marshall Plan. Taft, possibly with an eye on the presidential nomination process only a few months away and fearful of challenging an overwhelmingly popular program, ultimately voted for the ERP. He could not get himself to do so in person, however, and cast his vote in absentia. The House of Representatives followed suit two weeks later, passing the ERP by a margin of over 250 votes.

The conservative right's isolation was unsurprising. Their argument rested on principle alone. The economic data did not support their position; neither did the press or public opinion. Nothing suggests that, at this stage, the nationally held belief about U.S. global obligations and the intensifying fear of global Communism would lead to American hesitancy. On the contrary, the threat appeared increasingly real. In the midst of the Senate debate, the Alsops relayed a telling anecdote from a recent visit with an Italian minister. Deeply concerned about the Italian Communists and, by extension, Soviet domination of his country, he presented the two reporters with a rundown of Italy's few remaining hard assets, showing that the country's dollars, gold, and grain supplies had all been expended, with only half enough to last through the winter. He "threw up his hands in sudden emotion and confessed his bitter trouble: 'It all depends on you. Without your help . . . the government will be finished on the day we have to cut bread rations . . . after that the communists in full control.'" In light of that threat, they concluded—and all indications are that the American public concurred—that "Fate had suddenly imposed upon the United States the staggering responsibility of leadership of the West."[49]

In the middle of the ERP Senate negotiations in Washington, conditions some 4,000 miles away exposed the validity of the Italian fear. The Czechoslovakian coalition government had survived the previous summer's dressing-down by Stalin. As the ERP loomed in Western Europe, however, Moscow extinguished any hope Prague may have had that it might be able to position Czechoslovakia as a kind of halfway house between the East and the West. In 1946, the national Communist Party had received almost 40 percent of the vote, the most anywhere in Europe. A year later, it was clear that the Soviet Union's refusal to permit ERP participation was weakening the Communists' appeal. The "party knew its candidates would be lucky to receive 20 percent." This reality, combined with the willingness the government had already demonstrated to stray away from Moscow's control, became Prague's misfortune. In late February 1948, an internal debate between the governing parties brought an end to the Prague government. By March 1, an exclusively Communist government emerged. Jan Masaryk, the pro-Western Foreign Minister who had so bitterly accepted Stalin's heavy-handed dismissal of Prague's desire to join the Marshall Plan, was dead. He had either jumped or was pushed from his third-floor window. Had he survived, he likely would have fallen victim to the show trials and political arrests that soon gripped his country. By the end of the year, politics across Eastern Europe was "something that happened not between several parties, but within a single party."[50] Prague would not hold another free election for more than four decades.

Stalin's move against Czechoslovakia did not come as a surprise to American officials. While U.S. guarantees of aid had temporarily halted the political advance of Communist parties in Western Europe, as Marshall told the Cabinet in November of 1947, Moscow could be expected "to consolidate its hold on Eastern Europe." He expected the Kremlin to "clamp down completely on Czechoslovakia, for a relatively free Czechoslovakia could become a threatening salient in Moscow's political position." However predictable the outcome in Prague might have appeared to the Truman Administration, Marshall's calm was not mirrored in American or European public responses. In part, this likely reflected an element of historical shame given the Western democracies, failure to come to Czechoslovakia's aid against Hitler a decade earlier. There was plenty of newfound alarm as well, however. *Life's* headline, "U.S. Foreign Policy Takes a Licking," reflected a shared national mood that the Communist victory was a major Cold War defeat. The *Saturday Evening Post* argued that while America hesitated, the Communist empire was on the move: "The longer we are taking making up our minds, the more powerful the Communist appeal in Europe." A month later, the journal predicted that as "more lights go out in Europe, it is time Americans began asking themselves how much this country [the United States] has been softened up for a future communist coup." This was the zero-sum game attitude of the Cold War: a victory for the Communist world anywhere was considered a loss for the free world everywhere.[51]

The events in Czechoslovakia had repercussions in Europe too. In a cable home to Washington on March 5, Clay wrote from Berlin, that for

> many months, based on logical analysis, I have felt and held that war was unlikely for at least ten years. Within the last few weeks, I have felt a subtle change in Soviet attitude which I cannot define but which now gives me the feeling that *it may come with dramatic suddenness.*[52]

A similarly eerie feeling existed elsewhere as well. Throughout the spring, rumors swirled across Scandinavia that, following the Czechoslovakian *modus operandi*, the Soviet Union would seek to force Norway and Denmark into their sphere of influence next. At the very least, Moscow would levy political pressure aiming to pry Oslo and Copenhagen away from the kind of Western identity that appeared to be developing among the non-Communist countries. The Kremlin had already done so to Finland, which at the end of the war had been forced to accede to Moscow's foreign policy positions. Many even deemed war likely in Scandinavia. Josiah Marvel, Jr., the U.S. Ambassador to Copenhagen, informed Washington in early March that the Danish government was displaying an "acute nervousness" about domestic Communist moves in advance of a "possible Soviet invasion." Deeply scarred by their quick surrender to Hitler's invading army on April 9, 1940, the Danes even petitioned the Americans for arms for self-defense. "April 9, never again," became the Danish cry. It has been ever since. During the Easter days, the small Danish military even began to mobilize, preparing for the worst. At the time Copenhagen still remained hopeful, though, that it could steer a middle course between the emerging ideological blocs. In light of this, Prime Minister Hans Hedtoft made clear to Marvel that while Denmark would not join *any* non-aggression pact or sign *any* agreement with the Soviet Union, he would, for now, not commit to a role in a Western European regional defense pact either if such an organization were to materialize (on European regional defense see Chapter 4). For now, Hedtoft told Marvel, Denmark would await the international impact of Italy's April elections.[53] Every event across the continent now seemed to be connected.

In Washington and across Europe, governments shared Danish concerns for the outcome of the Italian elections. Buoyed by American support, Alcide De Gasperi had been able to contain Communist influence through May of 1947, but the Communist Party's popularity was once again on the rise. For the first time since early postwar France, there was real concern that a European Communist Party might emerge victorious at the ballot box. Many in Washington believed that a failure to keep Italy in the democratic camp could endanger the entire Marshall Plan and, with that, Western Europe's future. The concern proved to be unfounded. Efforts by the Catholic Church, private lobbying groups in the

Denmark's Easter Crisis

The apprehension felt in Denmark reached its peak during April 1948. Danish Prime Minister, Hans Hedtoft, spent Easter in a castle outside of Copenhagen. So tense was the situation that he ran to wake up his security detail people early in the morning when he mistook loud agricultural machinery for an imminent Soviet invasion.

The Italian Job of 1948

The Italian election of April 1948 was a close affair. Many observers believed the continuing socio-economic difficulties and the slow postwar recovery favored the Communists against the moderate Christian Democratic Party. Caught in the middle of the Cold War, it was also an election in which both superpowers sought to influence the outcome.

From the left, the Cominform initiated strikes in cities across the country, promoted attacks on newspapers, town halls, and opponent party headquarters. Rumors swirled about a possible militant insurrection assisted by Communists from the Balkans.

The United States, aiming to shore up Alcide De Gasperi, also intervened. The interim aid package approved by the U.S. Congress to hold over its allies until the formal arrival of the Marshall Plan was, for example, in large part inspired by the Communist strikes and the fear that labor unrest and deteriorating conditions would undermine the government. The Christian Democrats also received support from the newly created American Central Intelligence Agency. The Italian job was the CIA's first major covert operation. It involved the organization of economic and political support for the political right, while messages broadcast on Voice of America highlighted the benefits of American aid that would accompany a defeat of the PCI and the absence of aid in the event of a Communist victory. The U.S. also urged the Vatican to intervene on the side of De Gasperi and convinced U.S. private Catholic organizations to lend financial and other support to non-Communists. At the height of American concerns, President Truman's National Security Council (NSC) went so far as to suggest that, if necessary, the U.S. should use military power to prevent Italy from falling "under the domination of the USSR either through external armed attack or through [national] Soviet-dominated Communists movements." This was never a likely outcome, but the suggestion reflects the tension the election instilled among Americans and how great Washington believed the stakes to be.

Military intervention proved unnecessary. On April 18, De Gasperi claimed 48.5 percent of the vote. The Communists slipped to a surprising 31 percent, down almost 10 percent from the 1946 election. The American role in the election outcome was important, but not decisive. Of far greater importance were Pope Pius XII's denunciations of Communism and the role played by local priests in convincing the Italian public that their future was in the Western bloc.

In Washington, the CIA's status soared. Less than three weeks after the coup, George Kennan concluded a report fittingly entitled "The Inauguration of Political Warfare." At the highest levels of government, employing all means short of war—political and psychological warfare, as it would soon come to be known—hereafter became an integral part of U.S. national security policy. By June of 1948, the NSC created the Office of Special Projects—later the Office of Policy Coordination—a loosely joint CIA and State Department venture. The goal was to create an organization that could protect the rollout of the Marshall Plan and authorize operations for which the U.S. government could not formally take credit.[1]

Note

1   Kaeten Mistry, *The United States, Italy and the Origins of the Cold War* (Cambridge University Press, 2014); "The Inauguration of Political Warfare," May 4, 1948, *FRUS 1945–1950: Emergence of the Intelligence Establishment*, 668–672.

U.S., and covert operations launched by the U.S. Central Intelligence Agency (CIA) defeated the Communist vote. On April 18, De Gasperi's Christian Democrats claimed victory and went on to form a government without Togliatti's Communist Party.

"An Aroused Italy Chooses Freedom," *Life* declared. The last bastion of hope for freedom in Eastern Europe might have fallen in Czechoslovakia, but Communism had been beaten back in Western Europe.[54]

★   ★   ★

On April 3, 1948, President Truman signed the Economic Corporation Act of the Foreign Assistance Act into law. It allocated $4 billion for the first 12 months with the anticipation that the program would run until June 1952. Aid would be amended each year as needed. In total, close to $13 billion would find its way into Western Europe.[55]

Table 3.1 provides the breakdown for each nation. Great Britain would receive the most, followed by France and West Germany. In a clear sign that the Marshall Plan was about more than postwar reconstruction, even nations only marginally touched by the Second World War would benefit from the ERP as well.

Like the New Deal before it, the European aid program was not a handout. In 1933, FDR's plan to beat the depression rested on the three "Rs": Relief, Recovery, and Reform. The Marshall Plan, with a similar trio of goals in mind, contained various stipulations regarding the use of funds and American oversight over the distribution and targets. To oversee its development and execution, Marshall Plan legislation called for the establishment of the Economic Cooperation Administration (ECA). While the original proposal would have granted the State Department almost total control over the program, a political compromise instead led to the creation of the ECA as a special non-partisan ad hoc body. As its head, Truman chose automobile industry executive Paul G. Hoffman. Hoffman did not want the job. He was a Republican with commitment to the Studebaker Motor Company and had no interest in giving up his private role to work for Harry Truman. The President did not take no for an

Table 3.1 Table of aid breakdown from the Economic Corporation Act of the Foreign Assistance Act

Country	1948/49 ($ millions)	1949/50 ($ millions)	1950/51 ($ millions)	Cumulative ($ millions)
Austria	232	166	70	468
Belgium and Luxembourg	195	222	360	777
Denmark	103	87	195	385
France	1,085	691	520	2,296
West Germany	510	438	500	1,448
Greece	175	156	45	376
Iceland	6	22	15	43
Ireland	88	45	0	133
Italy and Trieste	594	405	205	1,204
Netherlands	471	302	355	1,128
Norway	82	90	200	372
Portugal	0	0	70	70
Sweden	39	48	260	347
Switzerland	0	0	250	250
Turkey	28	59	50	137
United Kingdom	1,316	921	1,060	3,297
Totals	4,924	3,652	4,155	12,731

answer. Hoffman had been a key participant on the Harriman committee that during the autumn of 1947 investigated the prospects of the Marshall Plan, and had testified during the Senate Foreign Relation Committee Hearings at the start of 1948. He came highly recommended and was popular on both sides of the political aisle. When he turned down Truman's offer, the President settled the issue by simply publicly announcing Hoffman's appointment.[56]

Apart from the decision to make Marshall Secretary of State, Truman probably did not make a smarter personnel choice than the appointment of Hoffman. Dean Acheson later remarked that some people insisted that Paul Hoffman "missed his calling: that he should have been an evangelist. Both statements miss the truth. He didn't miss his calling and he was . . . an evangelist."[57] As head of the ECA he preached the American message with conviction and clarity and he often played a key role in bringing Europeans onboard specific programs and in forcing them to accept American conditions.

Hoffman

Hoffman became one of the most respected government officials of his time but he was not pleased at Truman's decision to simply appoint him to a job he had turned down. It did not help that the announcement was delivered over loud speakers just as Hoffman was delivering a briefing at the Pentagon.

On the other side of the Atlantic, a Paris office comprised of close to 600 staffers and largely led by the seasoned diplomat Averell Harriman, was set up to handle ECA affairs on the ground. In addition, independent missions were established in the recipient countries to ensure close cooperation with local governments and to oversee the flow of funds. Per the agreement, a European counterpart to the ECA, the Organization for European Economic Cooperation (OEEC), would maintain European unity and thereby fulfill one of the most persistent American demands: the vision of a collaborative, liberalizing continent. The role of the OEEC did not always sit well with the Europeans who, as Hoffman recalled it, often "felt that they should have the right to deal directly with the USA." He was adamant, however,

> that if this were done, many misunderstandings would result. As a consequence, we insisted that every one of the sixteen recovery programs should be screened by the OEEC and further, that the OEEC should have the responsibility of recommending to us the amount of assistance that should be given to each country.[58]

European reluctance to grant the OEEC complete control meant that it never quite lived up to Hoffman and Harriman's hopes that it would efficiently further economic and political integration. Nonetheless, when compared to Europe's divided and militaristic past, the new organization was remarkably effective. It began the slow process of cooperation among Europeans and it helped form the idea of a Western identity unified by liberalism. On a more practical level, the OEEC also became, in time, a crucial vehicle for smoothening Marshall Plan operations. It conducted analyses of local economic conditions and needs, made recommendations regarding investment projects, and played a key role in the promotion of freer trade among the European powers.[59]

The ECA's role was multifaceted. It helped lock in prices and exchange rates, thereby stabilizing trade conditions and ensuring market flow. It also provided dollar assistance to Europe to procure food, machinery, and fuel, supported infrastructure projects, and engaged in public works projects. Its perhaps most important function was to help recipient nations close the dollar gap, an issue that by 1948 loomed as the most glaring example of Europe's economic problems. The inability to import goods and services without draining reserves was exhausting the European nations' capacity to buy products in the United States. To help rectify this, the ECA created the so-called counterpart funds—the counterpart of the U.S. dollars provided through the ERP—which authorized the use of local currency for Marshall Plan projects. Each recipient nation matched U.S. contributions in its local currency. This currency was placed in a fund that could only be released for the approval of specific projects recognized by the ECA. Behrman describes the process as such:

> A French farmer who needed a tractor manufactured by a U.S. company would go to a local dealer. He would pay for it in French francs. The ECA and the French government had a clearing mechanism that established a reasonable price and exchange rate for the tractor. Instead of going from the French farmer to the American tractor manufacturer, though, the French francs went back to the French central bank. The ECA and the French government would then work together to devise a strategy for the deployment of those counterpart funds to advance French recovery. The U.S. tractor manufacturer was paid with funds appropriated from the Marshall Plan, allowing the French farmer's francs to go to the French government.[60]

In this manner, counterpart funds could become available for the construction of electrical plants and projects, agriculture, national housing projects, canals, railroads, airports, and many other areas without exacerbating the French balance-of-payments deficit, while local currency could be spent on national recovery. As infrastructure rebounded, industrial and agricultural production recovered, and bottlenecks cleared, the need for continued U.S. assistance would decline. The program was brilliant in its simplicity and allowed the United States considerable control over European development projects and how its aid was being spent.

On April 14, the *New York Times* reported, the Bi-zonal area completed the first purchase "with funds expected from the ERP [for] . . . $3,000,000 of fruits and vegetables contracted for with Italy." On the same day, ships in American ports began taking onboard tons of grains, fuel, and other much-needed products destined for Western Europe. Two days later, with the first ships already heading east across the Atlantic, the European Foreign Ministers met in Paris to sign the final approval of the ERP. The plan admitted the German zones to the program and thus moved the entire Western half of the continent toward a solution to the problem regarding Germany's future.[61]

In the eyes of Hoffman, the goal of the ERP was to get Europe to help itself. From the beginning, that had always been the mission. Like other Marshall planners, however, he, too, pushed for the introduction of American ideals to reform Europe. This was never merely an economic aid program. In a long article in the *New York Times* released shortly after aid began shipping to Europe, Chester Bowles, who would go on to become one of the most astute thinkers on U.S. foreign aid, reminded Americans that postwar foreign policy was not about halting Communism, but about the globalization of American ideas and values. Bowles summoned Americans to "take our stand unequivocally beside the hungry and oppressed people all over the world." He believed the Marshall Plan was just the beginning.

> The spotlight of history is upon us. . . . A bold program of economic, social and political democracy skillfully conceived and aggressively programmed is the one means by which America can continue to develop as a symbol of hope in a world of two billion people who are determined not to go back [to colonialism and oppression].[62]

This supposition should not, as left-leaning critics did then and as revisionist historians have done since, be simplistically confused with imperialism. Ideology was at the heart of it. The "one-world" dream had undoubtedly died in 1947, but the vision of spreading American ideas to Europe in a mutually beneficial partnership was very much alive.

The American experience provided the impetus for the development and execution of the Marshall Plan. Americans had always believed the proliferation of their values, ideas, and methods would better the lot of humankind. Leading policymakers, intellectuals, businessmen, and diplomats shared the view that the export of American modernization ideas would revive Europe. Drawing on their own past—especially the interwar experience—many of the New Deal social scientists that came onboard to work on the ERP deduced that by breaking down the nationalistic barriers blocking the movement of capital, trade, and peoples, and by introducing effective methods of controlling the economies, Europe's recovery could proceed along a very American path.[63] This would take place in a different context from the even more ambitious perspective Americans envisioned during the war, but it contained the same teleological course and idealistic mission that had dominated postwar preparations during the first half of the 1940s. Once modernized, Americans expected that European nations would assume the role intended for them in the Bretton Woods system and move towards a far more Americanized and liberalized world. The Marshall Plan was at the heart of this enduring vision. As it fell into place, European hopes would begin to return.

Even so, Europe was not in the clear. On June 21, *Life* warned that the continent's future remained uncertain. The magazine concluded

> The West's recent political victories in France and Italy did more to allay the fear of Communism in the U.S. than in Europe, where nobody was surprised when French Communists set off a short-lived but ominous wave of strikes at the end of last week. The dread of invasion by the Red Army is still a real and present thing.

The invasion never came, but the Communist threat persisted. Three days after the *Life* article appeared in print, Stalin played his final Western European card, this time in Germany.

CHAPTER 4

The Marshall Plan in Action and the Emergence of European Unity, 1948–1951

Ever since the end of the war, Germany had been at the heart of the European dispute between Washington, London, Moscow, and Paris. Every American initiative seeking to revive the German economy and provide for greater political independence was met with strong opposition from the French and the Soviets. After Secretary of State Byrnes' Stuttgart speech in September, 1946, however, this Franco-Soviet obstruction slowly began to erode as the Truman Administration took ever more aggressive steps in pursuit of Western unity. These American initiatives, including the passage of Marshall Plan legislation, isolated the Soviet Union and severely strained the collaborative efforts of the Four Power Allied Control Council in Berlin. When American ERP administrators met with British, French, and Benelux officials in London in 1948, the Americans pushed through a series of measures aimed to bring Germany back into the fold of European unity. Perhaps more than any event in the immediate postwar period, the London conference demonstrated the extent of U.S. dominance over its partners. The accord finalized the merger of the French zone into the Anglo-American Bi-zone, established the Deutsche Mark as a new currency in the Western-controlled half of Germany, and authorized the German delegates to begin drafting a constitution for an independently run political entity in the three Western zones. These steps, which would lead to the formal division of Germany a year later, were the product of the post-1918 realization that a defeated enemy could not be expected to embrace a supportive role and accept punishment simultaneously. They were made necessary by the increasingly untenable situation across the Western zones, where hoarding had become rampant, black-marketeering flourished, and the existing currency had become worthless.

The Deutsche Mark currency reform was the heart of this American effort. It set the rate of exchange of "old money for new [fixed issues of] old debts, contracts, wage scales, social insurance, and other forms of insurance."[1] Combined with the promise of Marshall Aid, it brought confidence back to the German economy. The creation of the Tri-zone and the step toward a German-run state, similarly, reflected the American belief that as the principal productive and consumptive area in Europe, Germany was crucial to continental recovery. By 1948, Washington was no longer willing to wait to secure this reality. If anything, as Marshall wrote a friend in August,

> we have wrestled for three years in an effort to bring Russia to some form of agreement with respect to Germany and we could be criticized much more justly for our delay in acting as we did at the London Conference than for the manner of our actions.[2]

Moscow condemned the London accord. Stalin wanted either a unified Communist Germany or a neutral one. Instead, he faced the prospect of a West German state bankrolled by Washington's Marshall Plan and closely linked politically and economically to the West. Unwilling to accept this development, on June 24, 1948, the Soviet Union blocked all highway, railroad, and water access routes to the Western sectors of Berlin. This move, made possible by the city's location deep inside the Soviet zone (see Figure 4.1), sealed off the 2.2 million inhabitants in the Western half of the city from the outside world and, in violation of all previous agreements between the former wartime allies, severely restricted British, French, and American officials from entering their zones. The blockade also prevented food and fuel from coming through. Whether the Soviets specifically hoped to bring the Western powers to renege on German recovery and the creation of a West German state, or whether they viewed the blockade as the most expedient path to bring an end to the unnatural presence of Western forces and officials in Berlin, remains unclear. The goal was likely all of the above. There is no doubt, however, that Moscow saw the presence of West Berlin as "an annoying aberration, and a reminder of the Russian failure to complete their consolidation of power in Eastern Germany." Critics of American foreign policy believe that Stalin's actions were quite natural; "the only means at his disposal," Offner insists. They praise Stalin's pacific attitude insisting that the Soviets merely wanted to bring the Western powers back to the negotiation table to bring a halt to the creation of a West German state.[3] Stalin probably did hope for such an outcome but it was his own obstruction during the preceding two years that had led to this moment. From Washington's perspective, the time for negotiation had passed. Whatever Stalin's specific motivations, he miscalculated. Shortly before the blockade began, Lucius Clay had explained to Washington that while there was "no practicality in maintaining our position in Berlin. . . . We are convinced that our remaining in Berlin is essential to our prestige

> ## Munich
>
> Churchill's mentioning of "Munich" referred to the British and French attempt to appease Hitler in 1938. It has become ever since a metaphor for the belief that aggressors cannot be mollified through diplomacy. They must be countered by force. In American parlance, the term was used by Presidents about the wars in Korea, Vietnam, Iraq, and more recently about U.S. policy toward Iran and Russia.

in Germany and in Europe. Whether for good or bad, it has become a symbol of American intent." Just a few days later he defiantly explained that, "they cannot drive us out of Berlin by any action short of war."[4] Addressing a crowd of one 100,000 in Luton, Winston Churchill emphatically concurred. The former Prime Minister considered the issue of "Berlin as grave as Munich," and was certain that "the Communist government of Russia has made up its mind to drive us . . . and other allies out . . . and turn the Russian zone in Germany into one of the satellite states under the role of totalitarian terrorism."[5]

Ernest Bevin, the Foreign Office, and, most importantly, Harry Truman shared this view. On the issue of Berlin, Truman demonstrated the kind of decisiveness that would win him admirers in Washington and beyond. "I formed a particular kind of respect for him because of his willingness to take the decisions that involved some risk, but by doing so avoid greater risk later on," Clay recalled.

Reacting almost instantly to the Soviet blockade, Truman, in collaboration with the British government, ordered an airlift to deliver food, fuel, and medical supplies to the trapped citizens of Berlin. No effort of its kind had even been undertaken. At the time, no one was even sure it could be done. Advisors informed the president that in order to deliver the daily 1,700 calories per citizen needed for survival, it would require a supply of 1,500 to 2,000 tons of food to the city every single day. Meat, fish, potatoes, salt, flour, cereals, coffee, fats, oil, fruits, and vegetables were all needed. Also required were 2,500 tons of coal and gasoline—a total of 4,000 tons per day.

The Allies' C-47 transport plane was capable of carrying only three tons. On June 26, the first day of the airlift, only 80 tons of aid arrived. Truman was undeterred and the situation, in any case, improved once

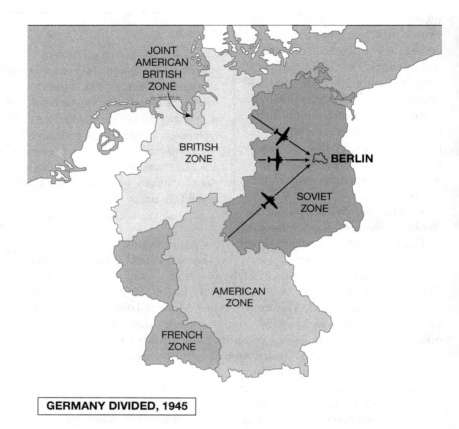

GERMANY DIVIDED, 1945

Figure 4.1 The Berlin Crisis

The presence of Berlin deep inside Soviet-controlled East Germany caused one of the major early Cold War confrontations when the Soviets blocked the agreed-upon Western access routes to the Western zones of the city.

larger C-54 transport planes arrived on the scene. The C-54 could carry three times the load of the C-47, and, combined with improved coordination, aid soon began arriving in massive quantities.[6] On September 9, egged on by the Broadcasting Service in the American Sector, 300,000 West Berliners—some sources list the number at half a million—protested the Soviet blockade. Addressing them was the Mayor Ernst Reuter. Reuter was a Communist, but unlike so many Western European Communist leaders who had pledged their loyalty to Moscow, he stood firmly on the side of his people. "You peoples of the world. You people of America, of England, of France, look on this city, and recognize that this city, this people must not be abandoned—cannot be abandoned," Reuter declared. Stalin's blockade of Berlin confirmed what Americans had believed since Marshall's Moscow meetings the previous spring: The Soviet Union was content to let Europeans starve in order to accomplish its goals. The Marshall Plan made it clear that Americans were not going to allow that to happen. In that sense, Berlin, as it would for the remainder of the Cold War, symbolized a battle of wills.

The Berlin Airlift ranks alongside the Truman Doctrine and the Marshall Plan as the most significant early U.S. Cold War initiatives. It confirmed that the American commitment to Western Europe was never exclusively about financial recovery. After all, if the principal concern were the recovery of the European economies due to their connections to the American market, the logical step would have been to abandon West Berlin to Soviet control. Truman, Marshall, and Clay never seriously entertained that idea. Three days before the blockade was initiated, Truman, conscious that trouble was brewing, wrote in his diary: "We'll stay in Berlin—come what may." Three weeks into the crisis, the President reiterated to the Cabinet his "firm determination" to save the city.[7] The Germans felt this ideological American commitment, too. The combination of the airlift and the Marshall Plan "gave the German people the feeling that they were no longer written off by the rest of the world [and] that they could take part in the process of the free world," as the former Director of the Economic Council in the Bi-zone and later Minister for Economic Affairs in the Federal Republic of Germany, Ludwig Erhard explained it.[8] To reiterate that support, Truman dispatched B-29 bombers to England. The United States neither anticipated nor wanted a war over Berlin, but the message sent by the presence of U.S. aircrafts in Europe—the same aircraft that had dropped the atomic bombs on Japan—was unmistakable. By the end of July, Marshall explained to the Cabinet that, in his view, the situation in Berlin was a response to Moscow having lost face politically, particularly in Italy and France. The blockade, the Secretary of State concluded, was a sign of Soviet "desperation in the face of success of the ERP."[9] The conclusion was understandable. The weight of the 11-month-long airlift that would continue to supply Berliners with American support until May of 1949, combined with the expansion of the Marshall Plan, drew West Germany into the Western orbit and united the non-Communist world more firmly. From this followed the creation of a united Western Europe.

★   ★   ★

Between 1948 and 1951, the Marshall Plan's goal for relief, recovery, re-construction, and European integration proceeded with remarkable success.

In a manner scarcely imaginable when viewing the still and moving images of Europe's destruction at the end of the war, Washington's partners would soon emerge as strong economic and political members of the West. This development owed less to the immediate economic impact of American aid and more to the manner in which Europeans and Americans joined to create a new and efficient Europe. Therefore, the ERP is best understood not simply as an economic rescue operation or a Cold War struggle, but rather as a way station in a process of development that began long before Marshall's speech and would continue long after he departed public life. By the 1950s and 1960s, this process came to be known as modernization among American social scientists looking to develop theories of social progress in underdeveloped countries. The economist Walt Rostow, chief among them, determined that progressive American socio-economic methods could be successfully applied elsewhere in the world. In his 1960 book, *The Stages of Economic Growth: A Non-Communist Manifesto*, Rostow would claim that societies' economic, social, and political changes were intimately connected. Modifications to one of these areas would inspire change in others, creating stages of growth that would eventually lead to the Americanization of Third World regions. Rostow insisted that U.S. technical assistance, guidance, and education would help decolonizing nations establish the industrial conditions needed for economic "takeoff" and eventually elevate them to a permanent plateau of "high mass consumption." As a high-level official in both the Kennedy and Johnson administrations, Rostow made this theory of modernization a core component of U.S. foreign aid policy.

While modernization theorists in the 1960s drew extensively on the domestic and international experiences of the 1930s and 1940s, including the New Deal and the Marshall Plan, the world they sought to develop differed noticeably from the Western European conditions that Hoffman, Marshall, and Harriman encountered during the ERP years. The underdeveloped regions targeted during the Kennedy and Johnson years, for example, possessed no record of Westernized socio-political structures. The nations that the Marshall Plan sought to uplift, in contrast, had a recent history of extensive bureaucratic structures, modern economic productivity, and political organization that mirrored the American experience to a far greater extent. In terms of intellectual rationale, however, the similarities between these programs were considerable. Both connected the traditional American mission to improve the weak and to stimulate democracy with the goal of saving countries from both Communism and their own economic and political quagmires. Both served ideological, economic, and national security purposes, and both were overwhelmingly inspired by a belief in the superiority of American methods and principles.[10]

In Europe, the ECA took the lead role in institutionalizing this expansion of American socio-economic ways and means. During the summer and fall of 1948, the key executive body of the ERP began to channel grants for commodity assistance and program financing. In the first year of recovery support alone, $1 billion of the total amount authorized was meant to be available only through loans, usually bearing an interest rate of 2.5 percent. As it became apparent that loans forced Marshall Plan recipients to accept further dollar obligations, thereby increasing the dollar gap the ERP aimed to close, a growing proportion of aid shifted to grants. By year two, only $150 million came through loans, while some $3.6 billion arrived in the form of grants. Like modernization programs in the 1960s, technical assistance programs supplemented these grants. In a manner reflective of many of Franklin Roosevelt's New Deal programs, Hoffman's technical assistance programs relied on top-down administrative procedures and training, and spanned a wide variety of sectors. The idea was that superior American business and production methods could be exported to Europe. The way to do so, Washington's technocratic elite concluded, was to educate Europeans in areas of industrial and agricultural productivity, marketing, worker utilization, public administration, tourism, infrastructure, and communications. In pursuit of this, vast sums were set aside to share ideas in these fields.

In the eyes of some American business owners, trade protectionists, and conservative Congressmen, the technical assistance program ran counter to American national interest. They believed that this kind of interaction with outsiders and the sharing of information and methods that Paul Hoffman and the ECA promoted would give away proprietary information and threaten American business interests at home and abroad because it strengthened America's most natural trade competitors, and might lead to a further expansion of the Federal government's power over private industry.[11] While these concerns were not entirely unjustified, they also reflected a failure to appreciate the purpose of the Marshall Plan. Despite the early decision to make the ECA independent of the normal State Department bureaucracy and regardless of the decision to place tough-minded corporate bourgeoisie officials such as Hoffman and Harriman in charge, the European Recovery Program was never designed nor run for the purpose of expanding American exports. While such an outcome was a likely and certainly welcome long-term possibility, the principal goal was to create a unified and modernized West. This required the establishment of a strong and vibrant European business culture and increased inter-European trade.

Whatever level of opposition to these programs did exist, most American businessmen, plant managers, factory owners, and corporations embraced technical assistance as both patriotic and necessary. By the time the Marshall Plan ended in 1951, more than 6,000 representatives of European industries, management, technicians, and workers had made the westward journey across the Atlantic to attend business seminars and to gain firsthand experience of American production methods and business management practices. Close to 5,000 U.S. plants, farms, and organizations took in visitors to share their techniques and operations, and to discuss labor-management relations. They were brought to the U.S., the State Department explained, "for a study of the 'climate' and the attitudes of American management and American labor that have made the United States the world's production leader." However, it went well beyond this. As Hoffman later recalled, even

> more important than what Europeans learned about latches and plows is what they learned about America. They learned that this is the land of full shelves and bulging shops, made possible by high productivity, good wages, and that its prosperity may be emulated elsewhere by those who will work toward it.[12]

Hoffman's reflection underlined the fundamental belief among American Marshall Planners that the inspiration of American ingenuity would vastly increase European production and would, at the same time, serve to tie their new partners far more closely to the United States. Technical assistance may only have accounted for less than one half of one percent of the total Marshall Plan expenditure, but this was vastly exceeded in terms of the kind of American influence it brought to the continent. As the program continued to grow, it became, in Hogan's view, a "cultural crusade on behalf of the 'American way' in Western Europe."[13] Combined with counterpart funds, technical assistance programs helped to create what Americans believed would be a far more efficient Europe. While the former ensured that the aid flowed to the proper projects, the latter sought to improve European know-how and proficiency.

Regardless of its level of success, critics back in Washington continued to publicly denounce the Marshall Plan even after it became law. The most common argument was that it was nothing more than a handout and a drain on American taxpayers. Joseph McCarthy, the rabid junior Senator from Wisconsin was—not for the first or last time—entirely out of line when, on the Senate floor in June 1951, he indicted George Marshall in scathing terms. The speech, later published as "America's Retreat from Victory: The Story of George Catlett Marshall," signaled the beginning of the end for McCarthy's anti-government crusade. Reversing reality —and certainly the reality experienced in Moscow—McCarthy asserted that rather than strengthening Western Europe, the ERP had, in fact, strengthened the Communist world. He dismissed the entire Plan as nothing more than a "massive and unrewarding boondoggle."[14] Never one to let facts get in the way of his narrative, McCarthy overlooked the plan's benefits to the United States. It was never a zero-sum game. The Marshall Plan provided benefits on both sides of the Atlantic. From the beginning, for example, the ERP encouraged the procurement of surplus goods from the United States while discouraging the acquisition of goods in short supply in the U.S. It mandated that surplus agriculture commodities be supplied by the United States, and that half of all goods would be delivered on ships flying the U.S. flag. As has been the case with the vast majority of foreign aid programs since, the result was positive for American businesses, food producers, manufacturers, and citizens more generally. By the time the Marshall Plan ended, over 80 percent of European ECA procurement dollars had been spent in the United States. Europeans were also not—accusations by McCarthy and others notwithstanding—simply benefiting from being on the American dole. The ECA had considerable leverage over recipients, and aid was conditioned upon participants committing to a series of demands that tied them to the inter-European American idea and pushed them to abandon nationalistic policies. Among the available steps was the opportunity to withhold large sums in counterpart funds, which could only be released with ECA approval and for specific purposes. This provided Americans leverage in certain cases, though most historians now accept that the ECA's power was, at times, deceptive because political circumstances on the ground often trumped economic ones.

Even if Europeans could occasionally evade American demands, the ECA's formal level of authority unsurprisingly did not sit well with recipient governments. French, Italian, and British officials, in particular, often resented the heavy-handed American influence. Given their previous status, this was to be expected. All three powers had been not only European powerhouses, but global actors with interests around the world. Hoffman's demands and the considerable extent to which these nations were now dependent on Washington and fearful of Moscow was only a further reminder of their declining status. They did not look kindly upon what many considered direct interference in internal matters. Because of this, Europeans frequently attempted to challenge Hoffman and his cadre of administrators. Most of this opposition came from politicians who traced their political roots to the left or center-left of the political spectrum. Old-time Trade Unionist Ernest Bevin, for example, who had spent his career pushing for a greater political welfare state, was of the opinion that "the British had 'little to learn' from American managers, whose methods of 'handling staff' impressed him as particularly 'dictatorial and unsuited for to European conditions.'"[15] Many French officials similarly attempted to convince American officials, including Harriman and David K. E. Bruce, the ECA's chief of mission in France and later U.S. Ambassador to Paris, that they knew best how to settle their nation's economic problems. Scenarios of a similar nature played out in America's relationship with Italy and with some, though not all, of the smaller recipient nations.

Defensive postures among Congressmen at home and Europeans abroad rarely persuaded American administrators to alter course. The rationale for the ECA's organization and the extent of its power on the ground was that Washington recognized local politicians would be tempted to use aid to solve short-term problems related to public morale. This could include disproportionately boosting wages or supporting excessive importation of consumer goods. While politically popular, such initiatives would only increase the dollar gap and threaten further inflation. They also ran counter to the American belief that long-term modernization programs, however austere they might appear, were crucial to eventual recovery. Lewis Douglas, the U.S. Ambassador to the United Kingdom and a key State Department Marshall Plan coordinator, noted, for example, that Paris had a "record of unsatisfactory fiscal policies" and he doubted that France would take appropriate steps without external pressure. As early as August 1947, U.S. Ambassador to Paris, Jefferson Caffery similarly suggested that the U.S. should be prepared to withdraw aid to ensure that the French "put their financial house in order."[16] In line with this belief, the ECA carefully monitored French spending plans and took active steps to contain these plans when they ran counter to American ideas of economic progress. They wanted to tie the release of counterpart funds to French containment of public spending and the pursuit of anti-inflationary policies. Of particular concern was the French government's apparent willingness to let consumer demands drive the level of imports with little to no regard for the subsequent depletion of the treasury's dollar and gold reserves. There was also concern that successive French governments between 1947 and 1949 were tempted to break the parliamentary-established 200 billion franc debt-ceiling rather than fund spending with tax revenues. Once Marshall Aid began flowing, Bruce and his administrators on the ground took strong steps to ensure that France complied, because they believed that if the French government asked parliament to raise the debt ceiling, it would indicate that the French economy was struggling to recover and the ECA was unable to control the situation. To keep the French government in line, the U.S. directly and indirectly made counterpart fund releases dependent on French commitments to monetary stability and a balanced budget.

An American Empire?

To some scholars, the manner in which the United States imposed its will and its ideas upon its new postwar partners resembles the behavior of an imperial power. In terms of the Marshall Plan this was a view held, of course, by Communists, who aimed to undermine American influence in Europe, but the argument has been revived in recent years by scholars, writing in response to the war in Iraq. Increasingly they have adopted William Appleman Williams' belief that the idea and reality of America is not even possible without empire.[1]

There is certainly no doubt that while the ERP may have been intended as a New Deal for Washington's allies, the strings attached to the program in many recipient countries made the U.S. appear to be more than just a benefactor. Historians Geir Lundestad and Charles Maier have explained the relationship more in terms of hegemony than traditional empire. In different contexts, Lundestad has, for example, defined the relationship between Washington and its new partners as both an "empire by invitation" and an "empire of integration." Whatever the appropriate moniker, it is clear that *if* this was indeed an American "empire," it was one that left an unusual degree of maneuverability to the supposed "victims." Always among the most perceptive observers of foreign policy, Walter Lippmann captured this remarkable new reality shortly after Truman signed the European Recovery Program into law in 1948. In Lippmann's words, it is not: "only this feeling that Russia is an intruder in Europe which possesses the nations of Europe. In a different way they feel also that their dependence upon America for sustenance, rehabilitation, and protection is, however necessary today, in the long run intolerable. If they cannot be slaves to Russian despotism neither can they be clients of the American republic." There were undoubtedly times between 1947 and 1951 when Europeans felt like American client states. In 1948, Sir Stafford Cripps warned the British cabinet that rejecting the terms of Marshall Aid would lead to a "number of violent shocks to the home economy at a number of separate points. The results to the structure of output, exports, investment, consumption and employment are extremely difficult to assess. We should be faced with an abrupt transition from a partially suppressed inflation to something not unlike a slump." To proud peoples such as the English, the status of dependency that Cripps described was uncomfortable at best. At the same time, it was a status that was far preferable to the one Moscow subjected its satellite states to in Eastern Europe or even to the one European powers had subjected their subjects to in the nineteenth and twentieth centuries in Africa and Asia.

Note

1 William Appleman Williams, *Empire as a Way of Life: An Essay on the Causes and Character of America's Present Predicament along with a Few Thoughts about an Alternative* (New York, Oxford University Press, 1980)

Despite this power to direct French policies, political conditions were a constant source of concern for David Bruce. In September, 1948, he informed Hoffman that the situation was "heading for a tragic climax." Bruce described a situation in which:

> Prices [are] still rising; uneasiness in rank non-Communist labor has made hold-the-line attitude of leaders nearly untenable in face of threatened strikes. . . . Demand for dollar and other hard currencies in black market depriving state of essential exchange. Retention of grain by peasants threatens collections. Unless checked soon, inflation will destroy gains painfully achieved during the first six months 1948.[17]

He considered the steady deterioration of confidence in the franc a menace "not only to [the] French economy but to [the] whole European recovery effort." When French Prime Minister Henri Queuille finally took steps to reform tax policy and curb government spending, the Americans deduced that their subtle pressure had forced the government to fall in line.

This counterpart diplomacy did not always work. As would be the case when Americans began providing aid to developing nations in the 1950s and 1960s, unanticipated local factors tended to overrule the ability to dictate uncompromising economic terms. When Communist strikes and street fighting between leftwing and rightwing protesters left over a hundred injured in France in late 1948, Bruce effectively warned Washington that economic austerity principles mattered little if the government fell. As a result, the ECA chose to release additional funds in an attempt to stabilize the government.[18]

Similar complications arose in Italy. After the Christian Democrats' 1948 election victory, American administrators were determined to stand firm and push Italy towards what they considered responsible economic modernization policies. As Walter Lippmann warned in the *Washington Post*, if Rome did not emphasize reconstruction, then "the electoral victory we are celebrating today will gradually become rancid."[19] The Rome government, however, did not appreciate the American New Deal-style belief that bridging traditional gaps between labor, business, and finance were prerequisites for recovery. Instead, Italy introduced conservative economic budgets to curb spending, stabilize the lira, tackle inflation, and cut government deficits. Rather than using counterpart funds for industrial modernization, the Italian government chose to pocket the money to build up currency reserves. These efforts helped stabilize the economy, but the lack of innovation and public works projects and the failure to introduce more Keynesian formulae led to high unemployment. In the long run some of these measures proved beneficial to Italian exports but the American ECA chief in Rome James Zellerbach was unimpressed at the time. He publicly criticized De Gasperi's government for what he considered an ineffective use of funds and opposed the Italian government's decision to side with management over labor. This policy undermined the attempt by the U.S. to move European labor unions away from their traditional leftwing political role and threatened to tie them to the still active Italian Communists. Despite their opposition to Italian steps, the Truman Administration overall struggled to force Italy to pursue expansionary fiscal policies or emphasize domestic consumption.[20] The American dilemma was that while they worried that high unemployment levels might cause social instability, there was equal concern in American circles that pressuring the Italian government or withholding counterpart funds might lead to its downfall. In light of the strong leftwing presence and the close nature of the April election, this was not a step Washington was willing to take. In hindsight, it appears Americans overestimated the extent of the Communist threat at this stage, but there is no doubt that it curbed the kind of demands the ECA was willing to place upon the Italians.

Great Britain was the largest and most important Marshall Aid recipient. Between 1948 and 1958, Britain's economic recovery was among the most impressive in Europe. Occasional setback aside, Britain's industrial output increased steadily during this ten-year period, inflation was under control when compared with the volatile preceding decade, unemployment dropped to between two and three percent, and her dollar and gold reserves increased. During the same period, Britain—in part pressured by the U.S. and by the cost of upkeep—began the dismantlement of its global empire; first on the Indian Subcontinent and then in the Middle East.[21] At the same time, as we have seen, Britain handed over its costly involvement in Greece to the United States and managed to pass on some of its expenses in Germany to the Americans after the fusion of the two zones in 1946.

Despite her relative success, like the French and the Italians, the British also, at times, engaged in fierce debates with the Americans over the proper course for recovery. Due to the particular nature of the British economy, including the role of the Commonwealth, and the absence of a domestic leftwing political threat, London had more freedom regarding the spending of Marshall Aid. As a result, her fiercest clashes with the Americans arose not over spending programs but were, rather caused by from British recalcitrance to European integration after 1947 and over currency concerns.

The latter problem was closely related to Britain's deliberate commitment to maintaining the high level of imports desired by the population and its increasingly expansive welfare state. The result was vast expenditure on domestic services and consumer goods from abroad. Between 1947 and 1948 alone, 75 percent of wheat and tobacco, 50 percent of corn, barley, and oats, 40 percent of cotton, meat, bacon, sugar, oils and fats for food industries, came from the U.S. dollar area.[22] The vast expenses associated with the welfare state, including the Labour government's commitment of medical support for all from cradle to grave further strained London's position. In 1949, Lewis Douglas warned the State Department that Britain faced its first major economic crisis since the beginning of Marshall Aid.[23] Despite Washington's overall push for greater European integration, much of the British economy targeted the Commonwealth. British production methods and avenues suffered from a lack of innovation and many of its goods were either of too low a quality or too expensively produced to make them competitive on the global market. This soon led to decreasing exports at a time when Britain, as shown above, was pursuing high imports. By mid-summer of 1949, Britain's gold and dollar reserves had slipped dramatically. The U.S. Embassy in London cautioned that a continued drain on these reserves would result in a deep financial crisis and would likely lead to the collapse of the Labour government. As a result, the ECA began to increasingly push for a currency devaluation to get the situation under control and to increase exports. Sir Stafford Cripps opposed the measure as did other British advisors. A devaluation of sterling, they reasoned, would increase the cost of American imports which they deemed vital not only to the national recovery but also to help boost British public morale. While some Americans shared Cripps' concern and also worried that tough unpopular measures might lead Britain in a more protectionist direction, there was a growing belief that devaluation and a curbing of some welfare state costs were necessary.[24] Ultimately no alternative existed as the postwar balance of deficits continued to climb. Under pressure from Hoffman, the British government in September of 1949 devalued the pound by 30 percent to stem the drain on reserves. This effort, along with improved economic conditions in the United States, led to an increase in British exports and steadied the U.K.'s financial ship. When Marshall Aid to Great Britain ended in December of 1950—well ahead of schedule and a year earlier than on the continent—the British economy was strong and growing once again. Although it accounted for only two percent of GNP, Marshall Aid played a crucial role in this recovery, though perhaps not as great a role as the immediate and more urgent American postwar loan provided to Great Britain in 1945 and 1946.

But not even this recovery could disguise the fact that Britain's use of Marshall Aid and loans was not always prudent. The heavy investment in products intended to lift the public spirits meant that the path to recovery came at a cost. Unlike France, Great Britain possessed no national plan for industrial modernization, nor did it have anywhere near the kind of carefully balanced approach to return the country to its prewar status exhibited by West Germany over the next decade. The lack of postwar attention to modernization of infrastructure and industries meant that while Germany and Japan emerged as modern economic powerhouses, Britain lingered, struggling to define its own position as a welfare state and still, at times, clinging to the illusion that it was a world power. The year Marshall Aid ended, Britain's investment in infrastructure and industry stood under ten percent, while West Germany committed almost 20 percent of GNP. West Germany's industrial output soared, particularly in machinery and manufactured output, including cars. Its autobahns would soon become revered as the principal connecting points of Western European trade and movement of people and its railroads would become electrified at a time when Britain still operated with semaphore signaling and clapped-out rail tracks. Perhaps it was worth the sacrifice by Britain to, in historian John Killick's words, "add a little color to a drab world," but the price was a permanent secondary status to Germany in Europe.[25]

The growing American influence was felt in smaller recipient nations as well, but while many of these countries similarly resented interference, the need for aid made most willing to surrender to ECA terms. In Denmark, for example, Hans Hedtoft's Social Democratic government largely welcomed the organized, planned economic approach, especially because it granted the sitting government a considerable national role in the distribution of aid and helped strengthen the party already in power. Furthermore, the Social Democrats had won the election on a program that tied recovery to industrialization. They were prepared to lessen income redistribution and wage growth in return for the kind of long-term economic progress which the ECA targeted. Recent research implies that the Marshall Plan's impact on the Danish economy was fairly limited and mostly indirect; its chief effect was the manner in which Europe's overall recovery helped reopen agricultural markets for Danish exports. The direct benefit to Denmark's resource-rich neighbors Sweden and Norway was, in financial terms, likewise limited. Norway's Atlantic borders and shipping industry generated considerable industrial output and helped keep unemployment low, while timber and pulp played an essential role in securing Sweden's recovery. Natural resources rather than decisions made by the ECA appear to have been key to Oslo and Stockholm's recovery. Ideologically, however, the ERP's impact in Scandinavia was significant, as it helped draw Norway and Denmark permanently into the U.S.-designed West; a path it is not at all evident that Copenhagen would otherwise have followed. Traditionally neutral, Sweden, of course, recoiled from this. At times, Sweden—far more so than Denmark—also vehemently opposed ECA pressure for inter-European commitments. Further to the south, Belgium relied less on Marshall Aid than most of the other war-torn countries. Prior to Germany's recovery, Brussels was one of the principal suppliers of coal on the continent, which helped strengthen her economy in the early postwar years. The ERP's principal importance here lay in the stimulus it delivered to the modernization of a wide variety of economic sectors, but it did not play an overwhelming role in the national recovery.

Among the smaller nations, the European Recovery Program played its most critical part in the Netherlands and Austria. The Second World War destroyed much of Dutch traditional trade, and it signaled the beginning of the end of her Far East Empire. By 1949, the Dutch were forced to grant independence to Indonesia, but not before a costly conflict that they could ill afford to fight. In the absence of aid, the government would have been forced to tighten the belt and lower national con-sumption. Financially, they likely could have weathered the storm, but as was the case in Italy and France, it appears likely that political instability would have ensued had it not been for American support. Austria faced one of the most precarious situations on the continent at the end of the war. Divided into four occupation zones, the nation, which had quite willingly allowed itself to be annexed by Hitler in 1938, was low on much-needed short-and long-term resources. As a proportion of GDP, the Vienna government received more aid than any other nation, and it was put to good effect. Counterpart funds helped import foods and, more importantly in the long run, were used to rebuild industries in utilities and infrastructure. Chief among these was the hydroelectric power plant at Kaprun near Salzburg, which played a key role in Austrian modernization. In Austria more so than in other recipient countries, Marshall Plan dollars were also spent on the creation of a tourism enterprise. Spas, hotels, resorts, ski lifts, and tourist towns received extensive support to make tourism Austria's most significant modern industry. The fact that the Soviet occupation zone, in stark contrast, was run largely as a colony during this period only helped ensure that Austria, even after it was forced to declare itself neutral in the Cold War in 1955 following the U.S.–Soviet agreed Austrian State Treaty, always leaned to the West.[26]

In small and large nations alike, the ECA's pressure met with varying success. It is beyond the scope of this study to examine this in great detail, but because many scholars in recent years have gone to great lengths to emphasize the limitations of American persuasiveness, it has become fashionable to interpret U.S. economic policy in Europe as a case of the "tail wagging the dog," to use a metaphor often invoked by scholars discussing the Soviet Union's limited ability to control its client states in the post-Stalin years. The Marshall Plan, one scholar tersely argues, was nothing but a "feeble weapon."[27] It is worth noting, however, that those who reach this conclusion do so because they invariably interpret the Marshall Plan through a narrow Cold War lens. As stated in Chapter 1, American plans for the postwar economic order long predated the Cold War and many of the principles the Marshall Plan aimed to sustain were already in place by the time aid began flowing in 1948. This is a reminder that the conflict with the Soviet Union did not create the need for U.S. involvement, though it did strengthen it. As we have already seen, ideological visions for the world, of which economic liberalization was a part, heavily influenced how Washington dictated conditions to Britain between 1941 and 1945 and planned for the postwar order during the Second World War.

The case of U.S.-French policy provides a potent example of why the Marshall Plan should not be interpreted solely through a Cold War era prism. As in the case of Great Britain, American pressure to reorganize France's economic role in the world began long before the Cold War. Between 1944 and 1946, Washington went to great lengths to dictate Paris' economic policy to an extent that diverged dramatically from the goals of French wartime leaders such as General Charles de Gaulle. Not unlike his British conservative counterparts, de Gaulle mistakenly believed that, once the war ended, France would be able to return to its former glory. France, General de Gaulle believed, "could not be France without greatness." He expected that she would recover her empire and her independence on the European continent, and he was willing to cede little ground in the pursuit of those goals. This attitude helps explain why the French shared Britain's hesitation and concern regarding the Bretton Woods system and why Paris, in 1944 and 1945, appeared a far more likely candidate to opt out of IMF and World Bank participation than Moscow. It was, of course, an unrealistic scenario. As in the case of Great Britain, the France of yesteryear no longer existed. Economist Jean Monnet understood as much; a veteran of the interwar economic difficulties, Monnet endorsed the idea of European integration over a strong postwar nationalistic stance as early as 1943. While the U.S., the Soviet Union, and the British Empire could fall back on other resources and markets, Monnet explained, France was "bound up in Europe. She cannot escape." European peace and productivity demanded a single free trade area. Monnet was willing to surrender a degree of sovereignty for the sake of peace and prosperity; de Gaulle was not. In the General's view, a "United States of Europe" could only become a "Europe of the United States." Washington's influence, he believed, would rise at the expense of French independence.[28] In the end, events would prove both men right. French recovery required an interdependent Europe as Monnet predicted, but it undeniably led to a considerable degree of U.S. influence.

In 1944, Monnet headed the French Supply Mission to Washington to request U.S. Lend-Lease aid. Here he would secure $3.2 billion for France, but as had been the case for Britain three years earlier, Paris, under Article VII of the agreement, had to commit to the dismantling of trade barriers and to move France towards a more liberal economic order. France's dependence on the Americans became even clearer when Truman terminated Lend-Lease in August of 1945. The effect of the abrupt cancellation of financial aid was even more devastating in Paris than in London. Heavy fighting on French soil had destroyed vast parts of the country, while the nation's status as an at times occupied and at times collaborative power excluded France from the Allied postwar conferences to decide Europe's future. Combined with the fact that the French economy was considerably smaller than Britain's, this limited any leverage Paris might otherwise have enjoyed. Economic data bears out this reality. By the time the war ended, French industrial production stood at two-thirds of the prewar level while food supplies were less than half. The budget deficit had tripled during the war, public debt quadrupled, and foreign debt was almost five times as high as at the start of the war. It only compounded the matter that comparatively these numbers were actually deceptively good. The Great Depression makes 1930s data a poor barometer for comparison, since France's 1938 GDP was comparable to pre-First World War levels. By the time the Second World War ended it was evident to all but the most fervent nationalists that the era of French great power was over. Left with no other options, on December 31, 1945, deadline day, Paris ratified the Bretton Woods agreements, thereby signaling the extent to which de Gaulle's nationalistic ambitions had surrendered to the American-designed world order. There was no realistic alternative. As Finance Minister René Pleven explained to the Constituent Assembly, choosing to withdraw from world affairs to seek an independent path to reconstruction would demand unparalleled sacrifices. It was an echo of the statements delivered in parliaments and foreign ministries across Europe. Two years earlier, Monnet had told de Gaulle: "you speak of greatness . . . but today the French are small."[29] Nothing symbolized this better than the French attempt to obtain credits from the U.S. in the spring

Jean Monnet and the Monnet Plan

The destruction caused by the Second World War severely limited France's potential as a future international power. The Nazi invasion in 1940 and the subsequent Allied invasion after D-Day in 1944 devastated the nation's industrial and agricultural capacities and left large parts of the country in ruins. The country also faced monetary and political crises. During the war, it became clear to economists, including Jean Monnet, that France's recovery would require outside assistance. "The liberation had given us back our freedom" but "those who believed that the Liberation would bring prosperity [who] had lived on idealized memories or impatient hopes . . . the basis of the prosperity they dreamed of had been forgotten for too long to be restored so quickly."[1] As Monnet documented in his memoir, a return to its prewar status as a world imperial power was no longer possible.

Monnet understood that foreign loans would be needed, and that only the United States would be able to provide the necessary injection of support. His wartime observations in Washington persuaded him of the effective ways in which government could mobilize society and reconstruct economies. In January 1946, Monnet drafted a *Plan de Modernisation et d'éuipment* (PME), the so-called "Monnet Plan" which targeted a five-year recovery program. The motto of the plan was "modernization or decadence."[2] To Monnet, it was that simple:

> The whole nation must join in these efforts. People will accept the measures to be taken, but only in so far as they know and understand the real situation. The proposed plan is not only a tool for the administration and the public authorities. It concerns all Frenchmen. It will give them the facts about where we stand, and directives to guide them in their own individual decisions.

The government would run the PME. Its aims were (1) to develop national production and foreign trade; (2) to increase productivity; (3) full employment of manpower; (4) to raise the standard of living and improve the conditions of national life.

It selected specific sectors and targets for recovery. Its core purpose was to rebuild French industries, to bring production levels to the pre-1929 era, and then, by 1950, expand exports. Monnet recognized the hard choices ahead. The PME targeted areas that would ensure output and deliberately avoided those that in the short term might raise the public's morale but were of limited long-term value. They targeted coal, hydro-electricity, and the building of tractors. The goal was to ensure enough coal and steel to make France second to none on the continent. America's commitment to Germany's recovery made this necessary. In that sense, the modernization plan targeted not only the reconstruction of France's productive capacity, but also aimed to ensure that France would overtake Germany as the principal industrial producer in Europe. French strength was to be measured against German strength. The Monnet Plan was an attempt to create a permanent solution to the strategic threat posed by their neighbor to the east who had brought war to France three times in the past seventy years.

Throughout 1946 and into 1947, the PME met stiff resistance from Maurice Thorez and the French Communist Party. Their opposition to French recovery only further helped isolate them, until, in May of 1947, it led to their ousting from government. The Monnet Plan, designed in France and supported in large part by American Marshall Aid, would help make France a permanent and productive member of the West on the world stage. By 1950, the ideas and the men behind them would help make France the principal unifying factor on the continent and the leading advocate for European unity and new economic and political organizations.

Notes

1 Jean Monnet, *Memoirs* (New York: Doubleday, 1978), 233–234.
2 Ibid., 255.

of 1946. In exchange for a loan of $650 million and the write-off of close to $2.25 billion in Lend-Lease debt, the French team led by Leonard Blum "pledged to abandon protectionist import quotas; to confine all discrimination to its period of 'convalescence'; to adopt reasonable *ad valorem* tariffs; and to limit nationalism." Capturing the American ideological mood of the early postwar period, the *New York Times* succinctly referred to the collective British and French loans not as a financial agreement, but rather as an American "investment in a system of government and a way of life."[30] The ECA may never have been as adept at enforcing its will on Paris after 1948 as they had hoped, but when viewed on the long axis, the American ideological influence of French economic policy was considerable.

The 1946 economic plan that Jean Monnet designed to help orchestrate France's postwar recovery further symbolized this American influence. Fascinated by the New Deal's reliance on planning and the American ideology of progress and growth, Monnet's Plan, in stark contrast to the recovery approach taken in London, sought to rebuild and modernize French industries at the expense of the importation of goods to support public spirit. As Hitchcock explains, this allowed France to make better use of Marshall Aid than perhaps any other country. The purpose of the Monnet Plan mirrored Marshall's call a year later for a cure and not a palliative. It channeled investments into crucial industrial sectors whose productive output helped fuel other areas. Steel, coal, electricity, infrastructure and transportation, housing, and agriculture took priority. The result was a remarkable turnaround. When Marshall Aid ended in 1951, France's industrial output exceeded the 1938 productivity level by over 40 percent.[31]

★ ★ ★

By the end of 1948, the ECA reported that "great strides had been made in the reconstruction of the economies of Western Europe." The United States and the Harry Truman Administration could, as Arthur Schlesinger pointed out at the time, consider itself "engaged in the most staggering and portentous experiment in the entire history of our foreign policy."[32] Eighteen months after the Truman Doctrine, the President could feel positive about events at home and abroad. In November 1948, Republicans paid the price for the internal political struggles Lodge had so publicly exposed in the preceding two years. Despite strong leads in the national polls throughout the election season, the GOP candidate Thomas Dewey lost heavily to Harry Truman, who could now finally consider himself president in his own right. He would have to go on without George Marshall, however. Marshall had rarely slowed down professionally since the outbreak of the Second World War. He had postponed surgery at the onset of the Berlin Crisis the previous June, but in December 1948 he finally had a kidney removed. Ready to move on to retirement, Marshall submitted his resignation in early January to a reluctant Harry Truman. The fact that Truman turned to Dean Acheson, the man he, prior to the appointment of Hoffman, had originally tapped to head the ECA two years earlier, sent a clear signal that the relationship between aid and foreign policy would continue to figure heavily in Truman's second term.

Harry Truman was a true believer in an American global mission. Like so many Americans who came to maturity in the early twentieth century, his international political education began in April 1917 when Woodrow Wilson's rhetoric inspired the formation of his global views. The Wilsonian quest to make the world safe for democracy had left Truman enthusiastically feeling "like Galahad after the Grail."[33] Like his predecessor in the oval office, he believed that "Americanism . . . was so very sensible, logical, and practical that societies would adopt those values and systems if only given the chance." As he entered his second term in office, he was ready to expand that chance around the world. Like the modernization theorists who would define much of American thinking about the world a decade later, Truman envisioned a commitment that went well beyond the already revolutionary nature of the Marshall Plan.

By the time of the 1948 election, fragmentary ideas for permanent American foreign aid programs had been circulating in Washington for several years. Walter S. Salant of the Council of Economic Advisers to the Executive Office and the State Department's Benjamin Hardy played key parts in this. Salant had been one of the principal economists involved in assessing U.S. resources, funds, and productive capacity prior to the execution of the Marshall Plan, while Hardy had considerable experience working emergency assistance operations during the war.[34] Both men viewed aid as something much more than an anti-Communist measure; it was a vehicle to promote and export American values of ingenuity, industry, and support. In late 1948, at the request of the White House, they formulated the earliest ideas of an American global assistance program. They suggested that, given the "almost universal yearning for better conditions of life throughout the world," the U.S. should "convert the instrument of America's immense technological resources . . . to the rest of the world." Americans needed to demonstrate how "the application of techniques and procedures that have proved themselves in this country can directly benefit [underdeveloped nations], through increased production of . . . clothing, housing and other consumer goods, better public health, social conditions, etc." Their core argument was the need for a new initiative to absorb the strengths of the Marshall Plan and expand upon its success. From Salant and Hardy's perspective,

> [the] ERP is an emergency operation that provides a shot-in-the-arm of immediate consumption of goods and means boosting production in a short time. The new program, expected to operate effectively on less than fifty million dollars annually, would enable the peoples we aid to use their own efforts to continue these short-term benefits indefinitely.

Emphasizing science and technology, they called for making

> full and affirmative use of one of the resources in which the U.S. is the richest and the Soviet Union the poorest. Our overwhelming superiority in a field of constructive effort would be apparent to even the most backward and illiterate people.[35]

On January 20, Truman laid out the plan in his inaugural address. Picking up where FDR had left off during the war, he declared that the

> "old imperialism-exploitation for foreign profit has no place in our plans. What we envisage is a program of development based on the concepts of democratic fair-dealing. . . . Democracy alone can

supply the vitalizing force to stir the peoples of the world into triumphant action, not only against their human oppressors, but also against their ancient enemies—hunger, misery, and despair."

Capturing the ideological mood of the Cold War, he summoned Americans to reverse a global situation where more than half the people of the world were victims of disease and lived with scarce food supplies. "For the first time in history," the President insisted,

humanity [possesses] the knowledge and skills to relieve the suffering of these people. The United States is pre-eminent among nations in the development of industrial and scientific techniques. The material resources which we can afford to use for the assistance of other peoples are limited. But our imponderable resources in technical knowledge are constantly growing and are inexhaustible. I believe that we should make available to peace-loving peoples the benefits of our store of technical knowledge in order to help them realize their aspirations for a better life. And, in cooperation with other nations, we should foster capital investment in areas needing development. Our aim should be to help the free peoples of the world, through their own efforts, to produce more food, more clothing, more materials for housing, and more mechanical power to lighten their burdens.[36]

What he called for was a modernization program for the doctrine that already bore his name. In his diary, David Lilienthal cheered Truman's speech. As a former director of the TVA, Lilienthal was one of the most qualified thinkers on aid policy and the execution of aid programs. He concurred with the President's assessment that there was an urgent need to pursue "great development undertakings throughout the world, based upon a sharing of our technical skills and resources." Lilienthal, noting that Truman echoed the words and ideas expressed in his 1944 book *Democracy on the March*, considered the "great address . . . an *effective* (italics in original) alternative to Communism."[37]

As if to underline the importance the President attached to this ambitious aid program, it took the name Point Four because it came fourth on the list of priorities included in his speech: it followed the U.N., the Marshall Plan, and NATO. Good company indeed. As in the case of the ERP, Point Four's purpose extended beyond benevolence. As one advisor later explained, "Financial assistance was closely linked to the achievement of . . . political and security objectives." In addition to uplifting poor nations, economic aid programs could serve to contain Communism because they could make the reestablishment of "normal economic trading relationships between" America's current and potential allies and "areas under Soviet domination" unnecessary.[38]

The national reception of the Point Four program was overwhelmingly positive among reporters and the public. The *New York Post*, in an article ostentatiously entitled "Our World," wrote that just

> as the 19th century was Britain's greatest, so the 20th century is to be America's greatest . . . the world will be shaped by the outflow from us . . . from the now unexplored jungles of Africa to the now unchartered parts of the Far East, from . . . South America to the vastly productive areas of the Middle East. Europe will become secondary.

Much like the Marshall Plan, Point Four was designed "to build, not simply to 'contain.'" The *Watertown Daily Times* declared that Truman had plotted "the new world role of the United States," asking American capital "to invade new areas . . . [to] raise the living standards of millions and provide rich markets for American products." Only the U.S. could "light a beacon to pierce the darkness . . . we continue our crusade for peace."[39] Nothing summed up the national feeling better than the *Washington Post's* excitement at the project. In a long front-page article, the paper highlighted just how "Roosevelt's dream" had now finally become a formal "U.S. objective." Truman, the columnist insisted,

> has given the whole concept a push such as it never had before. He has dramatized it to the hundreds of millions, abroad and at home, who read or heard his inaugural address. He has thrown the whole weight of the Presidency into getting the problem of back-ward areas out of the realm of talk and into the realm of action.[40]

Point Four sought to make ideas the core of America's message overseas. It reflected, as Scott Lucas argues in a different context, that the Cold War was not simply a contest of national security or economics, but "a clash of cultures and ideologies."[41] It built on New Deal and Marshall Plan experiences and it highlighted the American belief that unlike the Soviet model, which was always followed by authoritarian control, the U.S. model promoted modernization along with the development of popular government.

Point Four never lived up to these inflated expectations. Unlike the ERP, it lacked extensive Congressional support and a bureaucracy capable of implementing its ambitious agenda. Not until 1961 would the U.S.

have a permanent bureaucratic organ to handle aid policy and in the absence of a global ECA, Point Four was from the beginning at a distinct disadvantage. Because of these shortcomings, historians until recently either neglected or treated Point Four with scorn; it is, at best, a footnote in most scholarship on the early Cold War. This dismissal is unfortunate. When considered on the long axis, Point Four's real significance is not that it never managed to create a fully sustainable recovery program for the underdeveloped world, but that it represented an attempt to encourage world development and, for a short period, showed great promise and inspired great ideas. Its importance is that it was suggested in the first place.

The next step in the internationalization of American commitments came three months after the announcement of Point Four. This time the focus was Western security. In the past, the United States had always shunned the idea of military guarantees. In his 1796 Farewell Address to the nation, George Washington warned Americans about the danger of, on principle alone, favoring one nation too highly over another. Thomas Jefferson echoed that sentiment in his Inaugural Address when he urged the United States to steer clear of entangling alliances. This principle of unilateralism in foreign affairs had largely been sacrosanct ever since, interrupted only by *temporary* wartime alliances.

On the issue of postwar security, it was the Europeans who took the first step. By 1947, fear of Soviet intervention and the scars of two world wars led to some of the earliest talks among Western Europeans about a loose defense coalition. From the beginning, the key participants were Great Britain, France, the Netherlands, Luxembourg, and Belgium; the principal Western victims of Hitler's aggression. Unsurprisingly, they courted the United States as well. While the Truman Doctrine had informally devoted the United States to the protection of democracy against totalitarianism, and the Marshall Plan committed the U.S. to European socio-economic recovery, there was no formal military promise to safeguard Europe against aggressors. Seeking to obtain just such a commitment, Bevin broached the idea of American military support during conversations with the State Department's Director of the Office of European Affairs John Hickerson in December 1947. The British Foreign Secretary presented Hickerson with an unfinished illustration of circles outlining a hypothetical military relationship. As Hickerson later recalled it, there was one circle, a tight one. Then they wanted another circle taking in the [eventual] Brussels Pact countries and the U.S. and Canada, not quite as tightly drawn, but still a circle to bring us into a collective defense arrangement.[42]

When Washington hesitated, the Europeans pressed on by themselves. In March 1948, Britain, France, and the Benelux countries concluded the

Brussels Pact to form the Western Union Defence Organization, which pledged that members would defend each other from external military action. By the fall of 1948, Arthur Schlesinger had determined that the stark difference between the American Marshall Plan and Soviet methods in Czechoslovakia and its aggressive tactics in Western Europe finally destroyed any "fantasy" among Europeans that neutrality was possible in the Cold War.[43] In reality, the Brussels Pact was worth little. Even united, the democracies' depleted militaries stood no chance of holding the line in a potential war against the several hundred Soviet divisions stretched across Eastern Europe's frontier. It took events in Prague and Berlin in 1948 for the U.S. to get onboard with Bevin's request.

In April of 1949, a month before Stalin finally gave up his siege of West Berlin, the United States, Canada, Belgium, Denmark, France, Iceland, Italy, Luxembourg, the Netherlands, Norway, Portugal, and the United Kingdom met in Washington to sign the North Atlantic Treaty to create NATO. The signatories agreed that:

> an armed attack against one or more of them in Europe or North America shall be considered an attack against them all and . . . if such an armed attack occurs, each of them, in exercise of the right of individual or collective self-defence recognised by Article V of the Charter of the United Nations, will assist the Party or Parties so attacked by taking forthwith, individually and in concert with the other Parties, such action as it deems necessary, including the use of armed force.[44]

Despite the formal commitment to the principles of the United Nations, the Treaty only further underlined Washington's transition from a one-world vision toward the principle of the West. Even countries like Italy—which could hardly claim to be an "Atlantic" nation—joined the alliance. As would later be the case when Greece and Turkey entered the alliance, the inclusion of Rome as a security partner was a crucial American signal that no Western partner would be left to fend for itself.[45]

Once again, conservative Republicans challenged the American expansion of commitments to its allies and once again they were rebuffed. A military alliance was

Article V

The purpose of NATO was to protect Europe from outside aggression. It is not without irony, therefore, that the only time that Article V has been invoked was in 2001, when the Europeans came to the protection of the United States in the aftermath of the Al Qaeda attacks on September 11.

needed, Hickerson maintained, regardless of "whether entangling alliances have been considered worse than original sin since George Washington's time." New Secretary of State Dean Acheson shared Hickerson's view. The opinion of these two men reflected, as historian Robert Beisner explains, the intensifying belief within the United States that it was no longer enough for the West to be "strong enough to *contain* [italics in original] the Kremlin." Americans wanted the West to win the Cold War.[46] When conservative Republicans objected to NATO, it was once again Henry Cabot Lodge, Jr. that challenged them. In a town hall debate with Utah Republican Senator Arthur Watkins, Lodge dismissed the common conservative GOP argument that NATO was unnecessary. "It all depends," Lodge claimed,

> on whether you think the attempt of international communism to set up a Godless world dictatorship is a threat to the United States. If you do not think it is a threat . . . then the Marshall Plan, the North Atlantic Pact, and none of the things we have been doing make sense.[47]

By 1949, few believed that. Far from being merely an effort to save the Europeans, U.S. policy was now a series of "conscious and comprehensive attempts at changing Europe in the direction of U.S. ideas and models."[48]

★ ★ ★

Moscow was the catalyst that inspired the creation of NATO, but there is, at the same time, no doubt that the new alliance emerged within a culture of growing Western unity. Shortly after Marshall's speech in 1947, Jean Monnet told Robert Schuman that,

> to tackle the present situation, to face the dangers that threaten us, and to match the American effort, the countries of Western Europe must turn their national efforts into a truly European effort. This will be possible only through a *federation* of the West.[49]

The idea grew in the coming years. Designed in Paris, encouraged in Washington, desired in The Hague, Brussels, Rome, and elsewhere, and accepted in many other capitals, it brought Western Europe closer together. In 1948, European leaders, including soon to be West German Chancellor Konrad Adenauer, former British Prime Minister Winston Churchill, Georges Bidault, De Gasperi, Schuman, and many others, convened in Holland. The conference produced little and, in hindsight, it is easy to dismiss it as insignificant, but the conversations on political integration were a powerful statement of intent. It was an early sign of a maturing idea.

European unity developed slowly over the next two years, but it was kept alive by the combined role of the OEEC, the Soviet threat, and the persistent ECA demands for inter-European trade and continent-wide connections. In 1949, the ECA and the OEEC began working on an agreement to get the Marshall Plan recipient nations to create a European Payments Union (EPU) that would support intra-European currency transferability and further promote the idea of free trade by breaking down quotas and tariffs. This system, under which participants would subject their reserves and economies to currency convertibility, merged with the principles inherent in the ERP's technical assistance program to increase specialized innovational skills across industries and make the European economies more globally competitive. This development would integrate economic collaboration to a far greater extent than ever before and decrease the need for imports from the dollar zone, thereby increasing the potential for growth. As the predecessor to the later European Monetary System, the EPU was a mechanism under which currencies could be freely exchanged among participants thereby ending the failed system of bilateral exchange controls in existence before the Second World War.

The EPU model fit a new mode of thinking among Europeans, though not all supported the idea with equal conviction or desire. Once again, Great Britain was particularly skeptical. London had always envisioned itself as something of a midwife between the United States and the European continent and had been consistently hesitant to commit itself to economic collaboration. NATO had already moved the British out of their traditional comfort zone, but while security had been considered a necessary evil, the kind of collaboration proposed under the EPU, Cripps believed, threatened the British Commonwealth and the sterling area. The Chancellor of the Exchequer hoped that a position could be found in which Britain would have one foot in the new payments union, but would maintain its bilateral trade relationships and preserve greater British economic independence. Hoffman rejected this flat out. European integration had always been a key component of the ERP and, as had become increasingly clear since the Second World War, Britain no longer had the authority or influence to counter U.S. policy. Hoffman considered the EPU vital to further integration and, when faced with British obstinacy, he threatened that a quarter of the following year's ERP aid would be made available only to nations willing to aggressively pursue continental integration. Likely conscious of the extensive ways in which Britain had attempted to evade American postwar designs ever since FDR and Churchill signed the Atlantic Charter, the ECA was unwilling to compromise. The issue "with the British . . . is not a mere difference of views as to the technical solution of the sterling problem, but rather a basic difference of choice between economic nationalism and economic internationalism," the ECA informed Secretary of State Acheson. The issue, as the ECA saw it, was whether Britain was willing "to participate fully in the European and in the world economies and thereby enjoy those eventual improvements in productivity and in the standard of living which members in a wide, freely-trading area can bring."[50] In May 1950, Britain consented to join the EPU as a full member. As they had done on previous occasions, the U.S. demonstrated flexibility—this time for sterling—but Britain had to accept the new principled European economic system. The EPU, Behrman accurately states, "revolutionized European trade." It ensured that trade could be made in any European currency, and its mechanisms effectively helped make "deficits and surpluses" meaningless "between any two members." The key issue was no longer bilateral, but each member's trading position with the collective group of nations. Over the next decade, the result was skyrocketing multilateral trade among members—just what the U.S. had sought from the very beginning.[51]

The EPU was only one example of a rapidly developing process. Even as negotiations over improved trade conditions were underway, Paris and Bonn began moving independently on a measure that would transform Europe's political and economic map to an even greater degree. As had been the case since the end of the war, the cause and solution to all the continent's problems lay in Germany. Germany's size made her the most important trade market for many European nations. As a result, German recovery was crucial because it was the artery through which the economic recovery of nations such as Denmark, Sweden, Austria, the Netherlands, and others flowed. The development of an economically strong Germany, however, had caused great concern in France since 1945. Germany's Rhine and Ruhr regions were home to the most important raw materials in Europe. These regions' coal and iron ore reserves, the two principal ingredients for the making of steel, were crucial for both economic productivity and for the machinery of war. Neither country felt secure unless it commanded those resources. By the spring of 1949, the threat of Germany starting another war appeared less likely as the conclusion of the Berlin blockade gave way to the creation of the democratic Federal Republic of Germany (FRG) in the west and the Communist German Democratic Republic (GDR) in the east. However, as the Soviet Union broke the U.S. monopoly on atomic weapons in August, and China fell to Communism in October, many in Europe and the U.S. feared that the next war might be over Germany. These changing realities gave both the French and the Germans an incentive to move closer together.

In early 1950, Foreign Minister Robert Schuman, working off of Jean Monnet's ideas and suggestions, reached out to German Chancellor Konrad Adenauer, the head of the FRG, to suggest close economic cooperation. Adenauer, eager to move Germany away from its wartime past, wholeheartedly embraced the proposal.[52] Born in the disputed territory of Lorraine, Schuman was German by birth and the ideal candidate to reach out to Adenauer. A skillful diplomat, Dean Acheson later reminisced, his proposal emerged most impressively at a time when "it was hard to have vision in France . . . [a nation] in the grip of an inferiority neurosis."[53] Adenauer similarly, had come to find that his place and West Germany's belonged in a community of nations. The Schuman Plan, as the idea the two men agreed upon came to be known, received American backing in late April during talks with Acheson and was presented to the public on May 9.[54] The bold venture intended to bring the two old enemies together in a union to produce coal and steel under one authority. It aimed to leave the past behind and bring about a new, productive, and unified Europe. When Acheson first learned of the plan in a private meeting with Schuman and David Bruce the idea appeared "so breathtaking a step toward the unification of Western Europe that at first I did not grasp it." The Secretary of State worried that a cartel, precisely the kind of institution American ERP-policy sought to break up, might emerge as a result of this venture. Schuman reassuringly dismissed this. The goal was a political conception: "the unification of Western European by economic means."[55] The French Foreign Minister called it "a leap in the dark," but to many it was a leap filled with intense optimism. Schuman's plan called for continental integration and the French and Germans openly sought the support and participation of other European powers, especially Great Britain. Already displaying the hesitation toward continental unity that has plagued Britain ever since, London opted out of the venture refusing to "buy a pig in a poke" as Bevin colorfully informed Acheson.[56] The history of Anglo-French unity against Germany had come to a close; a new Europe inspired by the Marshall Plan's success was emerging with France and West Germany at its heart.

By June 1950, close to $11 billion in ERP support had made its way into Europe. As conditions improved, strikes began to vanish, farmers made goods available for markets, and black markets lost their power. Communist parties, which had spent two years fighting the Marshall Plan as an example of American imperialism, were losing the propaganda war. All across the continent, public displays illustrating Marshall Aid dollars at work were on display while videos demonstrating its success were shown across Europe. UNRRA supplies, due to the far more neutral vision for global reconstruction envisioned by the U.S. under the 1944 and 1945 "one world" banner, were intended to be apolitical and had thus been shipped without defining the country of origin. In contrast, ERP goods carried a red, white, and blue emblem and they bore the slogan "For European Recovery: Supplied by the United States." A peaceful Europe was on the rise. Another full year of reconstruction aid was expected to further boost recovery. It all changed on June 25, 1950.

★ ★ ★

Five thousand five hundred miles east of Paris, the Cold War turned hot when North Korean Communist troops invaded South Korea. Although we now know that Stalin did not orchestrate the attack, in June of 1950 nobody in Washington doubted that Moscow was behind it. In an overhaul of U.S. national security strategy presented to Truman less than three months before the unexpected attack in Korea, the National Security Council defined the Soviet Union as an aggressive state intent on world domination. The world, the NSC told Truman, was between freedom and slavery and between light and darkness. Whereas there was "purpose" to American policy the Soviets possessed only scheming "designs."[57] Korea seemed to confirm this conclusion. As he had in Berlin, Truman instantly concluded that this kind of aggression would not stand against a Cold War ally. Backed by U.N. forces, the United States intervened militarily against the North Koreans, who would soon be aided by Mao's Chinese "volunteer" army.

Truman's decisive response did not reflect any particular strategic concern. At least, no more so than had West Berlin in 1948. As Deputy Defense Secretary Robert Lovett explicated, and Secretary of State Acheson, Secretary of Defense Marshall, the Joint Chiefs, and Director of Central Intelligence Walter Bedell Smith all agreed, "Korea is not a decisive area for us." Even if losing Korea meant jeopardizing America's ability to maintain Japan in the Western sphere, "Western Europe" was the "prime concern and we would rather see that result [the loss of Japan] than lose in Western Europe." Henry Cabot Lodge, Jr. encapsulated this atmosphere in Washington:

Korea

After the Chinese Communist Revolution in 1949, the United States refused to recognize Mao Zedong's People's Republic of China and to grant them a seat at the United Nations. In protest the Soviet Union was boycotting the U.N. Security Council when North Korea attacked in June of 1950. This prevented a Soviet veto and explains why the Korean War became a U.N. war against Communist aggression.

> the situation with regards to Europe is potentially a thousand
> times more portentous and dangerous than the situation in Korea.
> The point of the Soviet arrow is not aimed at Korea or at Formosa
> or at Indo-China or at Iran: It is aimed at West-Germany.[58]

Truman needed the best men he could get, and so in the early fall he forced out sitting Defense Secretary Louis Johnson and brought Marshall back to active duty, this time to head the Department of Defense.[59]

The connections between the Korean War and the global situation changed the Marshall Plan as well. Europe was entirely incapable of defending itself against the Red Army. As a firmer and more confrontational American policy replaced the policy of containment, Washington's European policy priorities shifted from aid for the purpose of economic stability to military security. As it did, the ECA's influence in government declined as well. It had always been an unusual agency. The ECA operated overseas but it was not entirely under the State Department and it did not answer directly to the Secretary of State. This reason for this division of influence was, in part, to secure a degree of independent oversight. It was, however, also closely connected to the likelihood of a Republican victory in the presidential election of 1948 as the traditional practices associated with a transition of administrations might seriously disrupt the ECA's operational ability. Korea demonstrated the limits of the ECA's authority and influence as Washington's focus shifted away from immediate reconstruction and toward militarization. "In retrospect more than at the time it happened, I recognize how profoundly the Korean War changed the goals and the character of the ECA," a senior Marshall Plan official recalled.[60] By September 1950, the ECA informed the European participants that, henceforth, an increasing proportion of aid would be allocated for rearmament purposes instead of reconstruction. Shortly after, counterpart funds were increasingly decoupled from production purposes. To counter inflation, which resulted from the shortage of a wide range of materials due to the war in Korea, the ECA began to release counterpart funds for the retirement of public debt instead. William Foster, who replaced Hoffman as head of the ECA, also began to promote greater European integration, a development Washington had always deemed crucial to Europe's ability to sustain itself in the future. It was fortunate that the Korean attack occurred so late in the program; after three years, European recovery was on a fairly solid footing and in terms of productivity well ahead of schedule in many countries. By the end of the year, Britain ended Marshall Aid on its own recognizance, almost a year early. Shortly after, aid ended for Portugal, Sweden, and Ireland as well. The Second World War's impact on the three latter nations had been indirect, and, as such, it was unsurprising that they would be among the first for whom Americans suspended aid. In more general terms, it signaled that the Marshall Plan was nearing its end. By 1951, the pressure of the changing situation led to the creation of the Mutual Security Agency (MSA) to effectively succeed the ECA. Headed by Averell Harriman, who made the transition from the ECA's Paris office, the MSA took over military and economic assistance programs except those operated by the Technical Corporation Administration. It reflected how much the situation had changed. Having spent three years supplying economic aid, Americans now instead took to reinforcing Europe. Speaking in front of the Senate in 1951, Secretary of Defense, Marshall made it clear that protecting the idea of America—a democratic, free, non-militarized United States— required the cementation of freedom and democracy in Europe. The fall of Europe to Communism would "put us in an extremely perilous position, I feel, and our national existence would be threatened."[61] Marshall referred to not merely a physical threat, but to one of values: the idea of America was reliant on a world in which its ideals were proselytized, at the very least in Europe. Before Korea, NATO was a paper alliance; after June 1950, Article V meant something more. The U.S. soon reversed its postwar withdrawal policy, and American troops were once again deployed to protect Europe. They have remained a presence on the European continent ever since.

★　★　★

The Marshall Plan was supposed to run until the summer of 1952, but ended six months early, having distributed close to $13 billion. It officially came to an end on December 31, 1951. In its wake, it left Europe in much better economic shape than it had been when the plan began. The overall industrial production aggregate among recipient nations was 41 percent above 1938 levels, while total GNP rose some 25 percent. Steel production and oil refining capacity was considerably above projections outlined when the program began, and the total dollar gap and gold deficit, which had stood at $8 billion in 1947, stood at just over $2 billion by 1952. From the start of the ERP, Americans had lobbied heavily for an increase in inter-European trade and a lowering of barriers. By 1949, the OEEC had helped secure a 50 percent reduction of quota restrictions, and, by 1951, close to 75 percent of import restrictions had been elim-inated. Western Europe had abandoned its intensely nationalistic policies. After three decades of war and depression, optimism had returned to the continent despite the threat of Soviet Communism.

The Marshall Plan's most impressive achievement was the manner in which it helped make Europe an entity in its own right. In 1949, Congress amended the European Recovery Authorization Act to formally encourage the unification of European states. Though it is unclear just how much of an effect the United States' effort had on inspiring or even creating the European Economic Community—and later, the European Union—it was certainly not insignificant. In May 1947, William Clayton suggested that a European Federation was needed to secure Europe's recovery. A united Europe tied to American ideals, he believed, would set the tone for growing American influence and the fulfillment of democratization on the continent. Washington was never able to remake Europe entirely in its own image, but the compromise that emerged between American liberalistic ideals and European social democratic visions for society had a lasting impact. After the Marshall Plan, collaboration on the continent became the norm. The idea of the "one world" had vanished. It was replaced by the idea of the West: the system of shared ideas that continues to intimately connect the United States and Canada to its Western European partners.

CHAPTER 5

Epilogue

The Marshall Plan and Memory

"When future historians look back upon the achievements of the Marshall Plan," Richard Bissel, the last administrator of the ECA, declared as the European Recovery Program neared its formal end in late 1951,

> I believe they will see in it the charge that blasted the first substantial cracks in the centuries-old walls of European nationalism—walls that once destroyed will clear the way for the building of a unified, prosperous, and, above all, peaceful continent.[1]

Bissell's comment proved prophetic. In the decades that followed, the ideas, desires, and accomplishments of the Marshall Plan assumed almost legendary status. In the United States, it allowed Americans to remember the government as a source of good, an image that had been difficult to maintain in the aftermath of Vietnam, Watergate, and support for rightwing dictatorships. In American memory, the Marshall Plan was a bright shining moment that helped fortify Americans' faith in the nation and in what the true purpose of the Cold War really was. Western Europeans, scarred by the memories of two world wars and the economic struggles and shortages of the interwar and immediate post-1945 periods, similarly embraced the mythology of the ERP. It is easy to understand why: after the end of the Marshall Plan, Western Europe experienced a period of unprecedented growth and material prosperity. Incomes rose and unemployment dropped. High-end consumer goods such as cars, televisions, refrigerators, vacuum cleaners, washing machines, and other electrical devices dominated a landscape once overshadowed by piles of rubble, destroyed infrastructure, poverty, and hunger. Democracy and liberal ideals became the norm as Western European collaboration replaced the dogmatic nationalism that had dominated earlier periods. This change was captured most dramatically by the creation of inter-European organizations and by West Germany's reentry into the new community of nations. As he departed the Chancellor's Office after serving 15 years in charge as head of the FRG, Konrad Adenauer, in 1964, took time to praise Harry Truman. He commended the president for having refused the temptation "in spite of her past . . . to simply efface Germany from history" and instead make her an equal partner in Europe.[2] The praise was well deserved; it was the power of the United States that forced the other Europeans to accept German recovery. By 1960, West Germany's economy was the third largest in the world by average value of GDP. Despite being roughly the seventeenth largest nation by virtue of population size, Germany's economy has remained among the four largest in the world ever since. In the eyes of Georges Bidault, the French Foreign Minister who had been present at the creation of the European Recovery Program in 1947, "American aid prevented the French economy from coming to a standstill. There has never been a finer more far-sighted gesture in history than the Marshall Plan."[3] It was a view echoed along the entire western side of the Iron Curtain.

The image of Marshall Plan dollars having rescued Europe made captives out of later generations. Its success and popularity inspired the Eisenhower, Kennedy, and Johnson administrations to think of foreign aid as a powerful political, economic, and ideological vehicle of change. When President Kennedy summoned Congress in 1961 to create a permanent agency and mission to globalize U.S. foreign aid, he recalled the Marshall Plan as "a towering and successful program to rebuild the economies of Western Europe and prevent a communist takeover." It was, Kennedy continued, followed "by Point 4—an effort to make scientific and technological advances available to the people of developing nations." To build a permanent aid agency, Kennedy went on, "we will need to renew the spirit of common effort which lay behind our past efforts— we must also revise our foreign aid organization, and our basic concepts of operation to meet the new problems which now confront us." Commemorating the Marshall Plan two years later, Kennedy again asserted that:

> we face another extraordinary challenge—the task of helping the awakening nations of Asia, Africa, and Latin America catch up with the 20th century. Here, once again, a half-hearted response

will not do—and I take heart in the knowledge that many of those who helped to win the great victory over 'hunger, poverty, desperation, and chaos' in Western Europe are still fighting a good fight for freedom.[4]

As described in the preceding chapters, the European Recovery Program undoubtedly provided a considerable economic, political, and, first and foremost, ideological injection to Europe in the 1940s and early 1950s. At the same time, the extent to which the Marshall Plan has since come to be fixed in American and global consciousness as a surgical instrument that can be replicated to solve economic and social crises is misleading at best. Scholars have long since become aware of this. They recognize that the ERP's actual impact was considerably more complicated on both a continent-wide scale and across individual countries. Two decades ago, Barry Eichengreen and March Uzan emphasized that, despite the tendency to invoke the Marshall Plan's impact on Western European economies, its chief contribution was not the stimulation of investments, the augmentation of imports, or even infrastructure repair. Rather, its greatest impact was its ability to rebuild the European market by instilling confidence in nations. It was confidence, these scholars maintain, that brought an end to the hoarding of consumer goods, generated political stability, increased worker efforts and ethics, and ended fears of economic chaos.[5] The problem with this argument is, of course, that the path to confidence is infinitely twisted. European confidence grew from many factors, even those that Eichengreen and Uzan believe the Plan undervalued. It is this complexity which also undermines Milward's argument that the ERP made no noticeable economic difference. The recovery was not merely one of productivity; it was one of belief. The recovery from the war's destruction was a human experience. The eminent historian of European affairs Tony Judt said it most succinctly: The postwar recovery, in his view, could be boiled down to "optimism plus milk." The Marshall Plan provided both.[6]

Nonetheless, Eichengreen and Uzan are undoubtedly correct in their view that the European Recovery Program is remembered nowadays as a metaphor for good rather than for its actual economic accomplishments. The danger of this myth is evident in the persistent belief that new Marshall Plans can and should be established to solve socio-economic crises related to poverty. As is evident from President Kennedy's moments of remembrance, such rhetoric and belief were not in short supply during the 1960s. They emerged at the heart of modernization theory as American economic advisors began thinking about how to recover and reform Latin America and other regions. Based on the experience in the 1940s and 1950s, Harvard economist Lincoln Gordon—who helped formulate the Marshall Plan—believed that,

> American values of freedom, responsible government, and equality of opportunity, together with American economic prosperity, would be more likely to flourish at home if they were widely shared abroad. We had benefited from the revival of Europe and Japan, and would benefit similarly from the modernization of the underdeveloped world.

In the words of modernization historian Michael Latham, the logic behind this was that if "the United States had rebuilt the economy of Western Europe . . . why couldn't it now fundamentally transform the politics, economy, and social life of the rest of its own hemisphere?"[7] The endurance of this belief and the frequency with which the Marshall Plan is introduced as an example to solve local, regional, national, and global problems is nothing short of remarkable. This is even more significant because it is not merely invoked in rhetorical journalistic attempts to inspire dramatic headlines or by politicians seeking to score cheap points by underscoring a national icon; the Marshall Plan is frequently highlighted by economists, historians, and political scientists as well.

The most dramatic example of this was the extensive call for a new recovery program to help rehabilitate and democratize Eastern Europe at the end of the Cold War. The downfall of the Berlin Wall, the reunification of Germany, and the collapse of the Soviet Union between 1989 and 1991 justified Western Cold War policy. It also inspired calls on both sides of the now-lifted Iron Curtain for a program that would restore economic viability and introduce democratic ideas to the former Soviet-dominated part of Europe. Writing in the *New York Times*, longtime public intellectual and Pulitzer Prize winner Anthony Lewis backed a suggestion by the new Czechoslovakian Foreign Minister, Jiri Dienstbier, for a united Europe—across East and West—and a renewed American financial effort to sustain it. A $16 billion investment, Dienstbier insisted, could resuscitate the Soviet Union and her former Eastern European partners, thereby bringing the former Communist nations closer to the European Community in the West. Historian Charles Maier, by then one of the great authorities on modern European economic and political history, concurred. In Maier's view, it was not only possible to launch a Marshall Plan for the democratizing former Communist world; it was required for the continent's revival. "Eastern Europe, with its educated labor force and possibilities for regional integration, provides a promising arena for creative American policy," he claimed. "The Marshall Plan was a keystone of the democratic stability West Europeans have enjoyed for more than 40 years. It would be fitting if we now provided similar benefits for those who could not participate the first time round."[8] Maier's was not an uncommon call.

In the 1940s, the Truman Administration approached the Marshall Plan with ideological, strategic, and economic concerns. As we have seen, these concerns overlapped throughout the 1940s, as they would for the duration of the Cold War; but what about the post-Cold War era? Was there a similar sense of urgency to reconstruct and redevelop the other half of Europe? Those who answered in the affirmative heralded the moment as a second chance to bring the ideals of the United Nations and World Government to the global community. Most academics, however, were less optimistic. The failures of the U.N. during the preceding half century scarred many who, in 1945, had been ready to declare victory for global democracy. However, Johns Hopkins University political scientist, Francis Fukuyama, did not count himself among them. He believed that the end of the Cold War symbolized the victory of liberal ideals over the forces of totalitarianism. Fukuyama's most famous article—and later, book—*The End of History,* implied that the international forces and circumstances had worked themselves out over the course of the twentieth century. The decisive Cold War victory on behalf of Western values and visions had brought the evolution of human society to its zenith, and it was only a matter of time before the rest of the world followed. Although Fukuyama did not call for a democratizing crusade around the world, he backed the idea that the U.S. should stimulate a faster track toward democratization and liberalization wherever possible.[9] Though he later recanted, Fukuyama was a child of the neo-conservative movement that extended this logic to its fullest in Iraq in 2003, as it set out to democratize the Middle East. Few may be willing to draw comparisons between the revered Marshall Plan and the despised Iraq War, but a similar kind of ideology inspired both. Both allowed Americans to dream big. This helps explain why ideology matters when we talk about America's place in the world.

As for Eastern Europe, debate raged among academics, journalists, and policymakers over a potential reconstruction program throughout the 1990s. Writing in 1994, the doyen of modern realism, Henry Kissinger, convincingly claimed that an American investment in Russia's recovery might well be worthwhile. He made the cautious but prophetic statement, however, that if the United States were to provide aid to assist in the recovery of "post-Cold War Russia," there would be consequences "once Russia recovers economically" as its pressure on neighboring states begins "to mount." "This may be a price worth paying," he continued, "but it would be a mistake not to recognize that there is a price."[10] However prudent, such reflections may have been, they hardly slowed calls for American reform-policies. As late as 2000, Lech Walesa, the former Polish President and the man who led Solidarity against the Polish Communist regime in the 1980s, insisted that winning the Cold War was not enough for the forces of democracy. They needed to win the peace as well. According to Walesa,

> There was a clear understanding of this at the end of the Second World War. What we now need is a new Marshall Plan, in particular for Russia, Ukraine and Belarus, although this is a project that would require a large measure of vision and political will.[11]

In the end, there would be no Marshall Plan for Eastern Europe, though the U.S. and the eventual European Union would play an extensive role in the recovery of the former Communist world. Since then, Latvia, Lithuania, Estonia, the Czech Republic, Slovakia, Romania, Bulgaria, and Croatia have even entered the European Union. Several nations formerly under Soviet control have also become members of NATO, with more likely to follow suit over time. Many of these nations have done well for themselves. Fukuyama was quite right to insist that Communism had died as a result of the attractiveness of Western ideas, though it was also, as George Kennan argued in 1947, because Communism "carried within it, the seeds of its own destruction."[12] Despite these encouraging developments, Eastern Europe has never truly recovered, at least not in comparison to the recovery and reconstruction that the Western half of the continent experienced after 1948. East Germany has come closest to full recovery, but only because the newly reunited Germany bailed out the former German Democratic Republic. In many of the former Soviet Republics, conditions remain appallingly poor. Even in Russia, by far the most resource rich and powerful of these nations, socio-economic conditions and the standard of living lags far behind the Western world.

The failure to introduce a Marshall Plan in the former Communist world has not slowed down calls for plans elsewhere. In the mid-1980s, for example, Congressmen launched the so-called—if poorly named—"Mini-Marshall Plan for the Philippines." Since the turn of the century, James Hoge has made the case for a new ERP to solve the economic crisis that struck Europe in 2008, while Nicolaus Mills asserted that a Marshall Plan is needed to reshape the Middle East and undo the damage done by George W. Bush and Paul Bremer in Iraq. Closer to home, Ron Daniels maintains that we need a domestic Marshall Plan to transform America's ghettos, while others have queried that if we could rebuild Europe, why not Detroit?[13] In the decades since the Marshall Plan concluded, plenty of others have chimed in with similar proposals.[14] The idea that Secretary of State Marshall proposed at Harvard clearly continues to resonate with Americans. When President Barack Obama took the oath of office, national and international recovery was on the minds of many. As made evident by national commentary on his proposals, plenty of advocates believed that the name of the Obama–Biden White House's "Recovery Program" was not coincidental. At the very least it reached for the Democratic Party's glory days of the 1940s. Critics may see these programs as nothing more than an opportunity to increase the size of government, but to patrons they reflect a genuine belief in what the United States ought to represent in the world.

Given the extent to which Americans are enamored with their own can-do ability, these periodic calls for new recovery programs are unsurprising. They fit an image that helps define a mission in the world. The far more complex question is, of course, if it is even possible to recreate the Marshall Plan. Modernization theorists in the 1960s believed that it was, but they lived in a different time and place. Today, the nations and regions most in need of assistance do not compare well with the Western Europe of the late 1940s, nor do the circumstances facing them. Would Europeans have pursued integration without the combined threat of international Communism and American pressure? Monnet, Schuman, and Adenauer may have, but as demonstrated in the preceding chapter, Britain was a far less willing participant. It is also not at all clear that even Franco-German collaboration would have occurred without American economic and political pressure for continental unity. Particular conditions were, in other words, required for the plan to come to its fruition. In light of all of these issues, it is difficult to imagine that today's public or Congress would entrust the Federal government with a task of this magnitude. In an era of skepticism about big government, it is equally easy to forget how willingly Americans and others embraced the idea of a powerful state in the 1940s. The complete collapse of the West's economies during the Great Depression thoroughly undermined the prejudices against government spending and government intervention in national and global economies. If anything, it was the free market that appeared to be the culprit of the Depression. According to Judt, by the end of the Second World War,

> [the] faith in the state was at least as marked in poor lands as in rich ones—perhaps more so, since in such places only the state could offer hope or salvation to the mass of the population. And in the aftermath of depression, occupation and civil war, the

state—as an agent of welfare, security and fairness—was a vital
source of community and social cohesion.

Even those conservatives who opposed the New Deal had faith in the
functions of government. Ever since Watergate there has undoubtedly been
steadily increasing skepticism regarding "salvation-from-above. . . . But for
the generation of 1945 some workable balance between political freedoms
and the rational, equitable distributive function of the administrative state
seemed the only sensible route out of the abyss."[15] It is, of course, true that
the European Recovery Program was also run by the business elite and that
it recruited some of its most valuable people from the private sector, but
this was always overseen by government experts. No such comparable
operation is imaginable in the modern climate. This lack of confidence in
government intervention explains, in part, why nobody was willing to
provide a Marshall Plan for Eastern Europe in the 1990s. So, too, does the
fact that the Western European political leaders of the post-1945 era
already possessed a framework for collaboration and a sense of unity from
the wartime experience. They were also far better organized along parliamentary lines and were not, despite the chaos of depression and war, seen
as corrupt or dysfunctional. Few believed the same of the Eastern Europeans
when the Wall came down. Not only did Eastern European political
structures appear weak, their leaders had no experience with democracy
and the volatile conditions made constant shifts in power a constant menace
for any kind of large-scale reconstruction program. Even more alarming,
a new Marshall Plan, were it to follow the original script, would have sought
to bring all the Eastern European powers into the newly established European Union; after all, a core argument of the original plan was not simply
recovery and reconstruction, but integration as well. Given the uncertainty
of how integration would work, no Western European government was
willing to double the size of the EU with a stroke of a pen.

The same is the case for the Middle East today. However wise it might
be to use resources, technical assistance, and integration as a measure to
bring the Middle East closer to the West, few believe that it can be done
successfully on the scale envisioned by Hoffman, Harriman, Clayton, the
ECA, and State Department Administrators. Even fewer would consider
the regimes in a region marred by religious factionalism trustworthy or
collaborative enough to be part of such an effort. Add to that the fact
there today is a value-gap between the West and many regions of the
world that did not exist between Washington and its European partners
in 1947.

The lack of urgency when it comes to foreign aid is also evident in
the paltry sum that is now provided for this purpose. For Fiscal Year 2015,

European Integration

The European Union is, today, an organization made up of 28 nations, many of which come from behind the former Iron Curtain. The Marshall Plan helped underline the need for this effort. Robert Schuman's May 1950 proposal for a coal and steel community was the first step toward this European federation.[1] It rested on an idea that harkened back to the Roman Empire, to Victor Hugo, Immanuel Kant, and others, but which only emerged in a modern context after the Great War and then again after the Second World War. In 1951, France and West Germany united with Italy, the Netherlands, Belgium, and Luxembourg to establish the European Coal and Steel Community (ECSC). By the time the ECSC became operational a year later, this supranational association had a political organization to go along with the economic apparatus. This included a parliamentary assembly, an executive body, and a court of justice. In short order the ECSC had expanded its original goal of abolishing trade restrictions on coal and steel products to cover, at least in principle, all other economic sectors as well.

Problems would continue to fester over the role of West Germany, especially after the United States began pushing for German rearmament to help guard Europe against the Soviet Union. This rekindled French fears that the ECSC originally had hoped to quell. Intense debates over the issue of a militarized Germany eventually led to the 1954 Western European Union, a defense organization that enlarged the original Brussels Pact of 1948 to include Italy and West Germany. This was accompanied by a formal decision by Great Britain, the United States, and France to formally abandon the occupation role in West Germany and restore full sovereignty to Chancellor Konrad Adenauer's nation. This included the right to arm, though the Federal Republic of Germany had to pledge not to pursue the development or acquisition of atomic, biological, or chemical weapons. On May 9, a decade after Nazi Germany's surrender, the FRG joined NATO.

By 1957, the economic collaboration cemented in the Coal and Steel Community was expanded under the Treaty of Rome, which formally created the European Economic Community (EEC). In the short term, the result was a further lowering of restrictions on capital movement and eventually on labor movement. The long-term objective of political integration on the continent was furthered through the establishment of a Council of Ministers, a Commission, and a European Parliament. Great Britain chose once again to stand outside the European entity in large part because London feared membership would overshadow its relationship with Washington, would undermine its self-perceived status as the second most important power in the west, and would destabilize the relationship Britain maintained with members of the Commonwealth. By 1961, London, impressed by the economic strength of France and Germany and concerned by its own struggling economy, finally applied for membership. It was vetoed—twice—by Charles de Gaulle, who had returned to lead France. De Gaulle saw Europe as a continental concept and believed that Britain held a deep-seated hostility toward the idea of Europe. He did not want London to challenge Paris for leadership on the continent and he feared that Britain was a "Trojan horse" that would assist U.S. influence in Europe.[2] The French President's intransigence on the issue was a firm reminder why Americans had feared De Gaulle coming to power almost as much as they had the French Communists during the Marshall Plan era.

Along with the EEC and ECSC, the member states also founded the European Atomic Energy Community. In 1967, the three communities merged to become the European Community (EC) whose main focus was on cooperation in economic and agricultural affairs. By the early 1970s, De Gaulle having departed the scene, Great Britain finally managed to join the EC along with Denmark and Ireland. Greece joined in 1981, and Portugal and Spain followed in 1986. In 1991, The Treaty on European Union, signed at Maastricht in Holland, formally transformed the EC into the European Union. The project almost capsized when Denmark—always among the most Euro-skeptic countries—rejected Union membership in a national referendum. The Danes were appeased with a series of exemptions, some of which remain in place, and eventually helped smooth the transition towards a political union. Following Maastricht, the EU expanded into new areas, including the establishment of a loosely defined Common Foreign and Security Policy, a common policy on immigration, drugs, and eventually terrorism. EU citizenship followed as well, guaranteeing citizens of the Union the right to work, move, and live in any member country. The Maastricht Treaty also established a timetable for an economic and monetary union which would lead to the establishment of a common currency, known as the euro, at the expense of the national currencies. Once again, Denmark and the United Kingdom opted out when the euro was established in 1999, as did Sweden, which had joined the EU along with Austria and Finland in 1995.

Although the EU would not fund a Marshall Plan project for Eastern Europe after the collapse of Communism, the ruling powers in Brussels did clear a path towards membership for those countries which had escaped Moscow's domination after the collapse of the Soviet Union in 1991. In 2004, Cyprus, the Czech Republic, Estonia, Hungary, Latvia, Lithuania, Malta, Poland, Slovakia, and Slovenia joined the European Union. Three years later, Romania and Bulgaria became partners as well, while Croatia followed in 2013. Most of these would go on to join NATO, too, further highlighting the strength of the Western world built during the Truman years. The enlargement towards the east has caused numerous political and economic skirmishes in Brussels and in national capitals, particularly after the economic crisis that struck in 2008 and 2009. The movement of peoples has been of particular concern, which many Western European welfare states see as an infringement upon their territory in difficult economic times. Nonetheless, the European project that has its roots in the Marshall Plan era remains one of the most ambitious and effective political undertakings ever executed. It has created a collaborative community of nations that shares much with the United States and is intimately tied to the U.S. in terms of ideas, security, trade, culture, and values.

Notes

1 For the Schuman Plan, see, 159–161.
2 William R. Keylor, *A World of Nations: The International Order Since 1945* (Oxford University Press, 2009), 157–158.

The United States Agency for International Development's entire global budget stood at $35.6 billion. When adjusted for inflation, the ECA operated an annual budget several billion above that for Europe alone between 1948 and 1951. Even that number disguises the actual support provided by the Americans, since it does not factor in the billions of dollars in loans that flowed to Great Britain and France, the written-off Lend-Lease debt, the billions provided through UNRRA until it was shut down in 1946, or the vast sums paid out under special support accounts in the American zone in Germany. It also does not factor in the hundreds of millions of dollars in interim aid that was provided during the first six months of 1948. The reality is that despite its vast oil resources, vast parts of the Middle Eastern countries would require comparable amounts today, while amounts required by South East Asia or Africa for a similar plan would exceed it multiple times. This might have been possible if America's current economic health mirrored the surpluses of the 1940s, but in light of the deficit that has plagued the U.S. economy for decades, it is difficult to envision a financial commitment on the scale required.

On an even more practical level, the Marshall Plan depended not only on effective governments, but also well-developed private sectors through which large parts of the counterpart funds effectively flowed. These sectors generally do not exist in the areas most in need of foreign aid today. The alternative is to indiscriminately support the kind of leaders who have too often proven to be unreliable partners in foreign aid endeavors in the past. The Marshall Plan was also contingent upon recipients being willing to compromise on their national interests and join in a shared community of Westernized political and economic principles. Regardless of what the George W. Bush Administration may have believed, it seems highly unlikely that the idea of the West easily transfers to regions that are inherently culturally different. Beyond Europe the ideology of modernization which the Truman Doctrine and the Marshall Plan helped espouse has, Fukuyama's brief foray into that territory in the early post-Cold War period notwithstanding, long since vanished. The United States no longer possesses the status or reputation it did at the end of the Second World War. In 1945, Americans had played a crucial part in rescuing the world and were willing to build a new one. Few would trust the Washington bureaucracy to pursue a similar path in the twenty-first century. The belief that the Westernization of the world is possible or even desirable is gone. If anything, Rostow's visions of training and uplifting the rest of the world with American methods is now considered largely a none-too-subtle form of cultural or economic imperialism. It stimulates little international support and is met with a wall of opposition from conservative forces on the right opposed to American development policies *and* from groups on the left that, mostly on principle, oppose the World Bank, the International Monetary Fund, and free trade agreements. The European Union could perhaps, if it had the funds, pick up the mantle, but it does not possess the ideology necessary to engage in such an endeavor. These realities ought to be crucial to those policymakers, lawmakers, or intellectuals who make calls for renewed Marshall Plans. The effort launched by the Truman White House in 1947 was never merely an economic plan and never simply a strategic plan. It was part of an overwhelmingly powerful ideological vision to make the world more like the United States. That purpose might still be worth pursuing, but the prospects for success appear much dimmer in 2016 than they did in 1947 and 1948.

★   ★   ★

When the Marshall Plan came to an end in early 1952, Harry Truman could look back on it as the finest achievement of his presidency. Although his approval ratings collapsed in 1951 and 1952 as a result of the Korean War and over the Republican Congress's unwillingness to work with him on domestic issues, the President could take satisfaction from the fact that after close to four years and $13 billion spent, the European Recovery Program had played a crucial part in the reestablishment of the postwar world. The *Washington Post* hailed it as an

> idea that took vision and courage on the part of General Marshall, Mr. Harriman, Mr. Acheson, and the President himself; it was translated into law under the 'unpartisan' leadership of Senator Vandenberg and into action by the missionary drive of Mr. Hoffman.

The ERP's greatest accomplishment was that it had built "something more enduring than the old European 'firetrap' of the prewar years."[16] Success was only partial, the paper acknowledged. What had emerged, after all, was not the "one-world" that FDR, Truman, and so many Americans had yearned for after the Second World War came to a close in 1945. Still, the American effort, chiefly enshrined in the Marshall Plan, had kept

Western Europe at peace and seen her move rapidly toward recovery. The creation of the West was no small feat.

Americans were worthy of the acclaim lavished upon them, but plenty of praise belongs to the Europeans, too. The Marshall Plan worked because, just at the right time, elected officials and administrators at Whitehall and at the French Foreign Ministry at the Quay d'Orsay, and in the temporary West German capital in Bonn, understood the need to step back from the brink of nationalism. Ernest Bevin, Georges Bidault, Robert Schuman, Jean Monnet, and Konrad Adenauer all deserve much of the credit, as do many others. Historians still debate the extent to which the current European Union can be traced to the Marshall Plan years; it remains a question more worthy of curiosity than of empirical testing. If nothing else, what is worthy of reflection is the fact that the Western Europe that emerged after the Second World War was more united than ever before, to such an extent that today's students take the concept of *Europe* entirely for granted. Even if the economic crisis after 2008 shook the foundations of continental unity, and even if alarmists now speak of a declining Europe and the imminent collapse of the European Union, it should take nothing away from the fact that the American emphasis on inter-European relations has created the greatest period of peace, political stability, and prosperity the continent has ever known.

The Marshall Plan fell short of the Americanization of Europe just as later modernization endeavors failed to Westernize the underdeveloped world. Still, we should not be surprised that many of those involved in the Marshall Plan thought in such grandiose terms. Americans, far more so than to their allies, possess an enduring belief that ideas have consequences and, as intellectual historian Daniel Rodgers affirms, "that the course of history can turn on framing and agenda setting, on struggles on the intangible fields of the mind."[17] In light of this, there is, for better or for worse, little reason to suspect that grand ideas will not return to American foreign policy in the coming decades. For a country that perceives itself as an idea far more than a traditional nation, it can hardly be any other way. The bruising of the Iraq War and the economic collapse in the twenty-first century may well shelve ostentatious global ventures in the immediate future, but probably not for long. When Americans, whether it be the current or the next generation, eventually resume this mantle, it should not be with a desire to replicate the Marshall Plan, but rather a determination to learn from it. If they work with their partners in the West and if Americans can muster the will to bring to the poorest parts of the world "optimism plus milk"; it certainly would not be a bad place to start.

Documents

DOCUMENT 1

Truman and the United States in the World

By 1944, a vast majority of Americans and members of the Congress rallied to President Roosevelt's idea of a permanent American commitment to the postwar economic and political order. Conscious of the fact that the League of Nations would not be revived after the war, the call grew incessantly louder for U.S. global leadership. In this joint statement from the spring of 1944, three prominent Democratic Senators make their case for this role and for American superiority in the world. It is a telling example of the extent to which the idea of the American century reached the highest echelons of political life.

The Joint Statement presented by Mr. Thomas of Utah, on behalf of himself, Mr. Kilgore, and Mr. Truman is as follows:

As we prepare to strike the enemy with the decisive blows of the war we must also prepare the firm economic foundation for an enduring peace. These means are already at hand in the international economic collaboration developed during the prosecution of the war. On the continuance and expansion of such collaboration rests the hope of any lasting peace.

The United States cannot, nor does it wish to, shirk leadership in the post-war economic collaboration. Our own industrial accomplishments have nominated us as the Nation that must assume a position to guide others in the pathway of peaceful production. . .

To this end, we are introducing a resolution intended to foster and promote such international collaboration . . . [this] resolution advises that the executive branch of the Government begin immediately to explore with other nations the basic economic understanding upon which we must act to create a prosperous and progressive future for ourselves and for the world at large.

We have held at Hot Springs a great international meeting on food problems of the world.[1] We have held at Atlantic City a great international meeting on problems of relief for those who have suffered from the blight of Axis occupation.[2] The time has come to broaden the scope of such discussion among the United Nations to the postwar economic relations of all countries.

. . . We seek a joint study by the legislative and executive branches of the Government, and we seek mechanism whereby [these]. . .branches, acting in unity, will bring into counsel with them representatives of industry, labor, agriculture, and the consuming public. If, as all of us hope, the end of the war is to usher in an era of collaboration and unity among nations, then we must establish unity among ourselves which will enable us to invite across our threshold other nations with a common will to preserve the peace so costly won.

. . . The aggregate of facts and recommendations, called forth from the best minds in an effort to solve the most basic economic questions of our time, cannot fail to have great and abiding value to the President and to Congress in working out our Nation's fundamental foreign-economic policy.

The future peace depends on the abandonment of political nationalism and economic nationalism and autarchy. . . . The future peace depends on an economically healthy United States, and we cannot have economic health without a volume of foreign trade above and beyond anything we have ever had before. . . Our annual national output now equals $200,000,000,000, or twice that of 1940 when measured in dollars and cents, and more than 50 percent more in actual production when the total is corrected for price changes. . . . Our production of durable goods is three times what it was in 1929 and four times what it was in 1939. . . .

With this unparalleled productive apparatus, it becomes all the more incumbent upon this country, in our own interest and for the future of nations, to lead the world into a great era of productive peace. No other nation can match our preeminent responsibility, not Great Britain, whose industrial output is only one-fifth that of ours, nor Russia with its reconstruction and growth before it.

We cannot help but be sobered when we realize . . . that this country has within its grasp a leadership which will determine the happiness and prosperity not only of our own one-hundred-and-thirty-odd millions but of hundreds of millions of people in the years to come, that we can control a destiny which if unwisely used may bring depression and ruin, hunger and death to great numbers of the world's people.

. . . The author of Ecclesiastes said in his wisdom many years ago that the "profit of the earth is for all." We have an opportunity now to implement this bit of ancient wisdom, making the earth and the fullness thereof a boon instead of a war-causing burden upon the back of mankind.

Source: U.S. *Congressional Record*, 80th Congress, Senate (March 7, 1944), 2299–2300.

DOCUMENT 2

Europe's Coming Collapse

*H*arry *S. Truman became president on April 12, 1945, a month before the Second World War ended. Six years of conflict had left the territories of former friends and foes extensively damaged. Within his first month in office, several reports reached the White House warning Truman that the destruction of cities, infrastructure, industries, and agriculture, threatened the continent's ability to provide for its own citizens and its future political stability. In this April 26 assessment, Assistant Secretary of War John J. McCloy provides President Truman with one of the earliest descriptions of the dire conditions in Germany and Central Europe.*

Memorandum for the President, April 26, 1945

. . . President Roosevelt, who had the possibility of appointing a civilian as High Commissioner for Germany in mind, agreed as to the wisdom of permitting General [Dwight] Eisenhower to operate as the Military Governor of Germany in that part of it we controlled and as a representative on the Control Council for Germany without the appointment of a civilian commissioner at least for the initial period. This was done for several reasons.

The initial phase would be primarily a military operation anyway. There would be vast troop dispositions and adjustments to be made. Pacification operations would have to be carried on to some degree. The means of all supply and transportation would be in the hands of the Army. All fundamental elements during this period would be military or largely influenced by the military.

It was thought better that the initial impact on the German people should be military, and exclusively military. The Germans would understand it better . . .

. . . General Clay was selected to assist Eisenhower as deputy by reason of his general ability and his experience with matters of allocations, requisitioning of supply and industrial management and production problems—all matters which would be most important in connection with the administration of Germany.

. . . The destruction of the towns and facilities of Germany is immense. There is a complete economic, social, and political collapse going on in Central Europe, the extent of which is unparalleled in history unless one goes back to the collapse of the Roman Empire and even that may not have been as great an economic upheaval. The displaced persons are an enormous problem. Food is the greatest need—for the displaced persons, food for liberated Europe and food for the Germans. It looks very much as if there will be worse than general ill-nourishment in Germany—there will be actual starvation. Food and fuel and transportation are the great needs. The dissolution of society and its facilities are shocking.

. . . we are going to have to work out a practical relationship with the Russians. It will require the highest talents, tolerance, and wisdom in order to accomplish our aims. The need for topnotch men is painfully apparent. It may require assistance from the President in order to shake loose from the agencies and civilian life men of the quality, character, and strength needed. . . .

[France and Belgium] . . . are important and integral parts of our military system in Europe and thus bona fide entitled to receipts under our generous Lend-Lease policy. We are depending on France and Belgium for all sorts of facilities and help in order to redeploy as well as maintain our large forces. These countries also afford a stabilizing factor in Europe that does not elsewhere exist. Without some reestablishment of their economic life they too can very well be torn apart by the collapse now in effect over Middle Europe. If stimulated, they can afford the one remaining sector of Europe in which substantially large reserves of food and materials may be built up. France and Belgium have great potentials which can be realized on in a relatively short time if work is started quickly. This is a great need in the void of food, fuel, and materials which Europe now experiences.

Source: Harry S. Truman Presidential Library, Harry S. Truman Papers, President's Secretary's Files, Foreign Affairs Series, Germany: General, Folder 1.

DOCUMENT 3

Marshall to the People

*B*etween March and April 1947, George C. Marshall spent six weeks attending
the Conference of Foreign Ministers in Moscow. His meetings with his Soviet,
British, and French counterparts as well as with Joseph Stalin confirmed American
fears about Europe's future and the Soviet Union's position on the issue. Stalin's
willingness to allow Europe to collapse under the weight of its economic and industrial bottlenecks convinced Marshall that there was no prospect for meaningful
agreement between the former allies. The only path forward, Marshall explains
to the American public in this radio address shortly after his return home, was a
substantially increased American commitment to the Western European continent;
for the sake of America's allies and because it is in America's self-interest to see a
prosperous Europe.

Radio Address, April 28, 1947, Washington, D.C.

Tonight I hope to make clearly understandable the fundamental nature of
the issues discussed at the Moscow Conference of Foreign Ministers.

This Conference dealt with the very heart of the peace for which we
are struggling. It dealt with the vital center of Europe—Germany and
Austria—an area of large and skilled population, of great resources and
industrial plants, an area which has twice in recent times brought the world
to the brink of disaster. . . .

. . . Problems which bear directly on the future of our civilization
cannot be disposed of by general talk nor vague formulae—by what Lincoln
called "pernicious abstractions." They require concrete solutions for
definite and extremely complicated questions—questions which have to
do with boundaries, with power to prevent military ag[g]ression, with
people who have bitter memories, with the production and control of
things which are essential to the lives of millions of people.

. . . It is important to an understanding of the Conference that the complex character of the problems should be understood, together with their immediate effect on the people of Europe in the coming months. To cite a single example, more coal is most urgently needed throughout Europe for factories, for utilities, for railroads, and for the people in their homes. More coal for Allied countries cannot be mined and delivered until the damaged mines, mine machinery, railroad communications and like facilities are rehabilitated. This rehabilitation, however, depends on more steel, and more steel depends in turn on more coal for steel making. Therefore, and this is the point to be kept in mind, while the necessary rehabilitation is in progress, less coal would be available in the immediate future for the neighboring Allied states.

But less coal means less employment for labor, and a consequent delay in the production of goods for export to bring money for the purchase of food and necessities. Therefore, the delay necessary to permit rehabilitation of the mines so vitally affects France that the settlement of this matter has become for her a critical issue. All neighboring states and Great Britain and the Soviet Union are directly affected in various ways since coal is required for German production of goods for export sufficient to enable her to buy the necessary imports of foods, et cetera, for much of which the United States is now providing the funds.

. . . Regarding the character of the German economic system and its relation to all of Europe, the disagreements are even more serious and difficult of adjustment. German economy at the present time is crippled by the fact that there is no unity of action, and the rehabilitation of Germany to the point where she is self-supporting demands immediate decision.

.There is a declared agreement in the desire for economic unity in Germany but when it comes to the actual terms to regulate such unity there are wide and critical differences. One of the most serious difficulties encountered in the effort to secure economic unity has been the fact that the Soviet-occupied zone has operated practically without regard to the other zones and has made few if any reports of what has been occurring in that zone. There has been little or no disposition to proceed on a basis of reciprocity and there has been a refusal to disclose the availability of foodstuffs, and the degree or character of reparations taken out of this zone.

This unwillingness of the Soviet authorities to cooperate in establishing a balanced economy for Germany as agreed upon at Potsdam has been the most serious check on the development of a self-supporting Germany, and a Germany capable of providing coal and other necessities for the neighboring states who have always been dependent on Germany for these items. After long and futile efforts to secure a working accord in this matter, the British and American zones were combined for the improvement of the economic situation, meaning the free movement of excess supplies or produce available in one zone to another where there is a shortage. Our continuing invitation to the French and Soviets to join in the arrangement still exists. This merger is bitterly attacked by the Soviet authorities as a breach of the Potsdam Agreement and as a first step towards the dismemberment of Germany, ignoring the plain fact that their refusal to carry out that agreement was the sole cause of the merger. It is difficult to regard their attacks as anything but propaganda designed to divert attention from the Soviet failure to implement the economic unity agreed at Potsdam. Certainly some progress toward economic unity in Germany is better than none.

. . . The question of reparations is of critical importance as it affects almost every other question under discussion. . . . The results of the Versailles Treaty of 1919 regarding payment of reparations on a basis of dollars, and the difficulties encountered by the Reparations Commission appointed after Yalta in agreeing upon the dollar evaluation of reparations in kind convinced President Truman and his advisers considering the question at Potsdam that some other basis for determining reparations should be adopted if endless friction and bitterness were to be avoided in future years. They succeeded in getting agreement to the principle of reparations to be rendered out of capital assets—that is, the transfer of German plants, machinery, et cetera, to the Allied powers concerned.

It developed at the Moscow Conference that the Soviet officials flatly disagreed with President Truman's and Mr. Byrnes' understanding of the written terms of this agreement. The British have much the same view of this matter as the United States.

We believe that no reparations from current production were contemplated by the Potsdam Agreement. The Soviets strongly oppose this view. They hold that the previous discussions and agreements at Yalta authorize the taking of billions of dollars in reparations out of current production. This would mean that a substantial portion of the daily production of German factories would be levied on for reparation payments, which in turn would mean that the recovery of Germany sufficiently to be self-supporting would be long delayed. It would also mean that the plan and the hope of our Government, that Germany's economic recovery by the end of three years would permit the termination of American appropriations for the support of the German inhabitants of our zone, could not be realized. . . .

There is, however, general agreement among the Allies that the matter of the factories and equipment to be removed from Germany as reparations should be re-examined. They recognize the fact that a too drastic reduction in Germany's industrial set-up will not only make it difficult for Germany to become self-supporting but will retard the economic recovery of Europe. . .

Complicated as these issues are, there runs through them a pattern as to the character and control of central Europe which was to be established. The Foreign Ministers agreed that their task was to lay the foundations of a central government for Germany, to bring about the economic unity of Germany essential for its own existence as well as for European recovery, to establish workable boundaries, and to set up a guaranteed control through a four-power treaty. . . . Agreement was made impossible at Moscow because, in our view, the Soviet Union insisted upon proposals which would have established in Germany a centralized government, adapted to the seizure of absolute control of a country which would be doomed economically through inadequate area and excessive population, and would be mortgaged to turn over a large part of its production as reparations, principally to the Soviet Union.

. . . These issues are matters of vast importance to the lives of the people of Europe and to the future course of world history. We must not compromise on great principles in order to achieve agreement for agreement's sake. At the same time, we must sincerely try to understand the point of view of those with whom we differ.

In this connection, I think it proper to refer to a portion of a statement made to me by Generalissimo Stalin. He said, with reference to the Conference, that these were only the first skirmishes and brushes of reconnaissance forces on this question. Differences had occurred in the past on other questions, and, as a rule, after people had exhausted themselves in dispute, they then recognized the necessity of compromise. It was possible that no great success would be achieved at this session, but he thought that compromises were possible on all the main questions, including demilitarization, political structure of Germany, reparations and economic unity. It was necessary to have patience and not become pessimistic.

I sincerely hope that the Generalissimo is correct in the view he expressed and that it implies a greater spirit of cooperation by the Soviet Delegation in future conferences. But we cannot ignore the factor of time involved here. The recovery of Europe has been far slower than had been expected. Disintegrating forces are becoming evident. The patient is sinking while the doctors deliberate. So I believe that action cannot await compromise through exhaustion. New issues arise daily. Whatever action is possible to meet these pressing problems must be taken without delay.

Finally, I should comment on one aspect of the matter which is of transcendent importance to all our people . . . I [had] the invaluable assistance of Mr. Dulles, a distinguished representative of the Republican Party as well as a recognized specialist in foreign relations and in the processes of international negotiations and treaty-making. As a matter of fact the bi-partisan character of the American attitude in the present conduct of foreign affairs was clearly indicated by the strong and successful leadership displayed in the Senate during the period of this Conference by Senators Vandenberg and Connally in the debate over a development of our foreign policy of momentous importance to the American people. The fact that there was such evident unity of purpose in Washington was of incalculable assistance to me in Moscow. The state of the world today and the position of the United States make mandatory, in my opinion, a unity of action on the part of the American people.

Source: U.S. Department of State, *Bulletin* (May 11, 1947), 919–924.

Warning to Washington

*O*ver the course of 1947, American observers brought home increasingly alarming firsthand accounts of the European situation. Almost without exception these called for a growing American commitment to solve the crisis. In this memorandum the State Department's William Clayton, the former cotton baron turned government official, explains the rapidly deteriorating situation and calls for a dramatically expanded American role. He calls on the Administration to explain the European circumstances to the American people and insists that the U.S. is more than equipped to provide the required economic assistance.

Memorandum by Under Secretary of State for Economic Affairs William L. Clayton to Under Secretary of State Dean Acheson, May 27, 1947 (intended for George Marshall).

THE EUROPEAN CRISIS

It is now obvious that we grossly underestimated the destruction to the European economy by the war. We understood the physical destruction, but we failed to take fully into account the effects of economic dislocation on production—nationalization of industries, drastic land reform, severance of long-standing commercial ties, disappearance of private commercial firms through death or loss of capital, etc. . . .

Europe is steadily deteriorating. The political position reflects the economic. One political crisis after another merely denotes the existence of grave economic distress. Millions of people in the cities are slowly starving. More consumer goods and restored confidence in the local currency are absolutely essential if the peasant is again to supply food in normal quantities to the cities. (French grain acreage running 20–25%

under prewar, collection of production very unsatisfactory—much of the grain is fed to cattle. The modern system of division of labor has almost broken down in Europe.)

. . . *Only until the end of this year* [italics in original] can England and France meet [their] deficits out of their fast dwindling reserves of gold and dollars. Italy can't go that long.

. . . Before the war, Europe was self-sufficient in coal and imported very little bread and grain from the United States.

Europe must again become self-sufficient in coal (the U.S. must take over management of Ruhr coal production) and her agricultural production must be restored to normal levels. (Note: No inefficient or forced production through exorbitant tariffs, subsidies, etc. is here contemplated.)

Europe must again be equipped to perform her own shipping services. The United States should sell surplus ships to France, Italy, and other maritime nations to restore their merchant marine to at least prewar levels . . .

. . . Without further prompt and substantial aid from the United States, economic, social, and political disintegration will overwhelm Europe.

Aside from the awful implications which this would have for the future peace and security of the world, the immediate effects on our domestic economy would be disastrous: markets for our surplus production gone, unemployment, depression, a heavily unbalanced budget on the background of a mountainous war debt.

These things must not happen [italics in original]

How can they be avoided?

Mr. Baruch[3] asks for the appointment of a Commission to study and report on our national assets and liabilities in order to determine our ability to assist Europe.

This is wholly unnecessary.

The facts are well known.

Our resources and our productive capacity are ample to provide all the help necessary. . .

The problem can be met only if the American people are taken into the complete confidence of the Administration and told all the facts and only if a sound and workable plan is presented.

. . . It will be necessary for the President and Secretary of State to make a strong spiritual appeal to the American people to sacrifice a little themselves, to draw in their own belts just a little in order to save Europe from starvation and chaos (not from the Russians) and, at the same time, to preserve for ourselves and our children the glorious heritage of a free America.

Europe must have from us, as a grant, 6 or 7 billion dollars worth of goods a year for three years. With this help, the operations of the International Bank and Fund should enable European reconstruction to get under way at a rapid pace. Our grant could take the form principally of coal, food, cotton, tobacco, shipping services, and similar things—all now produced in the United States in surplus, except cotton. The probabilities are that cotton will be surplus in another one or two years. Food shipments should be stepped up despite the enormous total (15 million tons) of bread grains exported from the United States during the present crop year. We are wasting and over-consuming food in the United States to such an extent that a reasonable measure of conservation would make at least another million tons available for export with no harm whatsoever to the health and efficiency of the American people.

This three-year grant to Europe should be based on a European plan which the principal European nations, headed by the UK, France, and Italy, should work out. Such a plan should be based on a European economic federation on the order of the Belgium–Netherlands–Luxembourg Customs Union. Europe cannot recover from this war and again become independent if her economy continues to be divided into many small watertight compartments as it is today.

Obviously, the above is only the broad outline of a problem which will require much study and preparation before any move can be made.

Canada, Argentina, Brazil, Australia, New Zealand, Union of South Africa could all help with their surplus food and raw materials, but we must avoid getting into another UNRA. *The United States must run this show* [italics in original].

—W.L. Clayton

Source: U.S. Department of State, *Foreign Relations of the United States* 1947, III, 230–232.

DOCUMENT 5

Marshall at Harvard

Inspired by his own trip to Moscow earlier in the year and by the State Department's recommendations—including Clayton's memorandum (see Documents 3 and 4)—Marshall on June 5, 1947 addressed students, alumni, and faculty at Harvard University. The contents of his speech were known only to a few people in advance and it was delivered without extensive press in attendance. The speech was the culmination of a growing realization that the Soviet Union was unwilling to assist in Europe's general recovery and was in fact quite willing to let Western Europe collapse economically. Marshall was clearly not. This most famous speech by any Secretary of State laid out the American commitment to participate in Europe's recovery if the Europeans would be willing to take the lead. The speech was not the Marshall Plan—there was no plan in June of 1947—but it set the plan in motion.

Speech to the Harvard University Alumni, June 5, 1947

I need not to tell you that the world situation is very serious. That must be apparent to all intelligent people. I think one difficulty is that the problem is one of such enormous complexity that the very mass of facts presented to the public by press and radio make it exceedingly difficult for the man in the street to reach a clear appraisement of the situation. Furthermore, the people of this country are distant from the troubled areas of the earth and it is hard for them to comprehend the plight and consequent reactions of the long-suffering peoples, and the effect of those reactions on their governments in connection with our efforts to promote peace in the world.

In considering the requirements for the rehabilitation of Europe, the physical loss of life, the visible destruction of cities, factories, mines and railroads was correctly estimated, but it has become obvious during recent months that this visible destruction was probably less serious than the dislocation of the entire fabric of European economy. For the past ten years conditions have been highly abnormal. . . . Machinery has fallen into disrepair or is entirely obsolete. . . . Longstanding commercial ties, private institutions, banks, insurance companies and shipping companies disappeared, through loss of capital, absorption through nationalization or by simple destruction. In many countries, confidence in the local currency has been severely shaken. The breakdown of the business structure of Europe during the war was complete. Recovery has been seriously retarded by the fact that two years after the close of hostilities a peace settlement with Germany and Austria has not been agreed upon. But even given a more prompt solution of these difficult problems, the rehabilitation of the economic structure of Europe quite evidently will require a much longer time and greater effort than had been foreseen.

There is a phase of this matter which is both interesting and serious. The farmer has always produced the foodstuffs to exchange with the city dweller for the other necessities of life. This division of labor is the basis of modern civilization. At the present time it is threatened with breakdown. The town and city industries are not producing adequate goods to exchange with the food-producing farmer. Raw materials and fuel are in short supply. Machinery is lacking or worn out. The farmer or the peasant cannot find the goods for sale which he desires to purchase. So the sale of his farm produce for money which he cannot use seems to him an unprofitable transaction. He, therefore, has withdrawn many fields from crop cultivation and is using them for grazing. He feeds more grain to stock and finds for himself and his family an ample supply of food, however short he may be on clothing and the other ordinary gadgets of civilization. Meanwhile people in the cities are short of food and fuel. So the governments are forced to use their foreign money and credits to procure these necessities abroad. This process exhausts funds which are urgently needed for reconstruction. Thus a very serious situation is rapidly developing which bodes no good for the world. The modern system of the division of labor upon which the exchange of products is based is in danger of breaking down.

The truth of the matter is that Europe's requirements for the next three or four years of foreign food and other essential products—principally from America—are so much greater than her present ability to pay that she must have substantial additional help, or face economic, social and political deterioration of a very grave character.

The remedy lies in breaking the vicious circle and restoring the confidence of the European people in the economic future of their own countries and of Europe as a whole. The manufacturer and the farmer throughout wide areas must be able and willing to exchange their products for currencies the continuing value of which is not open to question.

. . . It is logical that the United States should do whatever it is able to do to assist in the return of normal economic health in the world, without which there can be no political stability and no assured peace. Our policy is directed not against any country or doctrine but against hunger, poverty, desperation and chaos. Its purpose should be the revival of a working economy in the world so as to permit the emergence of political and social conditions in which free institutions can exist. Such assistance, I am convinced, must not be on a piecemeal basis as various crises develop. Any assistance that this Government may render in the future should provide a cure rather than a mere palliative. Any government that is willing to assist in the task of recovery will find full cooperation. . . . Any government which maneuvers to block the recovery of other countries cannot expect help from us. Furthermore, governments, political parties or groups which seek to perpetuate human misery in order to profit therefrom politically or otherwise will encounter the opposition of the United States.

It is already evident that, before the United States Government can proceed much further in its efforts to alleviate the situation and help start the European world on its way to recovery, there must be some agreement among the countries of Europe as to the requirements of the situation and the part those countries themselves will take in order to give proper effect to whatever action might be undertaken by this Government. It would be neither fitting nor efficacious for this Government to undertake to draw up unilaterally a program designed to place Europe on its feet economically. This is the business of the Europeans. The initiative, I think, must come from Europe. The role of this country should consist of friendly aid in the drafting of a European program and of later support of such a program so far as it may be practical for us to do so. The program should be a joint one, agreed to by a number, if not all, European nations.

An essential part of any successful action on the part of the United States is an understanding on the part of the people of America of the character of the problem and the remedies to be applied. Political passion and prejudice should have no part. . . .

Source: Remarks by the Secretary of State, "European Initiative Essential to Economic Recovery," U.S. Department of State, *Bulletin* (June 15, 1947), 1159–1160.

Moscow's Response to the Marshall Plan

In the aftermath of Marshall's speech, the Soviet Union, at first, appeared willing to participate in a European-wide recovery effort. After only a few days of negotiations with the British and the French during the summer of 1947, however, the Soviets walked out. Soon they took a far more critical view of the American effort. In these two speeches, the Soviet Ambassador to the United Nations, Andrei Vyshinsky and the man by many at the time anticipated to succeed Stalin, Andrei Zhdanov forcefully demonstrated the extent to which Moscow had turned against it. While Vyshinsky used the floor of the United Nations General Assembly to publicly criticize the Truman Administration's policies, Zhdanov used a meeting of European Communist parties to effectively force them into the Soviet camp. Like Charles Bohlen (see Document 7), Zhdanov saw the world as divided into two camps. In the months that followed these speeches, nations on the eastern side of the Iron curtain felt the full effect of Sovietization as Moscow moved to establish complete control over local governments behind the Iron Curtain and destroyed those movements and individuals who hoped that a path to socialism could be found apart from Soviet control.

ANDREI VYSHINSKY, "A SOVIET CRITICISM OF THE TRUMAN DOCTRINE AND MARSHALL PLAN," SEPTEMBER 18, 1947

The so-called Truman Doctrine and the Marshall Plan are particularly glaring examples of the manner in which the principles of the United Nation are violated, of the way in which the organization is ignored.

As the experience of the past few months has shown, the proclamation of this doctrine meant that the United States government has moved towards a direct renunciation of the principles of international collaboration and concerted action by the great powers and towards attempts to impose its will on other independent states, while at the same time obviously using the economic resources distributed as relief to individual needy nations as an instrument of political pressure. This is clearly proved by the measures taken by the United States government with regard to Greece and Turkey which ignore and bypass the United Nations as well as by the measures proposed under the so-called Marshall Plan in Europe. This policy conflicts sharply with the principle expressed by the General Assembly in its resolution of 11 December 1946, which declares that relief supplies to other countries "should . . . at no time be used as a political weapon."

As is now clear, the Marshall Plan constitutes in essence merely a variant of the Truman Doctrine adapted to the conditions of postwar Europe. In bringing forward this plan, the United States government apparently counted on the cooperation of governments of the United Kingdom and France to confront the European countries in need of relief with the necessity of renouncing their inalienable right to dispose of their economic resources and to plan their national economy in their own way. The United States also counted on making all these countries directly dependent on the interests of American monopolies, which are striving to avert the approaching depression by an accelerated export of commodities and capital to Europe. . . .

It is becoming more and more evident to everyone that the implementation of the Marshall Plan will mean placing European countries under the economic and political control of the United States and direct interference by the latter in the internal affairs of those countries.

Moreover, this plan is an attempt to split Europe into two camps and, with the help of the United Kingdom and France, to complete the formation of a bloc of several European countries hostile to the interests of the democratic countries of Eastern Europe and most particularly to the interests of the Soviet Union.

An important feature of this plan is the attempt to confront the countries of Eastern Europe with a bloc of Western European states including Western Germany. The intention is to make use of Western Germany and German heavy industry (the Ruhr) as one of the most important economic bases for American expansion in Europe, in disregard of the national interests of the countries which suffered from German aggression.

I need only recall these facts to show the utter incompatibility of this policy of the United States, and of the British and French Governments which support it, with the fundamental principles of the United Nations.

ANDREI ZHDANOV, "THE INTERNATIONAL SITUATION," SEPTEMBER, 1947

The end of the Second World War brought with it big changes in the world situation. The military defeat of the bloc of fascist states, the character of the war as a war of liberation from fascism, and the decisive role played by the Soviet Union in the vanquishing of the fascist aggressors sharply altered the alignment of forces between the two systems—the Socialist and the Capitalist—in favor of Socialism.

What is the essential nature of these changes?

. . . The reactionary imperialist elements all over the world, notably in Britain, America and France, had reposed great hopes in Germany and Japan, and chiefly in Hitler Germany: firstly as in a force most capable of inflicting a blow on the Soviet Union in order to, if not having it destroyed altogether, weaken it at least and undermine its influence. . . This was the chief reason for the prewar policy of "appeasement" and encouragement of fascist aggression, the so-called Munich policy consistently pursued by the imperialist ruling circles of Britain, France, and the United States.

But the hopes reposed by the British, French, and American imperialists in the Hitlerites were not realized. . . .

The war immensely enhanced the international significance and prestige of the USSR. The USSR was the leading force and the guiding spirit in the military defeat of Germany and Japan. The progressive democratic forces of the whole world rallied around the Soviet Union. The socialist state successfully stood the strenuous test of the war and emerged victorious from the mortal struggle with a most powerful enemy. Instead of being enfeebled, the USSR became stronger. . . .

The war—itself a product of the unevenness of capitalist development in the different countries—still further intensified this unevenness. Of all the capitalist powers, only one—the United States—emerged from the war not only unweakened, but even considerably stronger economically and militarily. The war greatly enriched the American capitalists. The American people, on the other hand, did not experience the privations that accompany war, the hardship of occupation, or aerial bombardment; and since America entered the war practically in its concluding stage, when the issue was already decided, her human casualties were relatively small. For the USA, the war was primarily and chiefly a spur to extensive industrial development and to a substantial increase of exports (principally to Europe).

But the end of the war confronted the United States with a number of new problems. The capitalist monopolies were anxious to maintain their profits at the former high level, and accordingly pressed hard to prevent a reduction of the wartime volume of deliveries. But this meant that the United States must retain the foreign markets which had absorbed American products during the war, and moreover, acquire new markets, inasmuch as the war had substantially lowered the purchasing power of most of the countries. . . .

The purpose of this new, frankly expansionist course is to establish the world supremacy of American imperialism . . . the new policy of the United States is designed to consolidate its monopoly position and to reduce its capitalist partners to a state of subordination and dependence on America.

But America's aspirations to world supremacy encounter an obstacle in the USSR, the stronghold of anti-imperialist and anti-fascist policy, and its growing international influence, in the new democracies, which have escaped from the control of Britain and American imperialism, and in the workers of all countries, including America itself, who do not want a new war for the supremacy of their oppressors. Accordingly, the new expansionist and reactionary policy of the United States envisages a struggle against the USSR, against the labor movements in all countries, including the United States, and against the emancipationist, anti-imperialist forces in all countries.

Alarmed by the achievements of Socialism in the USSR, by the achievements of the new democracies, and by the postwar growth of the labor and democratic movement in all countries, the American reactionaries are disposed to take upon themselves the mission of "saviors" of the capital system from Communism.

The frank expansionist program of the United States is therefore highly reminiscent of the reckless program, which failed so ignominiously, of the fascist aggressors, who, as we know, also made a bid for world supremacy. . . .

The American imperialists regard themselves as the principal force opposed to the USSR, the new democracies and the labor and democratic movement in all countries of the world, as the bulwark of the reactionary, anti-democratic forces in all parts of the globe. Accordingly, literally on the day following the conclusion of World War II, they set to work to build up a front hostile to the USSR, and world democracy, and to encourage the anti-popular reactionary forces—collaborationists and former capitalist stooges—in the European countries which had been liberated from the Nazi yoke and which were beginning to arrange their affairs according to their own choice.

. . . The fundamental changes caused by the war on the international scene and in the position of individual countries has entirely changed the political landscape of the world. A new alignment of political forces has arisen. The more the war recedes into the past, the more distinct become two major trends in postwar international policy, corresponding to the division of the political forces operating on the international arena into two major camps; the imperialist and anti-democratic camp, on the one hand, and the anti-imperialist and democratic camp, on the other. The principal driving force of the imperialist camp is the USA. Allied with it are Great Britain and France. . . .

The cardinal purpose of the imperialist camp is to strengthen imperialism, to hatch a new imperialist war, to combat Socialism and democracy, and to support reactionary and anti-democratic pro-fascist regimes and movements everywhere . . .

The anti-fascist forces comprise the second camp. This camp is based on the USSR and the new democracies. It also includes countries that have broken with imperialism and have firmly set foot on the path of democratic development, such as Rumania, Hungary and Finland . . .

The successes and the growing international prestige of the democratic camp were not to the liking of the imperialists. Even while World War II was still on, reactionary forces in Great Britain and the United States became increasingly active, striving to prevent concerted action by the Allied powers, to protract the war, to bleed the USSR, and to save the fascist aggressors from utter defeat. The sabotage of the Second Front by the Anglo-Saxon imperialists, headed by Churchill, was a clear reflection of this tendency, which was in point of fact a continuation of the Munich policy in the new and changed conditions. . . .

The foreign policy of the Soviet Union and the democratic countries in these two past years has been a policy of consistently working for the observance of the democratic principles in the postwar settlement. The countries of the anti-imperialist camp have loyally and consistently striven for the implementation of these principles, without deviating from them one iota. . . .

It is known that the USSR is in favor of a united, peace-loving, demilitarized and democratic Germany. Comrade Stalin formulated the Soviet policy towards Germany when he said: "In short, the policy of the Soviet Union on the German question reduces itself to the demilitarization and democratization of Germany. The demilitarization and democratization of Germany is one of the most important guarantees for the establishment of a solid and lasting peace." However, this policy of the Soviet Union towards Germany is being encountered by frantic opposition from the imperialist circles in the United States and Great Britain.

The meeting of the Council of Foreign Ministers in Moscow in March and April 1947 demonstrated that the United States, Great Britain and

France are prepared not only to prevent the democratic reconstruction and demilitarization of Germany, but even to liquidate her as an integral state, to dismember her, and to settle the question of peace separately.
. . .

The crusade against Communism proclaimed by America's ruling circles with the backing of the capitalist monopolies, leads as a logical consequence to attacks on the fundamental rights and interests of the American working people, to the fascization of America's political life, and to the dissemination of the most savage and misanthropic "theories" and views. Dreaming about preparing for a new, a third world war, American expansionist circles are vitally interested in stifling all possible resistance within the country to adventures abroad, in poisoning the minds of the politically backward and unenlightened American masses with the virus of chauvinism and militarism, and in stultifying the average American with the help of all the diverse means of anti-Soviet and anti-Communist propaganda—the cinema, the radio, the church, and the press. The expansionist foreign policy inspired and conducted by the American reactionaries envisages simultaneous action along all lines:

1)   strategic military measures,
2)   economic expansion, and
3)   ideological struggle.

. . . In their ideological struggle against the USSR, the American imperialists, who have no great insight into political questions, demonstrate their ignorance by laying primary stress on the allegation that the Soviet Union is undemocratic and totalitarian, while the United States and Great Britain and the whole capitalist world are democratic. On this platform of ideological struggle—on this defense of bourgeois pseudo-democracy and condemnation of Communism as totalitarian—are united all the enemies of the working class without exception, from the capitalist magnates to the Right Socialist leaders, who seize with the greatest eagerness on any slanderous imputations against the USSR suggested to them by their imperialist masters. . . .

They would like to have in the USSR the bourgeois parties which are so dear to their hearts, including pseudo-socialistic parties, as an agency of imperialism. But to their bitter regret these parties of the exploiting bourgeoisie have been doomed by history to disappear from the scene.
. . .

The exposure of the American plan for the economic enslavement of the European countries is an indisputable service rendered by the foreign policy of the USSR and the new democracies.

It should be borne in mind that America herself is threatened with an economic crisis. There are weighty reasons for Marshall's official generosity. If the European countries do not receive American credits, their demand for American goods will diminish, and this will tend to accelerate and intensify the approaching economic crisis in the United States. Accordingly, if the European countries display the necessary stamina and readiness to resist the enthralling terms of the American credit, America may find herself compelled to beat a retreat.

Source: U.S. House of Representatives, *The Strategy and Tactics of World Communism* (Washington: Government Printing Office, 1948), 184–207.

The End of the One World Dream

*I*n 1947 the American commitment to the one-world vision finally came to an
end. The Truman Doctrine and the Marshall Plan committed the United States
to a new ideal that instead centered largely on the Western world. In this
memorandum and the included sub-annex, the State Department's Charles Bohlen
lays out the significance of this shifting ideal and maps out what the United States'
commitment to its allies in Western Europe must now be. The document also
highlights the extent to which Washington viewed Moscow as the obstacle to
European progress and the extent to which the U.S. would now have to go it alone.

MEMORANDUM OF CONVERSATION, BY THE COUNSELOR OF THE DEPARTMENT OF STATE (BOHLEN)

TOP SECRET   [Washington, August 30, 1947.]

Present:

Acting Secretary of State   Secretary of War
Mr. Salzman   Under Secretary of War
Mr. Bohlen   General Eisenhower
General Norstad
Admiral Wooldridge

The Acting Secretary of State said that he had suggested the meeting in
order that the top officials of the War Department might be kept up to
the minute on the thinking in the Department of State in regard to the
foreign situation as a whole.

At the Acting Secretary's request Mr. Bohlen then outlined certain basic aspects of the present critical world situation. . . . The Acting Secretary then related the basic considerations of the specific case of Western Europe and the implementation of the Marshall Plan. He pointed out that, in view of the fact that the world is definitely split in two, we must consider Europe west of the iron curtain as a whole and that we should apply our economic assistance to those sections of Western European economy which offered the best prospect of immediate and effective revival in an attempt to break the economic bottlenecks which were retarding the recovery of Western Europe as a whole. We should endeavor to keep in mind the concept of Western Europe rather than the individual countries and likewise short-term revival as against long-term complete reconstruction. . . . In the light of these concepts, the three Western zones of Germany should be regarded not as part of Germany but as part of Western Europe. It should be given proper weight as a factor in the economic recovery of Western Europe as a whole.

[Subannex]

MEMORANDUM BY THE CONSULAR OF THE DEPARTMENT OF STATE (BOHLEN)

TOP SECRET   [Washington, August 30, 1947.]

The United States is confronted with a condition in the world which is at direct variance with the assumptions upon which, during and directly after the war, major United States policies were predicated. Instead of unity among the great powers on the major issues of world reconstruction—both political and economic—after the war, there is complete disunity between the Soviet Union and the satellites on one side and the rest of the world on the other. There are, in short, two worlds instead of one. Faced with this disagreeable fact, however much we may deplore it, the United States in the interest of its own well-being and security and those of the free non-Soviet world must re-examine its major policy objectives in the light of this fact. Failure to do so would mean that we would be pursuing policies based on the assumptions which no longer exist and would expose us to the serious danger of falling between two stools. In furtherance of the policy based on the non-existent thesis of one world, the United States might neglect to take such measures as would make the non-Soviet world possible of existence. . . . In the Soviet world, which means those areas under direct Soviet control or domination in Europe and the Far East, the Soviet Government is proceeding on the exact opposite of the one world principle and is rapidly and, for the present at least, effectively engaged in consolidating and strengthening those areas under its control. . . .

In these circumstances, all American policies should be related to this central fact. It does not mean that as an eventual objective that the United Sates should discard forever a one world objective but rather bring its policies more into relation with reality as long as the condition described above continues to exist. Nor does it mean that the United States should endeavor to hermetically seal one world from the other. On the contrary, mutually profitable exchange of goods, in an endeavor to do good, can be carried on between the two worlds. But this could be done on a basis of equality and profit only if the non-Soviet world is able to face as a whole the areas dominated by the Soviet Union rather than as individual weak and disjointed units. . . .

On a short-term basis, all indications point towards a major political showdown crisis between the Soviet and non-Soviet world, which as a present correlation of forces means between the United States and the Soviet Union. There is virtually no chance of any of the problems existing between those worlds being settled until that crisis comes to a head and is met. Long-range plans of economic rehabilitation of even the non-Soviet world should not be allowed to obscure that almost inevitable fact. From present indications, this crisis will mature considerably earlier than has been expected. It is not a matter of several years in the future. It is more likely a question of months. . . . If it is to be solved short of war, it must result in a radical and basic change in Soviet policies. There is no sign as yet that any such change is to be anticipated or even if it is possible in view of the structure and character of the Soviet state. In anticipation of this global political crisis coming to a head in the not too distant future, the United States must do everything in its power to ensure the maximum degree of political support from the non-Soviet countries of the world. . . .

In relation to the present economic emergency in Europe, the logical consequence of the present state of the world is that measures of assistance envisaged by this Government should be consciously limited to Western Europe, based on the concept of the economic unity of Europe west of the Stettin-Trieste line.

Source: U.S. Department of State, *Foreign Relations of the United States* 1947, I, 762–765.

DOCUMENT 8

Toward a United Europe, The Schuman Plan, May 9, 1950

In May of 1950, French Foreign Minister Robert Schuman proposed the creation of a European Coal and Steel Community (ECSC), whose members would pool and coordinate the operation and development of vital industrial resources. The Marshall Plan's ideals and assets provided the basis for this endeavor, which united France, West Germany, Italy, the Netherlands, Belgium, and Luxembourg in a common market for coal, steel products, iron ore, coke, and scrap. As a result, members' trade in these commodities increased considerably in the 1950s. The plan was the first of a series of supranational European institutions that would be economic, political, and cultural in nature. A further crucial legacy of the Schuman Plan was France's acknowledgement of the Federal Republic of Germany as an equal partner and Germany's relinquishment of continental-wide ambitions. The new collaboration allowed Western Europe to leave the chaos of two world wars and instead chart a course that would eventually lead to the European Union.

. . . The contribution which an organized and living Europe can bring to civilization is indispensable to the maintenance of peaceful relations. In taking upon herself for more than 20 years the role of champion of a united Europe, France has always had as her essential aim the service of peace. A united Europe was not achieved and we had war. Europe will not be made all at once, or according to a single plan. It will be built through concrete achievements which first create a de facto solidarity. The coming together of the nations of Europe requires the elimination of the age-old opposition of France and Germany. Any action taken must in the first place concern these two countries.

With this aim in view, the French Government proposes that action be taken immediately on one limited but decisive point. It proposes that

Franco-German production of coal and steel as a whole be placed under a common High Authority, within the framework of an organization open to the participation of the other countries of Europe. The pooling of coal and steel production should immediately provide for the setting up of common foundations for economic development as a first step in the federation of Europe, and will change the destinies of those regions which have long been devoted to the manufacture of munitions of war, of which they have been the most constant victims.

The solidarity in production thus established will make it plain that any war between France and Germany becomes not merely unthinkable, but materially impossible. The setting up of this powerful productive unit, open to all countries willing to take part and bound ultimately to provide all the member countries with the basic elements of industrial production on the same terms, will lay a true foundation for their economic unification.

This production will be offered to the world as a whole without distinction or exception, with the aim of contributing to raising living standards and to promoting peaceful achievements. . . . By pooling basic production and by instituting a new High Authority, whose decisions will bind France, Germany and other member countries, this proposal will lead to the realization of the first concrete foundation of a European federation indispensable to the preservation of peace.

. . . The task with which this common High Authority will be charged will be that of securing in the shortest possible time the modernization of production and the improvement of its quality; the supply of coal and steel on identical terms to the French and German markets, as well as to the markets of other member countries; the development in common of exports to other countries; the equalization and improvement of the living conditions of workers in these industries. . . .

The movement of coal and steel between member countries will immediately be freed from all customs duty, and will not be affected by differential transport rates. Conditions will gradually be created which will spontaneously provide for the more rational distribution of production at the highest level of productivity.

In contrast to international cartels, which tend to impose restrictive practices on distribution and the exploitation of national markets, and to maintain high profits, the organization will ensure the fusion of markets and the expansion of production.

The essential principles and undertakings defined above will be the subject of a treaty signed between the States and submitted for the ratification of their parliaments. The negotiations required to settle details of applications will be undertaken with the help of an arbitrator appointed by common agreement. He will be entrusted with the task of seeing that the agreements reached conform with the principles laid down, and, in the event of a deadlock, he will decide what solution is to be adopted.

... The Authority's decisions will be enforceable in France, Germany and other member countries. Appropriate measures will be provided for means of appeal against the decisions of the Authority. . . . The institution of the High Authority will in no way prejudge the methods of ownership of enterprises. In the exercise of its functions, the common High Authority will take into account the powers conferred upon the International Ruhr Authority and the obligations of all kinds imposed upon Germany, so long as these remain in force.

Source: http://europa.eu/about-eu/basic-information/symbols/europe-day/schuman-declaration/index_en.htm

The End of the Marshall Plan

*B*y the end of December, 1951, the Marshall Plan came to an end. Over the course of the previous three and a half years it had funneled billions of dollars into Western Europe. In this press release, the European Cooperation Administration (ECA) assesses the plan, the American effort that went into its execution, and its accomplishments. The document, published in the State Department's official bi-weekly journal, provides valuable insight not only into the government's view of the plan but to how it intended for it to be remembered by later generations of Americans.

ECA SUMMARIZES EUROPEAN RECOVERY

The American people tomorrow close the books on the most daring and constructive venture in peacetime international relations the world has ever seen: The Marshall Plan.

It comes to an end tomorrow along with the Economic Cooperation Administration (ECA), the agency which built a fact out of the plan. While the Marshall Plan is thus marked complete exactly 6 months ahead of the June 30, 1952 schedule laid down by Congress, the legal powers and functions given to ECA are to finish out their allotted span under the newly created Mutual Security Agency (MSA). Into this new agency, with the new job of helping Europe to gird itself against possible Communist aggression, go also most of the U.S. Government workers who, for 3 years and 9 months, guided the program that changed not only the face of a continent but its whole state of mind.

. . . It has been said that "never in human history has so much been spent by so few with such great results." This has been accomplished without "hint of graft or cloud of scandal." The recovery of Europe from the chaos of 1947, when it was hungry, cold, disorderly, and frightened, can be measured in cold statistics: Industrial production, 64 percent above 1947 and 41 percent above prewar; steel production, nearly doubled in less than 4 years; coal production, slightly below prewar but still 27 percent higher than in 1947; aluminum, copper, and cement production, up respectively 69, 31, and 90 percent from 1947; food production, 24 percent above 1947 and 9 percent above prewar levels.

. . . And while production figures are impressive, the long-range benefits of what has been called "one of the most significant demonstrations of international cooperation in peacetime history" lie beyond these, according to Acting ECA Administrator Richard M. Bissell, Jr. . . . "When future historians look back upon the achievements of the Marshall Plan," Bissell said, "I believe they will see in it the charge that blasted the first substantial cracks in the centuries—old walls of European nationalism—walls that once destroyed will clear the way for the building of a unified, prosperous, and, above all, peaceful continent."

. . . The Economic Cooperation Administration has expended nearly 12 billion dollars in grants and loans in carrying out the European Recovery Program equal to nearly 80 dollars for every man, woman, and child in the United States. To this, the countries of Europe have added the equivalent of another 9 billion dollars in its own currencies to match the American grant-aid dollars. Of the U.S. funds, about 5.5 billion dollars have been used to purchase industrial commodities, mostly from the United States, and another 5.2 billion dollars for the purchase of food and other agricultural commodities such as cotton. Over 800 million dollars has alone gone into the cost of ocean freight for goods sent to Europe. The U.S. contribution to the setting up of the EPU was 350 million dollars and another 100 million dollars has been used since then to help the payments union over rough spots. In their turn, the Marshall Plan countries in the past 3 years completed or are pushing to completion a total of 27 major projects for the increase of power and 32 major projects for modernizing and expanding the production of iron and steel.

Major petroleum refining works number 11 and the volume of refining has quadrupled over prewar. Other industrial projects costing the equivalent of a million dollars or more bring the total of such projects to 132, costing the equivalent of over two billion dollars. About half a billion dollars of the U.S. commodity and technical aid has gone into these projects.

. . . Similarly vital to Europe's defenses has been the rehabilitation of the continent's run-down and war-smashed railway network, with approved projects for use of counterpart funds totaling more than the equivalent of half a billion dollars. Similarly, counterpart projects for the reconstruction of merchant fleets, port and shipping facilities, and inland waterways have been completed or are in the process of completion in the Marshall Plan countries. Airports, too, have been built or improved with ECA-generated local currencies. Through such double-barreled use of dollar aid and local funds, Marshall Plan nations, in less than 4 years, have rebuilt their economies to a point that could well persuade the Kremlin that the Europe which looked like such easy pickings in 1946 and 1947 is indeed a formidable bastion today.

. . . Overall, Europe's gross national product—the total sum of its production of goods and services—rose by nearly 25 percent in the less than 4 years of Marshall Plan aid to over 125 billion dollars in 1950. This is a 15 percent increase over prewar levels.

But Europe by no means considers its job finished. Member countries of the OEEC recently issued a manifesto declaring their intention to work for an expansion of total production in Western Europe by 25 percent over the next 5 years.

With her industrial plant rebuilt to better than prewar years, Europe's hope for meeting or surpassing this goal must rest on improved production methods and greater productivity—increased output of goods with the same amount of manpower, machines, and management.

Because it is in this field in particular that the United States far outstrips the rest of the world, it is in this field assistance to Europe is now being concentrated, and that priority aid will continue to be given to Free Europe through the Mutual Security Agency. Under the productivity and technical-assistance program of ECA, more than 6 thousand representatives of European industries—management, technicians, and workers—have come to the United States for varied periods of intensive studies of U.S. production methods. Nearly 5 thousand American industrial plants and organizations have thrown open their doors to these visitors and given freely of their techniques in everything from plant layout to labor-management relations.

. . . While it is still a potent force in some key areas of Europe, the expansion of communism in Western Europe has been abruptly halted and the tide sharply turned back in the years of the Marshall Plan. In country after country, free elections have seen the Communist Party overwhelmed almost to the point of extinction. In France and Italy, while Communist-dominated unions still hold the biggest bloc of workers, their membership losses have been staggering. In France, it is estimated that the powerful CGT has lost from half a million to three million members. In Italy, the Communist-dominated CGiL has lost about 2 1/2 million members.

While the growth of free trade-unions has not matched the losses in the Red-dominated unions, the declining strength of communism is evidenced In the failure, despite concentrated efforts, to close the ports of France and Italy to arms-aid shipments from the United States. There are still many dark spots in Europe's economic picture. Darkest of all is the widening dollar gap brought on by the inflationary pressures of the free world's rearmament effort. It is a dollar gap that makes mandatory continued economic aid to Europe through the burdensome period of rearmament. But the free world's leaders are convinced that the economic and moral foundation rebuilt by Europe in the past 4 years with the help of the American people through the Marshall Plan will hold firm.

. . . Tomorrow, that chapter of American history which made this possible—the Marshall Plan—is finished. Heavily criticized by some; labeled "the give-away program" by many, it has had the continuous support of the Congress, industry, labor, and nearly every other segment of American life. To them, the American people who have supported it, belongs whatever verdict is handed down by the unbiased eyes of future history.

Source: U.S Department of State, *Bulletin* (January 15, 1952), 43–45.

DOCUMENT 10

Marshall's Reflections

Interviews with General George C. Marshall
Present: Harry B. Price and Roy E. Foulke

In the years that followed the conclusion of the European Recovery Program, Marshall, like many other participants was interviewed several times about the effort. Because Marshall was of the belief that military men ought not to write memoirs, these interviews present historians with some of the most useful reminiscences regarding the program. The interviews below were conducted within two years of the plan's completion in the midst of the Korean War. They tell the story both of Marshall's speech at Harvard and how it came about.

INTERVIEW, OCTOBER 30, 1952

. . . The cardinal consideration during the period from the end of the Moscow Conference until my Harvard speech was to time properly the offer of U.S. assistance so as to assure domestic acceptance of the proposal. Our intention at all times was to "spring the plan with explosive force" in order not to dissipate the chances of U.S. acceptance by premature political debate. Little consideration was given to the European to [Europeans in] our proposal since it was believed that they were sufficiently desperate to accept any reasonable offer of U.S. aid. . . .

Originally I had planned to accept a degree from the University of Michigan [University of Wisconsin, May 24] in order to spring the "plan" in the heartland of expected opposition; however, this ceremony was cancelled because details of the plan could not be worked out in time. My second decision was to reveal the proposal during my acceptance of a degree from Amherst on June 16. However, a worsening of conditions in Europe and a full "realization of the dreadful situation in Europe" forced a stepping up of this schedule and I reversed an earlier decision not to accept a degree from Harvard on June 5th, 1947, in order to announce the U.S. proposal to assist Europe if they would work together cooperatively in devising means for making U.S. aid effective.

I took only a few intimate advisors into my confidence during the preparation of the European Recovery Program plan. I asked Kennan and Bohlen to present separate memoranda concerning means of meeting the European crisis. Kennan's was the most succinct and useful—this was during the embryo period of State's policy planning staff. . . .

As implied in the speech, I insisted that "the European countries come clean"—that is, that they come up with a workable plan for European recovery based on actual requirements, not what they thought the U.S. would give. For this reason I insisted that we not help Europe in the formulation of the European Recovery Program. I was subjected to heavy pressure from Clayton (then in Switzerland), Lew Douglas and others to let them consult with the Europeans and to let them advise the Europeans on the formulation of a plan for European recovery. However, I issued "an almost arbitrary, military-type command" that they were not to participate with the Europeans in the formulation of this plan. . . .

The plan had not been discussed with Europe in advance and Europe's prompt response represented quick foot work. Bevin and Bidault vied for leadership in the formulation of the ERP with Bevin generally winning out. The ability and character of Oliver Franks played a large part in the quality of the result. Getting Europe to agree that Britain should receive "such a large plug" of the total U.S. aid was one of the major problems. . . .

. . . In my opinion the Soviet Union and her bloc came close to associating themselves with the ERP. They changed their minds only after the Paris consultations.

INTERVIEW, FEBRUARY 18, 1953

On returning from the Moscow Conference I felt we couldn't let the European problem "fester any longer—the time for launching the boil was not [now?] at hand". There were undoubtedly a number of solutions to the European problem but the big problem was how to put it across. This was my greatest concern on how to win the battle. Kennan's memorandum, as I recall it, was probably the nearest thing to the basis for the ERP proposals, particularly in regard to the important [sic] of "how to do it". Largely as a result of prompt Bevin initiative in Europe, the criticism which we feared here in the United States did not develop until a month or so after my speech. . . .

. . . In 1947, many people in Europe were very timid about opposing the Soviet Union and I feared if we started our plan by throwing the Soviets out it would scare these people and perhaps keep some of the European countries out of the program. . . .

. . . The collaboration with Vandenberg started at the initial White House session with Congressional leaders. It was at this time that Vandenberg first suggested a committee which was the basis for the Harriman Committee. . . . Vandenberg stated that we would have to fight this out on an anti-Communist line. I did not want to fight it on this basis, I preferred to keep it more constructive, but Vandenberg was our principal adviser on the basic U.S. political problems. Lovett had many meetings with Vandenberg, as did I. I had to keep my meetings with Vandenberg rather quiet because some in the President's entourage were suspicious of Vandenberg—or perhaps jealous. I had to keep my relationship with Vandenberg quiet even though I was under heavy press attack for a failure to maintain bi-partisan policy. Actually we "couldn't have gotten much closer together unless I sat in Vandenberg's lap or he sat in mine."

. . . At the conclusion of the Moscow Conference, it was my feeling that the Soviets were doing everything possible to achieve a complete break-down in Europe. That is, they were doing anything they could think of to create greater turbulence. The major problem was how to counter this negative Soviet policy and to restore the European economy so that the Europeans "could live less like animals and more like people.". . .

During the debate over the administration of the ERP, the State Department was under a great deal of attack for wanting to control the program. Actually we didn't want to administer the program. What we did want was an opportunity to review or supervise the public statements which might come out of the new agency. The ECA people could have issued public statements and policy pronouncements that would have greatly disturbed our foreign policy and negated the State Department's role. It was to Hoffman's personal credit and understanding of this problem that such was never the case. Because of the people around Truman and the Executive position we could never admit publicly that we did not want to administer ERP—therefore in all my public statements I plugged for State Department control. Because of the position of Truman's entourage, I could never defend myself publicly against the charge that we wanted to administer ECA. As a matter of fact Lovett and I thought it would be an error for the State Department to undertake this administration.

Source: Harry. S. Truman Presidential Library, Independence, Missouri.

Notes

Introduction

1   George C. Marshall to James B. Conant, May 28, 1947 in Larry I. Bland and Mark Stoler (eds), *The Papers of George Catlett Marshall*, 6 (Johns Hopkins University Press, 2013), 141 (hereafter *GCMP*, followed by volume and page number).

2   George C. Marshall, Speech to the Harvard Alumni, June 5, 1947, ibid., 147–150. For Marshall's speech see Documents, 146–148.

3   Paul C. Light, "Government's Greatest Achievements of the Past Half Century," December, 2000, available online at www.brookings.edu/research/papers/2000/12/11governance-light (accessed December 4, 2015); History News Network, "What Are the Ten Most Important Documents in American History," available online at http://historynewsnetwork.org/article/150152 (accessed October 16, 2015). The poll intentionally excluded the Declaration of Independence and the U.S. Constitution because these were obvious first choices.

4   Arthur M. Schlesinger, Jr., *Journals: 1952–2000* (The Penguin Press, 2007), 765–766; William I. Hitchcock, "The Marshall Plan and the Creation of the West," in Odd Arne Westad and Melvyn P. Leffler (eds), *The Cambridge History of the Cold War*, I (Cambridge University Press, 2010), 154–174.

5   Roosevelt quoted in John S. D. Eisenhower, *General Ike: A Personal Reminiscence* (New York: Free Press, 2003), 99.

6   Charles Kindleberger, *Marshall Plan Days* (Boston: Allen and Unwin, 1987), 247; Ernest Bevin's speech is quoted in Alan Bullock, *Ernest Bevin: Foreign Secretary, 1945–1951* (Oxford University Press, 1983), 405; Blücher quoted in Greg Behrman, *The Most Noble Adventure: The Marshall Plan and the Time when America Helped Save Europe* (New York: Free Press, 2007), 334.

7   See, for example, Martin A. Schain (ed.), *The Marshall Plan: Fifty Years After* (New York: Palgrave, 2001).

8   Glenn Hubbard, "A Marshall Plan for the Middle East," *The Huffington Post*, February 28, 2011; Glenn Hubbard, "Think Again: A Marshall Plan for Africa," *Foreign Policy*, August 13, 2009; Niall Ferguson, "Dollar Diplomacy: How Much Did the Marshall Plan Really Matter?" *The New Yorker*, August 27, 2007.

9   Alan S. Milward, *The Reconstruction of Western Europe, 1945–1951* (London: Methuen, 1984) and his review of the scholarly debate on this issue, "Was the Marshall Plan Necessary," *Diplomatic History*, 13, 2 (1989), 231–252.

10   For essays on this scholarly debate see: John Lewis Gaddis, "The Emerging Post-Revisionist Synthesis on the Origins of the Cold War," *Diplomatic History*, 7, 3 (1983), 171–190; H.W. Brands, "Consensus Be Damned!" *Reviews in American History*, 22, 4. (December, 1994), 717–724; Michael H. Hunt, "The Long Crisis in U.S. Diplomatic History: Coming to Closure, *Diplomatic History*, 16, 1 (January, 1992): 115–140.

11   Kennan to the Secretary of State, February 22, 1946. *Foreign Relations of the United States* (hereafter *FRUS*), *1946*, VI, 696–709.

12   Thomas Bailey, *America Faces Russia: Russian-American Relations from Early Times to Our Day* (Cornell University Press, 1950); William H. Chamberlain, *America's Second Crusade* (Chicago: Henry Regnery Co., 1950); Herbert Feis, *Churchill, Roosevelt, Stalin: The War they Waged and the Peace they Sought* (Princeton University Press, 1967).

13   Feis, *Churchill, Roosevelt, Stalin*, 227–254; Joseph M. Jones, *The Fifteen Weeks* (New York: Harcourt, 1955).

14   William Appleman Williams, *The Tragedy of American Diplomacy* (New York: W.W. Norton, 1972 edition), 239.

15   For important revisionist works, see Walter LaFeber, *America, Russia, and the Cold War, 1945–2006* (New York: McGraw-Hill, 10th edition, 2007); Gabriel Kolko, *The Roots of American Foreign Policy: An Analysis of Power and Purpose* (New York: Beacon Press, 1969); Carolyn Eisenberg, *Drawing the Line: The American Decision to Divide Germany* (Cambridge University Press, 1998).

16   Important post-revisionist works include: John Lewis Gaddis, *The United States and the Origins of the Cold War, 1941–1947* (Columbia University Press, 1972); Vojtech Mastny, *Russia's Road to the Cold War: Diplomacy, Warfare, and the Politics of Communism* (Columbia University Press, 1979); William Taubman, *Stalin's American Policy: From Entente to Détente to Cold War* (New York: Norton, 1982); John Lewis Gaddis, "The Emerging Post-Revisionist Synthesis on the Cold War," *Diplomatic History* 7, 3, (July, 1983), 171–190; Robert A. Pollard, *Economic Security and the Origins of the Cold War* (Columbia University Press, 1985); Marc Trachtenberg, *A Constructed Peace: The Making of the European Settlement, 1945–1963* (Princeton University Press, 1999).

17   John Lewis Gaddis, *The Cold War: A New History* (New York: Penguin Books, 2005), 32.

18   Important corporatist works include: Thomas J. McCormick, "Drift or Mastery? A Corporatist Synthesis for American Diplomatic History," *Reviews in American History*, 10, 4 (December 1982), 323–329; Michael J. Hogan, "Corporatism: A Positive Appraisal," *Diplomatic History*, 10, 4 (October 1986), 363–372; Michael J. Hogan, *The Marshall Plan: America, Britain, and the Reconstruction of Western Europe, 1947–1952* (New York: Cambridge University Press, 1989). Also see Emily S. Rosenberg, *Spreading the American Dream: American Economic and Cultural Expansion* (New York: Hill & Wang, 1982).

19   Hogan, *The Marshall Plan*, 136. Melvyn Leffler echoed similar ideas in his *A Preponderance of Power: National Security, the Truman Administration, and the Cold War* (Stanford University Press, 1993), 182–237.

20   Charles S. Maier, "The Politics of Productivity: Foundations of American International Economic Policy after World War II," *International Organization*, 31, 4, (Autumn, 1977), 607–633.

21   Joan Hoff-Wilson, *Ideology and Economics: U.S. Relations with the Soviet Union, 1918–1933* (University of Missouri Press, 1974), 140; Michael H. Hunt, "Ideology," *The Journal of American History*, 77, 1 (June, 1990), 108–115.

22   For this definition I am particularly indebted to: Michael H. Hunt, *Ideology and U.S. Foreign Policy* (Yale University Press, 2nd edition, 2009); Herbert McClosky, "Consensus and Ideology in American Politics," *American Political Science Review*, 58 (June, 1964), 362; Willard A. Mullins, "On the Concept of Ideology in Political Science," *The American Political Science Review*, 66, 2 (June 1972), 498–510; Malcolm B. Hamilton, "The Elements of the Concept of Ideology," *Political Studies*, 35 (March 1987), 18–38; Lorenz M. Lüthi, *The Sino-Soviet Split: Cold War in the Communist World* (Princeton University Press, 2008), 8–12; Sasson Sofer, "International Relations and the Invisibility of Ideology," *Millennium: Journal of International Studies*, 16, 3 (1987), 489–521.

23   Reinhold Niebuhr, *The Irony of American History* (University of Chicago Press, 2008 edition), 71.

24   Gordon S. Wood, *The Idea of America: Reflections on the Birth of the United States* (The Penguin Press, 2011), 332.

25   Henry Kissinger, "Reflections on the Marshall Plan," *Harvard Gazette*, May 22, 2015, available online at http://news.harvard.edu/gazette/story/2015/05/reflections-on-the-marshall-plan/ (accessed October 4, 2015).

26   "Conant Sees Peace Depending Upon U.S.," *Washington Post*, June 9, 1947.

27   Odd Arne Westad, *The Global Cold War: Third World Interventions and the Making of Our Times* (Cambridge University Press, 2005), 9.

28   Odd Arne Westad, "The New International History: Three (Possible) Paradigms," *Diplomatic History*, 24, 4 (Fall 2000), 551–565.

29   Aristide Briand, "Speech Before the League of Nations," September 5, 1929 in Michael E. McGuire (ed.), *As It Actually Was: A History of International Relations Through Documents, 1823–1945*, (New York: McGraw Hill, 2008), 157–159.

30   Kissinger, "Reflections on the Marshall Plan."

31   Hitchcock, "The Marshall Plan," 154.

1 A New Deal for the World

1   Stokely W. Morgan, "American Policy and Problems in Central America," Lecture to the Foreign Service School, Department of State, January 29, 1926, quoted in Lars Schoultz, *Beneath the United States: A History of U.S. Policy Toward Latin America* (Harvard University Press, 1988), 326.

2   Woodrow Wilson, "American Neutrality—An Appeal By the President," August 19, 1914 in R.S. Baker and W.E. Dodd (eds), *The New Democracy: Presidential Messages, Addresses, and other Papers (1913–1917)*, I (New York: Harper and Brothers, 1926), 157–159.

3   See Walter Lippmann's articles: "A League of Peace," *New Republic*, March 20, 1915; "An Appeal to the President," *New Republic*, April 22, 1916; "Mr. Wilson's Great Utterance," *New Republic*, June 6, 1916; "The Great Decision," *New Republic*,

April 7, 1917. Also, "For Freedom and Civilization," *New York Times*, April 3, 1917.

4   On American progressives and the war see David Kennedy, *Over Here: The First World War and American Society* (Oxford University Press, 1980), 45–92.

5   John Dewey, "America in the World," (1918) in Jo Ann Boydston, (ed.), *The Middle Works 1899–1924* (Southern Illinois University Press, 1982), 11, 70–72; Ronald Steel, *Walter Lippmann and the American Century* (Boston: Little, Brown, & Company, 1980), 143.

6   Robert B. Westbrook, *John Dewey and American Democracy* (Cornell University Press, 1991), 203.

7   Dewey, "America in the World," 72.

8   Lippmann, "The World Conflict in Relation to American Democracy," *Annals of the American Academy of Political and Social Sciences* (July, 1917), 1–10; Lippmann, "What Program Shall the United States Stand for in International Relations?" *Annals of the American Academy of Political and Social Science* (July, 1916), 60–70; Steel, *Walter Lippmann*, 150–151.

9   Henry Kissinger, *Diplomacy* (New York: Simon and Schuster, 1994), 225–226.

10   Harry Truman, Election Eve Speech, Jackson County, MO, November 2, 1942, Harry S. Truman Papers, U.S. Senator and Vice President Collection, Box 287. Harry S. Truman Presidential Library, Independence, Missouri (hereafter HSTL).

11   Henry Cabot Lodge, Jr. Radio Address, WBZ, October 27, 1936. Henry Cabot Lodge, Jr. Papers I, Massachusetts Historical Society, Carton I (hereafter HCL Papers).

12   Elihu Root, "A Requisite for the Success of Popular Diplomacy," *Foreign Affairs*, 1, 1 (September, 1922), 3–10; George W. Wickersham, "The Senate and Our Foreign Relations," *Foreign Affairs*, 2, 2 (December, 1923), 177–192.

13   David Ekbladh, *The Great American Mission: Modernization and the Construction of an American World Order* (Princeton University Press, 2010), 25–39, 70–76. Eric Helleiner, *Forgotten Foundations of Bretton Woods: International Development and the Making of the Postwar Order* (Cornell University Press, 2014), 99–133.

14   For these plans, see, "Division the Study of Problems of Peace and Reconstruction, December 12, 1939," U.S. Department of State, *Postwar Foreign Policy Preparation, 1939–1945* (Washington, D.C., 1949), 453–454.

15   Walter Lippmann, "America and the World," *Life*, June 3, 1940.

16   George Gallup, (ed.), *The Gallup Poll: Public Opinion, 1935–1971*, I (American Institute of Public Opinion, 1972), 222; Norman Moss, *America, Britain, and the Fateful Summer of 1940* (New York: Houghton Mifflin Harcourt, 2003), 123–126.

17   Franklin D. Roosevelt, "Fireside Chat on National Security," December 29, 1940, in *Public Papers and Addresses of Franklin Roosevelt, 1940* (New York: Macmillan, 1941), 633–640.

18   "House Resolution 1776: A Bill Further to Promote the defense of the United States and for other purposes," January 10, 1941, 77th Congress, 1st Session.

19   Diary Entry, March 8, 1941 in Arthur H. Vandenberg, Jr. (ed.), *The Private Papers of Senator Vandenberg* (Boston: Houghton Mifflin, 1952), 9–11.

20   Lawrence Kaplan, *The Conversion of Senator Arthur H. Vandenberg: From Isolation to International Engagement* (University Press of Kentucky, 2015); Michael Holm, "Also

Present at the Creation: Henry Cabot Lodge, Jr. and the Coming of the Cold War," *The Journal of the Historical Society*, 10, 2 (June, 2010), 203–229.

21 David Reynolds, *From Munich to Pearl Harbor: Roosevelt's America and the Origins of the Second World War* (Chicago: Ivan R. Dee, 2001), 4.

22 "Stimson Hails Boys Facing Issues as they Enter the World's Darkest Hour," *New York Times*, June 15, 1940.

23 Henry Luce, "The American Century," *Life*, February 17, 1941.

24 Warren F. Kimball, *The Juggler: Franklin Roosevelt as Wartime Statesman* (Princeton University Press, 1991), 186. For a solid account on the postwar export of American human rights and international law values, see Elizabeth Borgwardt, *A New Deal for the World: America's Vision for Human Rights* (The Belknap Press of Harvard University Press, 2007).

25 William Appleman Williams, *Empire as a Way of Life* (Oxford University Press, 1980), 173; Emily S. Rosenberg, *Spreading the American Dream: American Economic and Cultural Expansion* (New York: Hill & Wang, 1982), 229.

26 Robert Dallek, *Franklin D. Roosevelt and American Foreign Policy*, (Oxford University Press, 1995), 281–282. For the official records and discussions, see *FRUS 1941*, I, 340–378.

27 "Adolf A. Berle, Jr. to Roosevelt, June 21, 1941," Franklin Delano Roosevelt Library, Hyde Park, N.Y. (hereafter FDRL), Franklin Delano Roosevelt Papers, President's Secretary File, State Department, 1941, Box 34.

28 "Nicholas Murray Butler to Franklin D. Roosevelt, August 27, 1941," FDRL, President's Secretary's File, Safe Files, "Atlantic Charter;" "Declaration of the Atlantic," *Saturday Evening Post*, September 27, 1941; "The Eight Great Points," *Washington Post*, August 25, 1941; Raymond Clapper, "Why Can't Americans Believe in America?" *Life*, October 27, 1941. Winant quoted in "Whose America," *Saturday Evening Post*, October 25, 1941.

29 "Fate and War," *Saturday Evening Post*, January 3, 1942; "- Shall Rule the World," *Saturday Evening Post*, March 7, 1942.

30 Office of War Information, *The United Nations Fight for the Four Freedoms* (August 1942).

31 Justin Hart, *Empire of Ideas: The Origins of Public Diplomacy and the Transformation of U.S. Foreign Policy* (Oxford University Press, 2013), 71–111.

32 Henry A. Wallace, *The Price of Free World Victory* (New York: L.B. Fischer, 1942).

33 James Reston, *Prelude to Victory* (New York: Random House, 1942), 134–139; "Our Own New Order," *Saturday Evening Post*, February 28, 1942.

34 Henry Luce, "America's War and America's Peace," *Life*, February 16, 1942.

35 For the State Department's plans on Human Rights, see, *Postwar Foreign Policy Preparation*, 84, 115–116, 365, 386. For the text of this "Bill of Rights," see, 483–485 and "The Charter of the United Nations (draft) August 14, 1943," 526–532.

36 Benn Steil, *The Battle of Bretton Woods: John Maynard Keynes, Harry Dexter White and the Making of a New World Order* (Princeton University Press, 2013), 99–124.

37 Memorandum by Welles of Conversation with Cadogan, August 9, 1941, *FRUS 1941*, I, 345–354. For the debate concerning the Ottawa System, see Memorandum of Conversation, by Welles, August 11, 1931, ibid., 356–363; Cordell Hull, *Memoirs* (New York: Macmillan, 1948), II, 1151–1152; Sir Alexander Cadogan, *The Diaries*

of Sir Alexander Cadogan, 1938–1945, David Dilks (ed.), (New York: G.P. Putnam's Sons, 1972), 431; Christopher D. O'Sullivan, *Sumner Welles, Postwar Planning, and the Quest for a New World Order* (Columbia University Press, 2009), 33–60; Edward R. Stettinius, Jr., *Lend-Lease: Weapon for Victory* (New York: Macmillan, 1944), 340–343; Richard. N. Gardner, *Sterling-Dollar Diplomacy in Current Perspective: The Origins and the Prospects of Our International Economic Order* (Columbia University Press, 1980), 54–68; For the official debate regarding Lend-Lease and Great Britain, see the accompanying online source collection.

38   "Roosevelt's World Blue Print," *Saturday Evening Post*, April 10, 1943. Sumner Welles insisted that FDR was certain "that communism would never prevail provided democracy became a living reality . . . [with a similar] self-sacrificing fervor shown by the Marxists in fighting for their creed." See Sumner Welles, *Seven Major Decisions that Shaped History* (London: Hamish Hamilton, 1951), 190.

39   For attempts to explain this new role in the world to the public, see Herbert Feis, "Restoring Trade after the War: A Suggested Remedy for Old Defects," *Foreign Affairs*, 20, 2 (January 1942), 282–292; Alvin H. Hansen and Charles P. Kindleberger, "The Economic Tasks of the Postwar World," *Foreign Affairs*, 20, 3 (April, 1942), 468–478; Alvin A. Hansen, "World Institutions for Stability and Expansion," *Foreign Affairs*, 22, 2 (January 1944), 248–255.

40   *Congressional Record*, 78th Congress, 1944, 2299–2300. For Truman et al., see Documents, 133–135.

41   Henry Morgenthau, Jr. to Harry D. White, April 1944 in John M. Blum (ed.) *From the Morgenthau Diaries: Years of War, 1941–1945*, 3 (Boston: Houghton Mifflin, 1967), 250.

42   "Message of the President," *New York Times*, July 2, 1944.

43   Diane Kunz, *Butter and Guns: America's Cold War Economic Diplomacy* (New York: The Free Press, 1997), 8–10.

44   For an overview of these discussions, see, U.S. Department of State, *Proceedings and Documents of United Nations Monetary and Financial Conference*, I–II. (Washington, D.C., 1948).

45   Georg Schild, *Bretton Woods and Dumbarton Oaks*, (New York: St. Martin's Press, 1995), 117–122.

46   Rosenberg, *Spreading the American Dream*, 194. For the House and Senate Debates see Armand Van Dormael, *Bretton Woods: Birth of a Monetary System* (New York: Holmes & Meier, 1978), 251–265.

47   Walter LaFeber, *America, Russia, and the Cold War, 1945–2006* (New York: McGraw-Hill, 10th edition, 2007) 11–12; Thomas G. Paterson, *Soviet-American Confrontation: Postwar Reconstruction and the Origins of the Cold War* (Johns Hopkins University Press, 1973), 147; Fred L. Block, *The Origins of International Economic Disorder: A Study of United States International Monetary Policy from World War II to the Present* (University Press of California, 1977); Joyce Kolko and Gabriel Kolko, *The Limits of Power: The World of United States Foreign Policy, 1945–1954* (New York: Harper & Row, 1972), 2.

48   Raymond F. Mikesell, "Negotiating at Bretton Woods," in Raymond Dennett and Joseph E. Johnson (eds), *Negotiating with the Russians* (New York: World Peace Foundation, 1951), 100–116.

49   "Speaking of Books," *New York Times*, April 18, 1943.

50   Wendell L. Willkie, *One World* (London: Cassell & Co., 1943); Wendell L. Willkie, *An American Program* (New York: Simon and Schuster, 1944); "Lord Halifax to Anthony Eden, August 31, 1943" in *British Documents on Foreign Affairs: Reports and Papers from the Foreign Office Confidential Print*, North America, III, January 1943–December 1943 (New University Press), 96.

51   Tentative Proposals, *FRUS 1944*, I, 655–670. See also, Department of State, *Postwar Foreign Policy Preparation* 595–606. The British plan was much vaguer, suggesting the organization acquire a role in "guarding the right of man to seek his freedom, and [support] increase in the well-being of human society," ibid., 671.

52   Memorandum by the Undersecretary of State to the Secretary of State, September 9, 1944, *FRUS*, I, 1944, 789–791; From Edward Stettinius, Jr. Diary, September 21, 1944, ibid., 831–834

53   "Declaration on Liberated Europe," *FRUS 1945*, The Conferences at Malta and Yalta, 977–978; Herbert Feis, *Churchill, Roosevelt, Stalin: The War they Waged and the Peace they Sought* (Princeton University Press, 1967), 549–550.

54   Robert E. Sherwood, *Hopkins and Roosevelt: An Intimate Story* (New York: Harper, 1950), 870.

55   For the DPL's role, see Oral History Interview with Assistant Secretary of State John S. Dickey, July 19, 1974. HSTL, Oral History Collection; Andrew Johnstone, "Creating a 'Democratic Foreign Policy': The State Department's Division of Public Liaison and Public Opinion, 1944–1953," *Diplomatic History*, 35, 3 (June 2011), 483–503.

56   Harry Truman, Address before a Joint Session of Congress, April 16, 1945, HSTL, Harry S. Truman Papers, President's Secretary's File, Box 23.

57   Address by Secretary of State Edward R. Stettinius Jr. at the opening of the United Nations Conference, at San Francisco on April 25, 1945, HSTL, Harry S. Truman Papers, President's Secretary's Files, Box 23.

58   Stettinius to Truman, April 23, 1945, HSTL, Harry S. Truman Papers, President's Secretary's File, Box 154. For the Secretary's evaluation of polls see, Stettinius to Truman, May 7, 1945, HSTL, Harry S. Truman Papers, President's Secretary's File, Box 121.

59   Harry S. Truman, Address at the Closing of The United Nations Conference, June 26, 1945. HSTL, Harry S. Truman Papers, White House Central Files, Official File, Box 85.

60   "United Nations Sign Charter," *Life*, July 9, 1945; "How it was Made," *Life*, July 23, 1945; "Words in the Charter," *Washington Post*, May 18, 1945; "Sage Counsel," *Washington Post*, June 26, 1945; For Arthur Vandenberg's endorsement of the Charter, see, "Text of Vandenberg's Senate Report," *Washington Post*, June 29, 1945.

61   Harry Truman, Address Before the Senate, July 2, 1945, HSTL, Harry S. Truman Papers, White House Central Files, Official File, Box 85.

62   Stephen C. Schlesinger, *Act of Creation: The Founding of the United Nations: A Story of Superpowers, Secret Agents, Wartime Allies and Enemies, and Their Quest for a Peaceful World* (Boulder, CO: Westview Press, 2003).

63   Kimball, *The Juggler*, 186.

64   Harry Dexter White quoted in Georg Schild, *Bretton Woods and Dumbarton Oaks*, 120.

65 Alonzo L. Hamby, *Man of Destiny: FDR and the Making of the American Century* (New York: Basic Books, 2015).

66 William H. Chamberlain, *America's Second Crusade* (New York: Henry Regnery Company, 1950), 232; Lord Halifax to Eden, December 1944 in *British Documents on Foreign Affairs: Report and Papers from the Foreign Office Confidential Print*, North America, January 1944–December 1944, 4 (University Publications of America, 1999), 274.

2 The World America Made

1 Memorandum from John J. McCloy to the President, April 26, 1945. HSTL, Harry S. Truman Papers, Box 178. Report of Samuel I. Rosenman to the President, "Civilian Supplies for the Liberated Areas of Northwest Europe," *Department of State Bulletin* (May 6, 1945), 860–862.

2 Harry S. Truman, "Letter to Heads of War Agencies on the Economic Situation in the Liberated Countries of Northwest Europe," May 22, 1945, *Public Papers of the Presidents, Harry S. Truman 1945* (Washington, D.C., 1961), Document 35, (hereafter *PPP Truman*).

3 "World Relief is America's Job," *Saturday Evening Post*, December 22, 1945.

4 Benn Steil, *The Battle of Bretton Woods: John Maynard Keynes, Harry Dexter White and the Making of a New World Order* (Princeton University Press, 2013), 276–287.

5 Marquis Childs, "Washington Calling: Loan to Britain," *Washington Post*, 16 February, 1945.

6 H.W. Brands, *Inside the Cold War: Loy Henderson and the Rise of the American Empire, 1918–1961* (Oxford University Press, 1991), 147.

7 Jean Edward Smith, *Lucius D. Clay* (Henry Holt and Company, 1980), 352–353, 357–358, 379, 384–389.

8 Secretary of State James Byrnes, "Restatement of U.S. Policy Towards Germany, Stuttgart, September 6, 1946," *Department of State Bulletin* (September 15, 1946), 496–501. See Byrnes speech in the online document collection. Arthur H. Vandenberg, Jr. (ed.), *The Private Papers of Senator Vandenberg* (Boston: Houghton Mifflin, 1952), 299; Smith, *Lucius D. Clay*, 388–389.

9 Richard Nixon, *Leaders* (New York: Warner Books, 1982), 136–137.

10 Alan S. Milward, "Was the Marshall Plan Necessary?" *Diplomatic History*, 13, 2 (1989), 231–252; Alan S. Milward, *The Reconstruction of Western Europe, 1945–1951* (London: Methuen, 1984), 55.

11 George H. Gallup (ed.), *The Gallup Poll and International Public Opinion Polls, Great Britain, 1937–1975*, I, 1937–1964 (New York: Random House, 1976), 135–136, 148–149, 160, 162, 164, 169, 181.

12 "The British Problem," *Washington Post*, February 11, 1947.

13 George H. Gallup (ed.), *The Gallup International Public Opinion Polls, France 1939, 1944–1975*, I (New York: Random House, 1975), 73–74, 87.

14 Alan Kramer, *The West German Economy, 1945–1955* (New York, 1991), 72–82; Stacy May, "Measuring the Marshall Plan," *Foreign Affairs*, 26, 3 (April, 1948), 457–469.

15   Eduard Mark, "October or Thermidor? Interpretations of Stalinism and the
     Perception of Soviet Foreign Policy in the United States, 1927–1947," *The American
     Historical Review*, 94, 4 (October, 1989), 937–962.
16   "The Test," *Time*, January 17, 1944.
17   "The Fight for Germany," *Life*, October 21, 1946; "U.S. Foreign Policy II," *Life*,
     January 13, 1947.
18   Robert Gellately, *Stalin's Curse: Battling for Communism in War and Cold War*
     (London: Vintage Books, 2013), 285.
19   On De Gasperi's visit to Washington see *FRUS 1947*, III, 835–859; Kaeten Mistry,
     The United States, Italy and the Origins of the Cold War (Cambridge University Press,
     2014), 48–53.
20   Ambassador Caffery to the Secretary of State, October 29, 1946, *FRUS 1946*, V,
     468–470.
21   The Tactics of the French Communist Part According to a Source Maintaining
     Close Contacts with Important Communists, November 23, 1946, *FRUS 1946*,
     V, 417–477; Smith to the Secretary of State, December 20, 1946, *FRUS 1946*, V,
     478–479.
22   Henderson to Byrnes and Acheson, October 21, 1946, *FRUS 1946*, VII, 240–245.
23   Records of UNSC, September 18, 1946, HSTL, Herschel V. Johnson Papers, Box
     16; Herschel V. Johnson, "Role of the Security Council," Delivered before the
     Foreign Policy Association, October 18, 1946. HSTL, Herschel V. Johnson Papers,
     Box 14.
24   "U.S. Severs Relations with Albania," *New York Times*, November 9, 1946; Oral
     Interview with Harry N. Howard, June, 1973. HSTL, Oral History Collection.
     Robert A. Pollard, *Economic Security and the Origins of the Cold War* (Columbia
     University Press, 1985), 115–116. See United Nations Security Council Meetings,"
     September–December 1946. HSTL, Herschel V. Johnson Papers, Box 16–17.
25   United Nations Security Council Meeting, December 13, 1946. HSTL, Herschel
     V. Johnson Papers, Box 17; "Greek Premier Coming to U.S. For U.N. Plea," *New
     York Times*, November 26, 1946.
26   Joseph and Stewart Alsop, "Crossed Fingers Toward Russia," *Washington Post*,
     December 15, 1946.
27   United Nations Security Council Meeting, December 19, 1946. HSTL, Herschel
     V. Johnson Papers, Box 17. "U.N. Council Votes Greek Investigation: Inquiry
     may Include Albania, Yugoslavia, and Bulgaria," *Washington Post*, December 19,
     1946.
28   "Big Power Harmony: The Council and the Greek Issue," *Washington Post*, Decem-
     ber 21 1946; Walter Lippmann, "Claims of Victory," *Washington Post*, December
     24, 1946.
29   Oral History Interview with Mark F. Ethridge, June 4, 1974. HSTL, Oral History
     Collection; Mark F. Ethridge to the Secretary of State, February 17, 1947, *FRUS
     1947*, V, 820–821; "Rift in U.N. Inquiry on Balkans Grows: Russian and Yugoslav
     Balk at Americans' Questions," *New York Times*, March 9, 1947.
30   "Porter's Three Choices in Greece," *Washington Post*, March 2, 1947.
31   David McCullough, *Truman* (New York: Simon and Schuster, 1992), 535.
32   Oral History Interview with Dr. Constantinos Doxiadis, May 5, 1964. HSTL, Oral
     History Collection.

33   "Threats to Greece," *Life*, March 17, 1947.

34   George C. Marshall, Speech at Princeton University, February 22, 1947, *GCMP*, VI, 47–50; Walter Lippmann, "Marshall at Princeton," *Washington Post*, February 25, 1947.

35   The British Embassy to the Department of State, Aide Memoire, February 21, 1947, *FRUS 1947*, V, 32–37. "Acheson's Statement on Plans to Aid Greece and Turkey," *Washington Post*, March 21, 1947.

36   Acheson to the Secretary of State, February 21, 1947, *FRUS 1947*, V, 29–31; Brands, *Inside the Cold War*, 157.

37   Report of the Meeting of the State-War-Navy Coordinating Committee Subcommittee on Foreign Policy Information, February 28, 1947, *FRUS 1947*, V, 66–67.

38   Eben A. Ayers, diary entries from the first two weeks of March. HSTL, Eben A. Ayers Papers, Box 20.

39   Joseph M. Jones to Loy Henderson, February 28, 1947. HSTL, Joseph M. Jones Papers, Box 6. Draft of Meeting Notes between Congressional leaders and the State Department February 27, 1945, ibid.; Denise M. Bostdorff, *Proclaiming the Truman Doctrine: The Cold War Call to Arms* (Texas A & M University Press, 2008), 68–72.

40   Will Clayton to Marshall, "Memorandum on the Creation of a National Council of Defense, March 5, 1947," in *Selected Papers of Will Clayton*, Fredrick J. Dobney (ed.), (The Johns Hopkins University Press, 1971), 198–200.

41   Memorandum on the Genesis of President's Truman's March 12 Speech, *FRUS 1947*, V, 121–123. John Lewis Gaddis, *George F. Kennan: An American Life* (New York: Penguin Press, 2011), 254–255.

42   George Kennan, Address at the Council on Foreign Relations, January 7, 1947, quoted in Michael Wala, *The Council on Foreign Relations and American Foreign Policy in the Early Cold War* (Providence: Berghahn, 1994), 80–81.

43   Harry S. Truman, "Annual Message to the Congress on the State of the Union, January 6, 1947," *PPP Truman, 1947*, 1–12; "U.S. Foreign Policy, III," *Life*, January 20, 1947.

44   Harry S. Truman, "Special Message to the Congress on Aid to Greece and Turkey: The Truman Doctrine," *PPP Truman, 1947*, Document 56.

45   For Truman's view of Stalin, see Robert H. Ferrell (ed.). *Dear Bess: Letters from Harry to Bess Truman* (New York: W.W. Norton and Co., 1983), 522.

46   Gellately, *Stalin's Curse*, 11–13.

47   Conversation between Monsieur Georges Bidault and General Marshall, March 13, 1947, *GCMP*, VI, 73–77; Conversation with Bevin, March 22, 1947, ibid., 82–85; George Marshall, "Statement to the Eighteenth Meeting of the Council on Foreign Ministers," March 31, 1947, ibid., 87–89.

48   Memorandum of Conversation with Generalissimo Stalin, ibid., 97–104; Forest C. Pogue, *George C. Marshall: Statesman, 1945–1959* (New York: Viking, 1987), 168–194.

49   Bevin to Attlee, April 16, 1945, quoted in Alan Bullock, *Ernest Bevin: Foreign Secretary, 1945–1951* (Oxford University Press, 1983), 388.

50   George Frost Kennan, *Memoirs, 1925–1950* (Boston: Little, Brown and Co., 1967), 325–327; Gaddis, *George F. Kennan*, 264–265.

51   George Marshall Radio Address," *GCMP*, 6, 113–122. For Marshall's radio address see Documents, 138–142.

52   Hearings Before the House Committee on Foreign Affairs, March 24, 1947, 80th Congress (1947), 63–69.

53   Henry Wallace, "The Fight for Peace Begins," *New Republic*, CXVI, March 24, 1947; Robert A. Taft, "Statement about Aid to Turkey and Greece, March 12, 1947," in Clarence E. Wunderlin (ed.), *The Papers of Robert A. Taft*, 3 (Kent State University Press, 2001), 260.

54   Arthur Vandenberg, "Senate Committee on Foreign Relations, April 2, 1947," HCL Papers, Carton 14.

55   Michael Holm, "Also Present at the Creation: Henry Cabot Lodge, Jr. and the Coming of the Cold War," *The Journal of the Historical Society*, 10, 2 (June, 2010), 213–214; "Our Foreign Policy Crisis," *Life*, March 17, 1947; John Foster Dulles, "Thoughts on Soviet Foreign Policy and What to Do About It, Part I," *Life*, June 3, 1946; John Foster Dulles, "Thoughts on Soviet Foreign Policy and What to Do About It, Part II," *Life*, June 10, 1946.

56   Enclosure to Kennan memo, May 23, 1947, *FRUS 1947*, III, 224–226, 228.

57   Steil, *The Battle of Bretton Woods*, 311.

58   Marshall, Speech to the Harvard Alumni, 147–150.

59   Available online at http://harvardmagazine.com/1997/05/marshall.speech.html (accessed October 11, 2015).

3 Creating the European Recovery Program, 1947–1948

1   Forest C. Pogue, *George C. Marshall: Statesman, 1945–1959* (New York: Viking, 1987), 217; Interview with Paul Hoffman, January 28, 1953. HSTL, available online at www.trumanlibrary.org/whistlestop/study_collections/marshall/large/index.php (accessed December 4, 2015).

2   Dean Acheson, *Sketches from Life: Of Men I have Known* (New York: Harper & Brothers, 1961), 1–29.

3   George Frost Kennan, *Memoirs, 1925–1950* (Boston: Little, Brown and Co., 1967), 342. Charles E. Bohlen, *Witness to History, 1929–1969* (New York: Norton, 1973), 264; Summary of Discussion on Problems of Relief, Rehabilitation, and Reconstruction of Europe, May 29, 1947, *FRUS 1947*, III, 234–236.

4   Mikhail Narinsky, "Soviet Foreign Policy and the Origins of the Cold War," in Gabriel Gorodetsky, ed., *Soviet Foreign Policy, 1917–1991: A Retrospective* (London: Frank Cass, 1994), 105–110.

5   "Hope of Soviet Cooperation?" *The Times* (London), June 24, 1947.

6   John Lewis Gaddis, *We Now Know: Rethinking Cold War History* (New York: Oxford University Press, 1997), 41–42; Robert Gellately, *Stalin's Curse: Battling for Communism in War and Cold War* (New York: Vintage Books, 2013), 303–304.

7   Robert Service, *Stalin: A Biography* (Belknap Press of Harvard University Press, 2004), 504–506.

8   Bernard Nover, "Choosing Sides: Europe's Testing Time," *Washington Post*, July 5, 1947.

9   "Record of Stalin's Conversation with the Czechoslovak Government Delegation on the issue of their Position regarding the Marshall Plan and the Prospects for

Economic Cooperation with the U.S.S.R.," Moscow, July 9, 1947 in Ralph B. Levering, Vladimir O. Pechatnov, Verena Botzenhart-Viehe, and C. Earl Edmonson (eds), *Debating the Origins of the Cold War* (London: Rowman & Littlefield, 2000), 169–172.

10 Arnold A. Offner, *Another Such Victory: President Truman and the Cold War, 1945–1953* (Stanford University Press, 2002), 226.

11 Gellately, *Stalin's Curse*, 308–312.

12 The Embassy in Poland to the Secretary of State, July 7 and July 10, 1947, *FRUS 1947*, III, 313, 320–322.

13 Carolyn Eisenberg, "Revisiting the Division of Germany," March 1, 2013, available online at www.newleftproject.org/index.php/site/article_comments/revisiting_the_division_of_germany (accessed November 6, 2015); Charles S. Maier, "The Marshall Plan and the Division of Europe," *Journal of Cold War Studies*, 7, 1, (Winter, 2005), 168–174.

14 Smith to the Secretary of State, July 11, 1947, *FRUS 1947*, III, 327. For Smith's memo, see the accompanying online source collection.

15 Memorandum by the Consular of the Department of State, August 30, 1947, *FRUS 1947*, I, 763–765.

16 Tizard quoted in Robert Pearce, *Attlee* (London: Routledge, 1997), 166.

17 Joseph Alsop, "Struggle Between de Gaulle and Communists Could End in Civil War," *Daily Boston Globe*, October 10, 1947.

18 "The Only Danger in Italy and France is Inaction in the Face of Need," *Daily Boston Globe*, October 17, 1947; Andrei Vyshinsky, Speech to the United Nations General Assembly, September 18, 1947, United Nations General Assembly, *Official Records*, Plenary Meetings (1947), 86–88. For Vyshinsky's speech see Documents, 149–150. Andrei Zhdanov, "The International Situation" in U.S. House of Representatives, Committee on Foreign Affairs, 80th Congress, *The Strategy and Tactics of World Communism* (Washington, D.C.: Government Printing Office, 1948), 211–230. For Zhdanov's speech see Documents, 151–155.

19 Anne Applebaum, *Iron Curtain: The Crushing of Eastern Europe, 1944–1956* (New York: Doubleday, 2012), 223.

20 Gellately, *Stalin's Curse*, 315–317.

21 William I. Hitchcock, *The Struggle for Europe: the Turbulent History of a Divided Continent, 1945–2002* (New York: Anchor Books, 2004), 89–90; Applebaum, *Iron Curtain*, 218–221.

22 Walter Lippmann, "Europe Revisited," *Washington Post*, November 4, 1947.

23 Walter Lippmann, "The Disorders in Western Europe," *Washington Post*, November 18, 1947.

24 Michael J. Hogan, *The Marshall Plan: America, Britain, and the Reconstruction of Western Europe, 1947–1952* (Cambridge University Press, 1989), 82–84.

25 Interview with General George C. Marshall, October 30, 1952. HSTL. Available online at www.trumanlibrary.org/whistlestop/study_collections/marshall/large/index.php (accessed December 4, 2015). For some of Marshall's efforts see: NBC Radio Speech, August 15, 1947, *GCMP*, VI, 195–197; Speech to the Congress of Industrial Organization, October 15, 1947, ibid., 225–228; Speech to the Herald Tribune Forum, October 22, 1947; and his Testimony on Interim Aid for Europe, November 11–12, 1947, ibid., 256–258; Michael Wala, "Selling the Marshall Plan

at Home: The Committee for the Marshall Plan to Aid European Recovery," *Diplomatic History*, 10, 3 (July, 1986), 247–265; Justin Hart, *Empire of Ideas: The Origins of Public Diplomacy and the Transformation of U.S. Foreign Policy* (Oxford University Press, 2013), 123–128.

26   "Lehman in Plea for Food—Warns on Chaos in Europe," *New York Times*, October 12, 1947.

27   Dean Acheson, *Present at the Creation: My Years in the State Department* (New York: W.W. Norton & Company, 1987), 239–241; Robert L. Beisner, *Dean Acheson: A Life in the Cold War* (Oxford University Press, 2009), 74–75.

28   Henry L. Stimson, "The Challenge to Americans," *Foreign Affairs*, 26, 4 (October, 1947), 5–14.

29   Michael J. Hogan, *A Cross of Iron: Harry S. Truman and the Origins of the National Security State, 1945–1954* (New York: Cambridge University Press, 1998), 90; Greg Behrman, *The Most Noble Adventure: The Marshall Plan and the Time when America Helped Save Europe* (New York: Free Press, 2007), 136.

30   *Congressional Record*, 80th Congress (March 12, 1948), 2645.

31   Joseph and Stewart Alsop, "The Evolution of Foreign Policy," *Washington Post*, June 15, 1947.

32   Michael Holm, "Also Present at the Creation: Henry Cabot Lodge, Jr. and the Coming of the Cold War," *The Journal of the Historical Society*, 10, 2 (June, 2010), 216–217.

33   "How Can We Combat Anti-American Propaganda in Europe," *Bulletin of Town Meetings of the Air*, 13, 33 (1947), 3–22.

34   "Russia and the West Cut German Nation in Half," *Life*, December 29, 1947.

35   George C. Marshall, "Address on the London Conference of Foreign Ministers," *GCMP*, VI, 297–302.

36   Henry Cabot Lodge, Jr. "Town Hall Speech," December 9, 1947. HCL Papers, Reel 3.

37   Harry S. Truman, "Special Message to the Congress on the Marshall Plan," *PPP Truman, 1947,* Doc. 238. For Truman's speech, see the accompanying online source collection.

38   "Plan of Action," *Washington Post*, December 20, 1947; "Let Us Raise A Standard," *New York Times*, December 21, 1947; "Truman Message Hailed: Non-Communist Newspaper in Western Europe Praise Plan," *New York Times*, December 21, 1947.

39   Eleanor Roosevelt to Harry Truman, December 23, 1947 in Steve Neal (ed.), *Eleanor and Harry: The Correspondence of Eleanor Roosevelt and Harry S. Truman* (New York: Scribner, 2002), 116–117.

40   Arthur H. Vandenberg, Jr. (ed.), *The Private Papers of Senator Vandenberg* (Boston: Houghton Mifflin, 1952), 383–386; Behrman, *The Most Noble Adventure*, 131–133; "Doctors Speak," *Life*, February 2, 1948; "Bi-Zonia's Troubles," ibid.

41   Statement to the Senate Committee on Foreign Relations, January 8, 1947, *GCMP*, VI, 309–320; Senate Testimony on the European Recovery Program, January 8, 1947, ibid., 321–323; Behrman, *The Most Noble Adventure*, 143–145.

42   Behrman, *The Most Noble Adventure*, 146–150.

43   Vandenberg, *Private Papers*, 385–386.

44   *Congressional Record*, 80th Congress, (February 3, 1948), 964; "ERP's Progress," *Life*, March 1, 1948.

45 *Congressional Record*, 80th Congress, (February 3, 1948), 965; Hogan, *A Cross of Iron*, 93–94.

46 For the most important floor debates see *Congressional Record*, 80th Congress, (March 2, 1948), 1961–1986; ibid., (March, 3, 1948), 2019–2052; ibid., (March 4, 2106–2135; ibid., (March 5, 1948), 2187–2220; ibid., (March 11, 1948), 2514–2548.

47 "ERP's Progress," *Life*, March 1, 1948.

48 William J. Miller, *Henry Cabot Lodge, Jr.: A Biography* (New York: Norton, 1967), 197–198.

49 Joseph and Stewart Alsop, "Must America Save the World," *Saturday Evening Post*, February 21, 1948.

50 Applebaum, *Iron Curtain*, 221–222

51 "U.S. Foreign Policy Takes a Licking," *Life*, March 8, 1948; "Stalin is Marching While We Drag Our Feet," *Saturday Evening Post*, March 20, 1948; "Is America Immune to the Communist Plague?" *Saturday Evening Post*, April 24, 1948; Melvyn Leffler, *A Preponderance of Power: National Security, the Truman Administration, and the Cold War* (Stanford University Press, 1993), 203–206.

52 Clay to Chamberlain, March 5, 1948 quoted in Jean Edward Smith, *Lucius D. Clay* (New York: Henry Holt and Company, 1980), 466.

53 Marvel to State Department, March 24 and March 27, *FRUS 1948*, III, 66–68; Bo Lidegaard, *I Kongens Navn: Henrik Kauffmann i Dansk Diplomati, 1919–58* (NB PrePress, 1996), 452–456.

54 "An Aroused Italy Chooses Freedom," *Life*, May 3, 1948

55 Adjusted for inflation, the equivalent amount for 2016 would be approximately $125 billion.

56 Paul G. Hoffman, Oral Interview, 1964, HSTL Oral History Collection. Available online at www.trumanlibrary.org/oralhist/hoffmanp.htm (accessed March 1, 2016).

57 Acheson, *Sketches from Life*, 19; Oral Interview with Paul G. Hoffman, October 25, 1964, HSTL, Oral History Collection.

58 Ibid.

59 Hogan, *The Marshall Plan*, 124–127.

60 Behrman, *The Most Noble Adventure*, 179.

61 Anthony Leviero, "First ERP Wheat Shipment Start Texas Loadings Today," *New York Times*, April 14, 1948; "Europe Aid Pact Set Up Machinery," *New York Times*, April 16, 1948

62 Chester Bowles, "We Need a Program *For* as Well as *Against*," *New York Times*, April 18, 1948.

63 Hogan, *Marshall Plan*, 1–25; Charles Maier, "The Politics of Productivity: Foundation of American International Economic Policy after World War II," *International Organization*, 31, 4 (Autumn 1977), 607–633.

4 The Marshall Plan in Action and the Emergence of European Unity, 1948–1951

1 "Third Currency Reform Law in Germany," *Department of State Bulletin* (August 1, 1948), 141–143.

2 Marshall to General Charles G. Dawes, August 3, 1948, *GCMP*, VI, 515.

3   William I. Hitchcock, *The Struggle for Europe: The Turbulent History of a Divided Continent, 1945-Present* (New York: Anchor Books, 2004), 93–94. Arnold A. Offner, *Another Such Victory: President Truman and the Cold War, 1945–1953* (Stanford University Press, 2002), 245–273.

4   Jean E. Smith, ed., *The Papers of General Lucius D. Clay: Germany, 1945–1949*, II (Indiana University Press, 1974), 677; "Soviet Bans Food, Milk Supplies for West Berlin," *Washington Post*, June 25, 1948.

5   Churchill quoted in A. Warren Dockter, *Winston Churchill at the Telegraph* (London: Aurum Press Ltd., 2015), 168–171.

6   Smith, *Lucius D. Clay*, 505; Hitchcock, *The Struggle for Europe*, 93–97.

7   David Pietrusza, *1948: Harry Truman's Improbable Victory and the Year that Changed America* (New York: Union Square Press, 2011) 274–275; "Marshall to the Embassy in the United Kingdom," *FRUS 1948*, III, 971.

8   Ludwig Erhard, *Wohlstand für Alle* (Düsseldorf: Econ-Verlag GMBH, 1957), 338.

9   Greg Behrman, *The Most Noble Adventure: The Marshall Plan and the Time when America Helped Save Europe* (New York: Free Press, 2007), 206.

10 Andrew David and Michael Holm, "The Kennedy Administration and the Battle over Foreign Aid: The Untold Story of the Clay Committee." *Diplomacy and Statecraft*, 27, 1 (March, 2016), 65–92.

11 For one scholar's unsuccessful attempt to display American business interests as largely anti-Marshall Plan see Jacqueline McGlade, "A Single Path for European Recovery? American Business Debates and Conflicts over the Marshall Plan," in Martin A. Schain (ed.), *The Marshall Plan: Fifty Years After* (New York: Palgrave, 2001), 185–204.

12 "Achievements of the Marshall Plan," *Department of State Bulletin* (January 14, 1952), 43–45; Behrman, *The Most Noble Adventure*, 311–314.

13 Michael J. Hogan, *The Marshall Plan: America, Britain, and the Reconstruction of Western Europe, 1947–1952* (Cambridge University Press, 1989), 143.

14 Behrman, *The Most Noble Adventure*, 319–321.

15 Hogan, *The Marshall Plan*, 143–145.

16 William Burr, "Marshall Planners and the Politics of Empire: The United States and France, 1948," *Diplomatic History*, 15, 4 (October, 1991), 504.

17 Burr, "Marshall Planners," 514–518.

18 Burr, "Marshall Planners," 515–519; "100 Injured in Paris Fights as Workers and Police Clash," *New York Times*, September 16, 1948; "Safety Crews Quit French Coal Mines; Troops Move in, Fight Strikers in Loire Valley," ibid., October 19, 1948.

19 Kaeten Mistry, *The United States, Italy and the Origins of the Cold War* (Cambridge University Press, 2014), 167.

20 Ibid., 169–170; John Killick, *The United States and European Reconstruction* (London: Routledge, 2000), 117–120.

21 Killick, *The United States and European Reconstruction*, 106–108.

22 Ibid., 108.

23 Douglas to Secretary of State, June 16, 1949, *FRUS 1949*, IV, 784–786.

24 Hogan, *The Marshall Plan*, 238–257, 261–263.

25 Killick, *The United States and European Reconstruction*, 101–102.

26 Bo Lidegaard, *Jens Otto Kragh, 1914–1961* (København: Gyldendal, 2001), 320–331;

Vibeke Sørensen, *Denmark's Social Democratic Government and the Marshall Plan* (Museum Tusulanums Forlag: University of Copenhagen, 2001); Fritz Hodne, *The Norwegian Economy, 1920–1980* (Kent, UK: Croom Helm, 1983), 130–179; Charles Silva, *Keep Them Strong, Keep Them Friendly: Swedish-American Relations and the Pax Americana, 1948–1952* (Stockholm: Akademitryck AB, 1999); Bernadette Whelan, *Ireland and the Marshall Plan 1947–1957* (Dublin: Four Courts Press, 2000); Günter Bischof, Anton Pelinka and Dieter Stiefel (eds), *The Marshall Plan in Austria* (New Brunswick, NJ: Transaction, 2000); Johan De Vries, *The Netherlands Economy in the Twentieth Century* (Assen: Van Gorchum, 1978), 63–64, 99–107; Killick, *The United States and European Recovery*, 123–133.

27 Chiarella Esposito, *America's Feeble Weapon: Funding the Marshall Plan in France and Italy, 1948–1950* (Westport: Greenwood, 1994).

28 Stewart Patrick, "Embedded Liberalism in France? American Hegemony, the Monnet Plan, and Postwar Multilateralism," in Schain, *The Marshall Plan*, 205–245.

29 Ibid., 221–225.

30 Ibid., 233; "Investment in Democracy," *New York Times*, May 30, 1946.

31 William I. Hitchcock, "The Marshall Plan and the Creation of the West," in Odd Arne Westad and Melvyn P. Leffler (eds), *The Cambridge History of the Cold War*, I (Cambridge University Press, 2010), 161.

32 Behrman, *The Most Noble Adventure*, 226–227.

33 Wilson D. Miscamble, *From Roosevelt to Truman: Potsdam, Hiroshima, and the Cold War* (New York: Cambridge University Press, 2007), 5–7.

34 Claude C. Erb, "Prelude to Point Four: The Institute of Inter-American Affairs," *Diplomatic History*, 9, 3 (Summer, 1985), 249–269.

35 Benjamin Hardy, "Use of U.S. Technological Resources as a Weapon in the Struggle with International Communism," November 23, 1948. HSTL, Walter S. Salant Papers, Box 2; "Memorandum for the President," December 20, 1948, ibid.; Walter S. Salant to David Lloyd, January 11, 1949, ibid. Oral interview with Walter S. Salant, March 30, 1970. HSTL, Oral History Collection.

36 Harry. S. Truman, Inaugural Address, January 20, 1949, *PPP Truman, 1949*, 112–116. Oral Interview with Clark M. Clifford, 1971–1973. HSTL, Oral History Collection.

37 Lilienthal, *The Journals of David E. Lilienthal*, vol. 2, *The Atomic Years, 1945–1950* (New York: Harper and Row, 1964), 448–449.

38 Memorandum: The Problem of the Future Balance of Payments of the United States, February 16, 1950, *FRUS 1950*, I, 838–841.

39 "Our World," *New York Post*, January 25, 1949; "Truman Maps our World," *Watertown Daily Times*, January 21, 1949; "Truman's Words Hearten Asian and African Colonists," *New York Post*, January 25, 1949; "Truman Plan for Needy Areas Stirs Europe and Washington: Scheme may Dwarf ERP," *Christian Science Monitor*, January 21, 1949. There were other more pessimistic views. Both Walter Lippmann and James Reston questioned whether Republicans in Congress would support this endeavor. See Walter Lippmann, "The Inaugural," *Washington Post*, January 24, 1949; James Reston, "Truman's Four Points have Wide Implications:

Washington is Analyzing the Speech Carefully as Criticism Begins," *New York Times*, January 23, 1949; David Ekbladh, *The Great American Mission: Modernization and the Construction of an American World Order* (Princeton University Press, 2010), 100–101.

40 "Roosevelt's Dream Now U.S. Objective," *Washington Post*, January 21, 1949.

41 Scott Lucas, *Freedom's War: The U.S. Crusade Against the Soviet Union, 1945–1956* (Manchester University Press, 1999), 2.

42 Oral Interview with John D. Hickerson, November 10, 1972. HSTL, Oral History Collection.

43 Arthur Schlesinger, "Europe Takes Hope from ECA," *New Republic*, November 8, 1948.

44 Article V, The North Atlantic Treaty, Washington, D.C, April 4, 1949, available online at www.nato.int/cps/en/natolive/official_texts_17120.htm (accessed January 6, 2016).

45 Mistry, *The United States and Italy*, 171–174.

46 Oral Interview with Theodore C. Achilles, November 13 and December 18, 1972. HSTL, Oral History Collection. Robert L. Beisner, *Dean Acheson: A Life in the Cold War* (Oxford University Press, 2009), 143.

47 Michael Holm, "Also Present at the Creation: Henry Cabot Lodge, Jr. and the Coming of the Cold War," *The Journal of the Historical Society*, 10, 2 (June, 2010), 222.

48 Odd Arne Westad, "The New International History: Three (Possible) Paradigms," *Diplomatic History*, 24, 4 (Fall 2000), 555.

49 Monnet, *Memoirs* (New York: Doubleday, 1978), 272–273.

50 Report by the Economic Cooperation Administration April 14, 1950, *FRUS 1950*, III, 646–652; Hogan, *The Marshall Plan*, 295–335; Alan Bullock, *Ernest Bevin: Foreign Secretary, 1945–1951* (Oxford University Press, 1983), 716–723.

51 Behrman, *The Most Noble Adventure*, 281.

52 Monnet, *Memoirs*, 282–298.

53 Dean Acheson, *Sketches from Life: Of Men I have Known* (New York: Harper & Brothers, 1961), 33.

54 For the Schuman Plan see Documents, 159–161.

55 Acheson, *Sketches From Life*, 36–37.

56 Hogan, *The Marshall Plan*, 368–372; Bullock, *Bevin*, 714–720.

57 A Report to the National Security Council on United States Objectives and Programs for National Security, NSC-68, April 14, 1950, available online at www.trumanlibrary.org/whistlestop/study_collections/coldwar/documents/pdf/10-1.pdf (accessed December 6, 2015).

58 Memorandum of Conversation, December 1, 1950, *FRUS 1950*, VII, 1276–1281; Holm, "Also Present at the Creation," 225.

59 Mark A. Stoler, "George C. Marshall and the 'Europe-First' Strategy, 1939–1951: A Study in Diplomatic as well as Military History," *Journal of Military History*, 79, 2 (April 2015), 309; Forest C. Pogue, *George C. Marshall: Statesman, 1945–1959* (New York: Viking, 1987), 420–440.

60 Behrman, *The Most Noble Adventure*, 303.

61 Stoler, "George C. Marshall and the 'Europe-First' Strategy," 314.

5 Epilogue

1 "Achievements of the Marshall Plan," *Department of State Bulletin* (January 14, 1952), 43–45.

2 Oral Interview with Konrad Adenauer, June 10, 1964. HSTL, Oral History Collection.

3 Greg Behrman, *The Most Noble Adventure: The Marshall Plan and the Time when America Helped Save Europe* (New York: Free Press, 2007), 334.

4 John F. Kennedy, "Special Message to the Congress on Foreign Aid, March 22, 1961," *PPP, John F. Kennedy, 1961*, Document 90. John F. Kennedy, "Message to the Guests at a Dinner Marking the 15th Anniversary of the Marshall Plan," ibid., 1963, Document 124.

5 Barry Eichengreen and Marc Uzan, "The Marshall Plan: Economic Effects and Implications for Eastern Europe and the Former USSR," *Economic Policy*, 7, 14, Eastern Europe (April, 1992), 13–75.

6 Tony Judt, *Postwar: A History of Europe Since 1945* (New York: Penguin Books, 2006), 335.

7 Michael E. Latham, *Modernization as Ideology: American Social Science and 'Nation Building' in the Kennedy Era* (University of North Caroline Press, 2000), 79.

8 Anthony Lewis, "Leveraged Investment," *New York Times*, May 22, 1990; Charles Maier, "Eastern Europe's Turn For a Marshall Plan," *New York Times*, June 6, 1990.

9 Francis Fukuyama, "The End of History," *The National Interest* (Summer, 1989); Francis Fukuyama, *The End of History and the Last Man* (New York: Free Press, 1992).

10 Henry Kissinger, *Diplomacy* (New York: Simon and Schuster, 1994), 272.

11 Lech Walesa at European ESC: "We need a new Marshall Plan for Eastern Europe" European Commission, Press Release, December 18, 2000.

12 "X" (George F. Kennan), "The Sources of Soviet Conduct," *Foreign Affairs*, 25, 4 (July, 1947), 566–582.

13 James Hoge, "Europe Needs a Marshall Plan," *The World Today*, 68, 2 (February/March 2012), 5; Nicolaus Mills, "A Marshall Plan for the Middle East," *World Policy Journal*, 25, 3, (Fall, 2008) 79–83; Ron Daniels, "A Domestic Marshall Plan to Transform America's 'Dark Ghettos': Toward a Martin Luther King—Malcolm X Community Revitalization Initiative," *The Black Scholar*, 37, 3, (Fall, 2007), 10–13; Larry Gabriel, "If We Rebuilt War-Torn Europe—Why Not Detroit?" *Detroit Metro Times*, January 14, 2009.

14 Bernard Braine, "A Marshall Plan for the Third World," *Third World Quarterly*, 1, 2, (April, 1979), 43–52; Richard N. Gardner, "Time for a New Marshall Plan," *New York Times*, June 3, 1967; Robert A. Pastor and Richard Feinberg, "U.S. Latin American Policy: A Marshall Plan for the Caribbean?" *Vital Issues*, 33, 1, 1984; Alan Cranston, "Let's Have a Marshall Plan for Philippines," *Los Angeles Times*, September 13, 1987; Irwin M. Stelzer, "A Marshall Plan for Eastern Europe?" *Commentary*, January 1990; "'Global Marshall Plan' Urged for Environment," *Washington Post*, May 3, 1990; "Mandela Urges Marshall Plan for South Africa," *Reuters,* May 22, 1996; "Kohl Proposes a New Marshall Plan for the Middle East," *Deutsche Presse Agentur*, January 25, 1996.

15 Judt, *Postwar: A History of Europe*, 76–77.

16 "Quality of the ECA," *Washington Post*, December 31, 1951.

17 Daniel T. Rodgers, *Age of Fracture* (The Belknap Press of Harvard University, 2011), 2.

Documents

1 In May and June 1943 representatives from 45 countries met in Hot Springs, Virginia to discuss global food and agricultural problems. The conference's ambitious goal, mirroring the globalization of FDR's Four Freedoms was to help secure freedom from want of food and to help secure adequate health around the world when the war ended.

2 Following up on the Hot Springs Conference, UNRRA held its world conference in Atlantic City in November. The goal was to discuss how most effectively to distribute food and relief supplies to prevent famine during and after the war.

3 Bernard Baruch was one of the chief financiers in the United States and a frequent political consultant to Presidents. Generally speaking when Baruch spoke, presidents and members of Congress listened.

Bibliography

PRIMARY SOURCES

Archives

Franklin Delano Roosevelt Presidential Library
President's Secretary's File: Atlantic Charter
President's Secretary's File: Lend Lease
Harry S. Truman Presidential Library
Personal Papers
Acheson, Dean
Ayers, Eben A.
Clayton, Will L.
Clifford, Clark M.
Elsey, George M.
Jones, Joseph M.
Kindleberger, Charles P.
Truman, Harry S.
Oral History Collection
Achilles, Theodore C.
Adenauer, Konrad
Arneson, R. Gordon
Clay, Lucius D.
Clifford, Clark M.
Dickey, John S.
Doxiadis, Constantinos
Elsey, George M.
Ethridge, Mark F.
Hoffman, Paul G.
Howard, Harry N.
Melby, John F.

Nitze, Paul H.
Salant, Walter S.
Massachusetts Historical Society
Personal Papers
Lodge, Jr., Henry Cabot

Personal and Government Papers

British Documents on Foreign Affairs: Reports and Papers from the Foreign Office Confidential Print.

Documents of the United Nations Conference on International Organization, San Francisco 1945.

Documentary History of the Truman Presidency. University Publications of America.

IMF History, vol. I–III. Washington, D.C., 1969.

The Papers of George Catlett Marshall, 1947–1949, 6, Johns Hopkins University Press, 2013.

Public Papers of the Presidents. *Harry S. Truman.* Multiple volumes.

Public Papers of the Presidents, *John F. Kennedy.* Multiple volumes.

The Public Papers and Addresses of Franklin D. Roosevelt. Multiple volumes.

U.S. Congress, *Congressional Record,* 1945–1950. Washington, D.C.

U.S. Congress, House. *Assistance to Greece and Turkey,* Hearings Before the House Committee on Foreign Affairs, March 24, 1947, 80th Congress, 1947.

U.S. Congress, House. Committee on Foreign Affairs. *Mutual Defense Assistance Act of 1949: Hearings on H.R. 5748 and H.R. 5895,* 81st Congress, 1949.

U.S. Congress, House. Committee on Un-American Activities. *Review of Scientific and Cultural Conference for World Peace.* Washington, D.C., April, 1949.

U.S. Congress, Senate. Committee on Banking and Currency. *Bretton Woods Agreements Act,* Hearing on H.R. 3314, 79th Congress, 1945.

U.S. Department of State, *Bulletin,* 1947.

U.S. Department of State, *Foreign Relations of the United States.* Government Printing Office. Multiple volumes.

U.S. Department of State, *Proceedings and Documents of United Nations Monetary and Financial Conference,* vols. I–II. Washington, D.C., 1948.

U.S. Department of State, *Postwar Foreign Policy Preparation, 1939–1945.* Washington, D.C., 1949.

U.S. House of Representatives, Committee on Foreign Affairs, 80th Congress, *The Strategy and Tactics of World Communism.* Washington, D.C.: Government Printing Office, 1948.

Media

Daily Boston Globe
Foreign Affairs
Harvard Gazette
Life

New Republic
New York Times
Saturday Evening Post
Time
Washington Post

Memoirs, Diaries, and Contemporary Accounts

Acheson, Dean. *Present at the Creation: My Years in the State Department.* New York: W. W. Norton and Co., 1969.

Acheson, Dean. *Sketches from Life: Of Men I have Known.* New York: Harper & Brothers, 1961.

Alsop, Joseph W. with Adam Platt. *"I've Seen the Best of It": Memoirs.* New York: W.W. Norton and Co., 1972.

Bernstein, Barton J. and Allen J. Matusow. *The Truman Administration: A Documentary History.* New York: Harper & Row, 1966.

Blum, John (ed.). *From the Morgenthau Diaries: Years of War, 1941–1945,* vol. 3. Boston: Houghton Mifflin, 1967.

Bohlen, Charles E. *Witness to History, 1929–1969.* New York: Norton, 1973.

Bullock, Alan. *Ernest Bevin: Foreign Secretary, 1945–1951.* New York: W.W. Norton, 1984.

Byrnes, James. *Speaking Frankly.* New York: Harper, 1947.

Campbell, Thomas M. and George C. Herring (eds). *The Diaries of Edward Stettinius, Jr.* Worthing: Littlehampton Book Services, 1975.

Cantril, Hadley. *Public Opinion 1935–1946.* Princeton University Press, 1951.

Chamberlain, Henry. *America's Second Crusade.* Chicago: Henry Regnery Co., 1950.

Churchill, Winston S. *The Grand Alliance: The Second World War.* New York: Mariner Books, 1986.

Clifford, Clark M. with Richard Holbrooke. *Special Counsel to the President: A Memoir.* New York: Random House, 1991.

Dennett, Raymond and Joseph E. Johnson (eds). *Negotiating with the Russians.* New York: World Peace Foundation, 1951.

Dilks, David (ed.). *The Diaries of Sir Alexander Cadogan, 1938–1945.* New York, G.P. Putnam's Sons, 1972.

Dobney, Fredrick J. *Selected Papers of Will Clayton.* The Johns Hopkins University Press, 1971.

Drury, Allen. *A Senate Journal, 1943–1945.* New York: McGraw-Hill, 1963.

Erhard, Ludwig, *Wohlstand für Alle.* Düsseldorf: Econ-Verlag GMBH, 1957.

Ferrell, Robert H. (ed.). *Off the Record: The Private Papers of Harry S. Truman.* New York: Harper & Row, 1980.

Ferrell, Robert H. (ed.). *Dear Bess: Letters from Harry to Bess Truman.* New York: W.W. Norton and Co., 1983.

Ferrell, Robert H. (ed.). *Truman in the White House: The Diary of Eben Ayers.* Columbia, MO: University of Missouri Press, 1991.

Gallup, George H. *The Gallup Poll: Public Opinion, 1935–1971*, vols. I–II. New York: Random House, 1972.

Gordon, Lincoln. "Recollections of a Marshall Planner." *Journal of International Affairs*, 41, 2 (Summer, 1988): 233–245.

Hull, Cordell. *Memoirs* vols. I–II. New York: Macmillan, 1948.

Jones, Joseph M. *The Fifteen Weeks*. New York: Harcourt, 1955.

Kennan, George, F. *American Diplomacy, 1900–1950*. Expanded Edition. University of Chicago Press, 1985.

Kennan, George, F. *Measures Short of War: The George F. Kennan Lectures at the National War College, 1946–1947*. Washington, D.C.: National Defense University Press, 1991.

Kennan, George, F. *Memoirs, 1925–1950*. Boston: Little, Brown and Co., 1967.

Kennan, George, F. *Memoirs, 1950–1963*. Boston: Little, Brown and Co., 1972.

Kindleberger, Charles. *Marshall Plan Days*. Boston: Allen and Unwin, 1987

Kramer, Alan. *The West German Economy, 1945–1955*. New York: Berg, 1991.

Lilienthal, David E. *The Journals of David E. Lilienthal*, vol. 2, *The Atomic Years, 1945–1950*. New York: Harper and Row, 1964.

Lippmann, Walter. *U.S. Foreign Policy: Shield of the Republic*. Boston: Little, Brown & Co., 1943.

Lippmann, Walter. *U.S. War Aims*. Boston: Little, Brown and Co., 1944.

Mikesell, Raymond F. *The Bretton Woods Debates: A Memoir*. Princeton University Press, 1994.

Millies, Walter (ed.). *The Forrestal Diaries*. New York: The Viking Press, 1951.

Monnet, Jean. *Memoirs*. New York: Doubleday, 1978.

Neal, Steve (ed.). *Eleanor and Harry: The Correspondence of Eleanor Roosevelt and Harry S. Truman*. New York, Scribner, 2002.

Niebuhr, Reinhold. *The Children of Light and the Children of Darkness*. New York: Scribner, 1944.

Niebuhr, Reinhold. *The Irony of American History*. University of Chicago Press, 2008.

Niebuhr, Reinhold. *Moral Man and Immoral Society*. New York: Scribner, 1932.

Nixon, Richard. *Leaders*. New York: Warner Books, 1982.

Reston, James. *Deadline: A Memoir*. New York: Random House, 1991.

Reston, James. *Prelude to Victory*. New York: Random House, 1942.

Schlesinger, Jr., Arthur M. *The Vital Center: The Politics of Freedom*. Boston: Houghton Mifflin Co., 1949.

Schlesinger, Jr., Arthur M. *Journals: 1952–2000*. New York: The Penguin Press, 2007.

Schlesinger, Jr., Arthur M. *A Life in the 20th Century: Innocent Beginnings, 1917–1950*. Boston: Houghton Mifflin, 2002.

Smith, Jean E. (ed.). *The Papers of General Lucius D. Clay: Germany, 1945–1949*, 2 vols. Indiana University Press, 1974.

Stettinius, Jr., Edward R. *Lend-Lease: Weapon for Victory*. New York: Macmillan, 1944.

Truman, Harry S. *Memoirs*, vol. 1, *Years of Decision*. New York: Signet Books, 1965.

Truman, Harry S. *Memoirs*, vol. 2, *Years of Trial and Hope, 1946–1952*. Garden City, NY: Doubleday and Co., 1956.

Vandenberg, Jr. (eds.) Arthur H. *The Private Papers of Senator Vandenberg*. Boston: Houghton Mifflin, 1952.

Wallace, Henry A. *Christian Bases of World Order*. New York: Abingdon-Cokesbury Press, 1943.

Wallace, Henry A. *The Price of Free World Victory*. New York: L.B. Fischer, 1942.

Welles, Sumner. *The Realization of a Great Vision*. Columbia University Press, 1943.

Welles, Sumner. *Seven Major Decisions that Shaped History*. London: Hamish Hamilton, 1951.

Welles, Sumner. *Where We Are Heading?* New York: Harper and Brothers, 1946.

Willkie, Wendell L. *An American Program*. New York: Simon and Schuster, 1944.

Willkie, Wendell L. *One World*. London: Cassell & Co., 1943.

Wunderlin Jr., Clarence E. (ed.). *The Papers of Robert A. Taft*, 3 vols. Kent State University Press, 2001.

SECONDARY SOURCES

Acacia, John. *Clark Clifford: The Wise Man of Washington*. University of Kentucky Press, 2009.

Applebaum, Anne. *Iron Curtain: The Crushing of Eastern Europe, 1944–1956*. New York: Doubleday, 2012.

Bailey, Thomas. *America Faces Russia: Russian-American Relations from Early Times to Our Day*. Cornell University Press, 1950.

Baratta, Joseph Preston. *The Politics of World Federation: From World Federation to Global Governance*. Westport, CT: Praeger, 2004.

Behrman, Greg. *The Most Noble Adventure: The Marshall Plan and the Time when America Helped Save Europe*. New York: Free Press, 2007.

Beisner, Robert. *Dean Acheson: A Life in the Cold War*. Oxford University Press, 2006.

Bischof, Günter, Anton Pelinka and Dieter Stiefel, (eds). *The Marshall Plan in Austria*. New Brunswick, NJ: Transaction, 2000.

Block, Fred L. *The Origins of International Economic Disorder: A Study of United States International Monetary Policy from World War II to the Present*. University Press of California, 1977.

Borgwardt, Elizabeth. *A New Deal for the World: America's Vision for Human Rights*. The Belknap Press of Harvard University Press, 2007.

Bostdorff, Denise M. *Proclaiming the Truman Doctrine: The Cold War Call to Arms*. Texas A & M University Press, 2008.

Brands, H.W. *Inside the Cold War: Loy Henderson and the Rise of the American Empire, 1918–1961*. Oxford University Press, 1991.

Brands, H.W. "Consensus Be Damned!" *Reviews in American History*, 22, 4. (December, 1994): 717–724.

Burr, William. "Marshall Planners and the Politics of Empire: The United States and France, 1948," *Diplomatic History*, 15, 4 (October, 1991): 495–522.

Casey, Kevin M. *Saving International Capitalism During the Early Truman Presidency: The National Advisory Council on International Monetary and Financial Problem.* New York: Routledge, 2001.

Costigliola, Frank. "After Roosevelt's Death: Dangerous Emotions, Divisive Discourses, and the Abandoned Alliance," *Diplomatic History,* 34, 1 (January, 2010): 1–23.

Costigliola, Frank. *Roosevelt's Lost Alliances: How Personal Politics Helped Start the Cold War.* Princeton University Press, 2011.

Craig, Campbell and Fredrick Logevall. *America's Cold War: The Politics of Insecurity.* Harvard University Press, 2009.

Craig, R. Bruce. *Treasonable Doubt: The Harry Dexter White Spy Case.* University Press of Kansas, 2004.

Dallek, Robert. *Franklin D. Roosevelt and American Foreign Policy.* Oxford University Press, 1995.

David, Andrew and Michael Holm. "The Kennedy Administration and the Battle over Foreign Aid: The Untold Story of the Clay Committee," *Diplomacy and Statecraft,* (March, 2016): 65–92.

De Vries, Johan De. *The Netherlands Economy in the Twentieth Century.* Assen: Van Gorchum, 1978.

Dockter, A. Warren. *Winston Churchill at the Telegraph.* Aurum Press Ltd., 2015.

Eckes, Jr., Alfred E. *Opening America's Market: U.S. Foreign Trade Policy Since 1776.* The University of North Carolina Press, 1995.

Eichengreen, Barry and Marc Uzan, "The Marshall Plan: Economic Effects and Implications for Eastern Europe and the Former USSR," *Economic Policy,* 7, 14, (April, 1992): 13–75.

Eisenberg, Carolyn W. *Drawing the Line: The American Decision to Divide Germany, 1944–1949.* Cambridge University Press, 1998.

Eisenhower, John S.D. *General Ike: A Personal Reminiscence.* Free Press, 2003.

Ekbladh, David. *The Great American Mission: Modernization and the Construction of an American World Order.* Princeton University Press, 2010.

Engerman, David et al. (eds). *Staging Growth: Modernization, Development, and the Global Cold War.* University of Massachusetts Press, 2003.

Erb, Claude C. "Prelude to Point Four: The Institute of Inter-American Affairs," *Diplomatic History,* 9, 3 (Summer, 1985): 249–269.

Esposito, Chiarella. *America's Feeble Weapon: Funding the Marshall Plan in France and Italy, 1948–1950.* Westport: Greenwood, 1994.

Feis, Herbert. *Churchill, Roosevelt, Stalin: The War they Waged and the Peace they Sought.* Princeton University Press, 1967.

Ferguson, Niall. "Dollar Diplomacy: How Much Did the Marshall Plan Really Matter?" *The New Yorker,* August 27, 2007.

Fousek, John M. *To Lead the Free World: American Nationalism and the Cultural Roots of the Cold War.* University of North Carolina Press, 2000.

Fukuyama, Francis. *The End of History and The Last Man.* New York: Free Press, 1992.

Gaddis, John Lewis. *George F. Kennan: An American Life*. New York: Penguin Press, 2011.

Gaddis, John Lewis. *The Cold War: A New History*. New York: Penguin Books, 2005.

Gaddis, John Lewis. *We Now Know: Rethinking Cold War History*. New York: Oxford University Press, 1997.

Gaddis, John Lewis. "The Emerging Post-Revisionist Synthesis on the Origins of the Cold War," *Diplomatic History*, 7, 3 (July, 1983): 171–190.

Gardner, Richard. N. *Sterling-Dollar Diplomacy in Current Perspective: The Origins and the Prospects of Our International Economic Order*. Columbia University Press, 1980.

Geertz, Clifford. "Ideology as a Cultural System," in David E. Apter (ed.), *Ideology and Discontent*. New York: Free Press of Glencoe, 1964: 49–76.

Geertz, Clifford. *The Interpretation of Cultures*. New York: Basic Books, 1973.

Gellately, Robert. *Stalin's Curse: Battling for Communism in War and Cold War*. London: Vintage Books, 2013.

Graebner, Norman A., Richard Dean Burns, and Joseph M. Siracusa. *America and the Cold War, 1941–1991: A Realist Interpretation*, 2 vols. New York: Praeger, 2010.

Gramsci, Antonio, *Selections from the Prison Notebooks of Antonio Gramsci*. New York: International Publishers Co., 1971.

Hamby, Alonzo. *Man of Destiny: FDR and the Making of the American Century*. New York: Basic Books, 2015.

Hamilton, Malcolm B. "The Elements of the Concept of Ideology," *Political Studies*, 35 (March, 1987): 18–38.

Harrington, Daniel F. *Berlin on the Brink: The Blockade, the Airlift, and the Early Cold War*. University Press of Kentucky, 2012.

Hart, Justin. *Empire of Ideas: The Origins of Public Diplomacy and the Transformation of U.S. Foreign Policy*. Oxford University Press, 2013.

Healey, Timothy. "Will Clayton, Negotiating the Marshall Plan, and European Economic Integration," *Diplomatic History*, 35, 2 (April, 2011): 229–256.

Helleiner, Eric. *Forgotten Foundations of Bretton Woods: International Development and the Making of the Postwar Order*. Cornell University Press, 2014.

Hitchcock, William I. *The Bitter Road to Freedom: The Human Cost of Allied Victory in World War II*. New York: Free Press, 2009.

Hitchcock, William I. *The Struggle for Europe: The Turbulent History of a Divided Continent, 1945–2002*. New York: Anchor Books, 2004.

Hitchcock, William I. "The Marshall Plan and the creation of the West," in Odd Arne Westad and Melvyn P. Leffler (eds.), *The Cambridge History of the Cold War*, I. Cambridge University Press, 2010: 154–174.

Hitchcock, William I. *France Restored: Cold War Diplomacy and the Quest for Leadership in Europe, 1944–1954*. University of North Carolina Press, 1998.

Hodne, Fritz. *The Norwegian Economy, 1920–1980*. Kent, UK: Croom Helm, 1983.

Hoff-Wilson, Joan. *Ideology and Economics: U.S. Relations with the Soviet Union, 1918–1933*. University of Missouri Press, 1974.

Hogan, Michael J. *A Cross of Iron: Harry S. Truman and the Origins of the National Security State, 1945–1954.* New York: Cambridge University Press, 1998.

Hogan, Michael J. *The Marshall Plan: America, Britain, and the Reconstruction of Western Europe, 1947–1952.* New York: Cambridge University Press, 1989.

Holm, Michael. "Also Present at the Creation: Henry Cabot Lodge, Jr. and the Coming of the Cold War," *The Journal of the Historical Society*, 10, 2 (June, 2010): 203–229.

Hubbard, Glenn. "A Marshall Plan for the Middle East," *The Huffington Post*, February 28, 2011.

Hubbard, Glenn. "Think Again: A Marshall Plan for Africa," *Foreign Policy*, August 13, 2009.

Hunt, Michael H. "Ideology," *Journal of American History*, 77, 1 (June, 1990): 108–115.

Hunt, Michael H. "The Long Crisis in U.S. Diplomatic History: Coming to Closure, *Diplomatic History*, 16, 1 (January, 1992): 115–140.

Hunt, Michael H. *Ideology and U.S. Foreign Policy.* Second Edition. Yale University Press, 2009.

Judt, Tony. *Postwar: A History of Europe Since 1945.* London: Penguin Books, 2006.

Kaplan, Lawrence. *The Conversion of Senator Arthur H. Vandenberg: From Isolation to International Engagement.* University Press of Kentucky, 2015.

Kennedy, David. *Over Here: The First World War and American Society.* Oxford University Press, 2004.

Kennedy, David. "What Would Wilson Do?" *The Atlantic Monthly* (Jan/Feb, 2010): 90–94.

Keylor, William R. *A World of Nations: The International Order Since 1945.* Oxford University Press, 2009.

Killick, John. *The United States and European Reconstruction.* New York: Routledge, 2000.

Kimball, Warren F. "Lend-Lease and the Open Door: The Temptation of British Opulence, 1937–1942," *Political Science Quarterly*, 86 (June 1971): 232–259.

Kimball, Warren F. *The Most Unsordid Act: Lend-Lease, 1939–1941.* The Johns Hopkins University Press, 1969.

Kimball, Warren F. *The Juggler: Franklin Roosevelt as Wartime Statesman.* Princeton University Press, 1991.

Kissinger, Henry. *Diplomacy.* New York: Simon and Schuster, 1994.

Knock, Thomas J. *To End All Wars: Woodrow Wilson and the Quest for a New World Order.* Princeton University Press, 1995.

Knock, Thomas J. *The Roots of American Foreign Policy: An Analysis of Power and Purpose.* Boston: Beacon Press, 1969.

Kolko, Gabriel. *The Roots of American Foreign Policy: An Analysis of Power and Purpose.* New York: Beacon Press, 1969.

Kolko, Joyce and Gabriel Kolko. *The Limits of Power: The World of United States Foreign Policy, 1945–1954.* New York: Harper & Row, 1972.

Kunz, Dianne. *Guns and Butter: America's Cold War Economic Diplomacy.* New York: The Free Press, 1997.

LaFeber, Walter. *America, Russia, and the Cold War, 1945–2006.* Tenth Edition. New York: McGraw-Hill, 2007.

LaFeber, Walter. *The Cambridge History of American Foreign Relations: The American Search for Opportunity, 1865–1913,* vol. 2. Cambridge University Press, 1995.

LaFeber, Walter. "NATO and the Korean War: A Context," *Diplomatic History,* 13, 4 (Fall, 1989): 461–478.

Lathman, Michael E., *Modernization as Ideology: American Social Sciences and "Nation Building" in the Kennedy Era.* University of North Carolina Press, 2000.

Leffler, Melvyn P. *A Preponderance of Power: National Security, the Truman Administration, and the Cold War.* Stanford University Press, 1991.

Leffler, Melvyn P. *For the Soul of Mankind: The United States, The Soviet Union, and the Cold War.* New York: Hill and Wang, 2006.

Levering, Ralph B., Vladimir O. Pechatnov, Verena Botzenhart-Viehe, and C. Earl Edmonson (eds). *Debating the Origins of the Cold War.* New York: Rowman & Littlefield, 2000.

Lidegaard, Bo. *I Kongens Navn: Henrik Kauffmann i Dansk Diplomati, 1919–58.* NB PrePress, 1996.

Lidegaard, Bo. *Jens Otto Kragh, 1914–1961.* København: Gyldendal, 2001.

Lucas, Scott. *Freedom's War: The U.S. Crusade Against the Soviet Union, 1945–1956.* Manchester University Press, 1999.

Lüthi, Lorenz M. *The Sino-Soviet Split: Cold War in the Communist World.* Princeton University Press, 2008.

McAllister, James. *No Exit: America and the German Problem, 1943–1954.* Cornell University Press, 2002.

McClosky, Herbert. "Consensus and Ideology in American Politics," *American Political Science Review,* 58 (June 1964): 361–382.

McCullough, David. *Truman.* New York: Simon and Schuster, 1992.

McGuire, Michael E. (ed.). *As It Actually Was: A History of International Relations Through Documents, 1823–1945.* New York: McGraw Hill, 2008.

Maier, Charles S. "The Marshall Plan and the Division of Europe," *Journal of Cold War Studies,* 7, 1, (Winter, 2005): 168–174.

Maier, Charles S. "The Politics of Productivity: Foundation of American International Economic Policy after World War II," *International Organization,* 31, 4 (Autumn 1977): 607–633.

Maier, Charles S. with Gunter Bishof. *The Marshall Plan and Germany: West German Development within the Framework of the European Recovery Program.* New York: Berg, 1991.

Maier, Charles S. "The Marshall Plan and the Division of Europe," *Journal of Cold War Studies,* 7, 1 (Winter, 2005): 168–174.

Mark, Eduard. "October or Thermidor? Interpretations of Stalinism and the Perception of Soviet Foreign Policy in the United States, 1927–1947," *The American Historical Review,* 94, 4 (October, 1989): 937–962.

Miller, William J. *Henry Cabot Lodge, Jr.: A Biography.* New York: Norton, 1967.

Millikan, Max F. and W.W. Rostow, *A Proposal: Key to an Effective Foreign Policy.* New York: Harper & Row, 1957.

Milward, Alan S. *The Reconstruction of Western Europe, 1945–1951* (London: Methuen, 1984).

Milward, Alan S. "Was the Marshall Plan Necessary," *Diplomatic History*, 13, 2 (1989): 231–252.

Miscamble, Wilson D. *George F. Kennan and the Making of American Foreign Policy, 1947–1950.* Princeton University Press, 1992.

Miscamble, Wilson D. *From Roosevelt to Truman: Potsdam, Hiroshima, and the Cold War.* New York: Cambridge University Press, 2007.

Mistry, Kaeten. *The United States, Italy and the Origins of the Cold War.* Cambridge University Press, 2014.

Morgenthau, Hans J. *A New Foreign Policy for the United States.* New York: Praeger, 1969.

Morgenthau, Hans J. *In Defense of the National Interest: A Critical Examination of American Foreign Policy.* New York: Knopf, 1951.

Morgenthau, Hans J. *Politics Among Nations: The Struggle for Power and Peace.* New York: Knopf, 1967.

Moss, Norman. *America, Britain, and the Fateful Summer of 1940.* New York: Houghton Mifflin Harcourt, 2003.

Mullins, Willard A. "On the Concept of Ideology in Political Science," *The American Political Science Review*, 66 (June 1972): 498–510.

Narinsky, Mikhail. "Soviet Foreign Policy and the Origins of the Cold War," in Gabriel Gorodetsky (ed.), *Soviet Foreign Policy, 1917–1991: A Retrospective.* London: Frank Cass, 1994.

Offner, Arnold A. *Another Such Victory: President Truman and the Cold War, 1945–1953.* Stanford University Press, 2002.

O'Sullivan, Christopher. *Sumner Welles, Postwar Planning, and the Quest for a New World Order.* Columbia University Press, 2009.

Paterson, Thomas G. *Soviet-American Confrontation: Postwar Reconstruction and the Origins of the Cold War.* Johns Hopkins University Press, 1973.

Patterson, James T. *Mr. Republican: A Biography of Robert A. Taft.* New York: Houghton Mifflin Co., 1972.

Pearce, Robert. *Attlee.* Routledge, 1997.

Pechatnov, V.O. "The Allies are Pressing on You to Break Your Will . . .': Foreign Policy Correspondence between Stalin and Molotov and other Politburo Members, September 1945–December 1946," *Cold War International History Project*, Working Papers no. 26 (Woodrow Wilson International Center, 1999): 18–32.

Pietrusza, David. *1948: Harry Truman's Improbable Victory and the Year that Changed America.* New York: Union Square Press, 2011.

Pogue, Forrest C. *George C. Marshall: Statesman, 1945–1959.* New York: Viking Press, 1987.

Pollard, Robert. *Economic Security and the Origins of the Cold War.* Columbia University Press, 1985.

Putnam, Robert D. "Studying Elite Political Culture: The Case of Ideology," *The American Political Science Review*, 65, 3 (September, 1971): 651–681.

Raack, Richard C. "The Cold War Revisionists Kayoed: New Books Dispel More Historical Darkness," *World Affairs*, 62, 2 (Fall 1999): 43–62.

Reinisch, Jessica. "'We Shall Rebuild Anew a Powerful Nation': UNRRA, Internationalism and National Reconstruction in Poland," *Journal of Contemporary History*, 43, 3 (July, 2008): 451–476.

Reynolds, David. *From Munich to Pearl Harbor: Roosevelt's America and the Origins of the Second World War*. Chicago: Ivan R. Dee, 2001.

Reynolds, David. "From World War to Cold War: The Wartime Alliance and Postwar Transitions, 1941–1947," *The Historical Journal*, 45, 1, (March, 2002): 211–227.

Rodgers, Daniel T. *Age of Fracture*. The Belknap Press of Harvard University, 2011.

Rosenberg, Emily. *Spreading the American Dream: American Economic and Cultural Expansion, 1890–1945*. New York: Hill & Wang, 1982.

Rostow, Eugene V. *A Breakfast for Bonaparte: U.S. National Security Interest from the Heights of Abraham to the Nuclear Age*. Washington, D.C.: National Defense University Press, 1993.

Rostow, W.W. *The Stages of Economic Growth: A Non-Communist Manifesto*. Cambridge University Press, 1960.

Schain, Martin A. (ed.). *The Marshall Plan Fifty Years After*. New York: Palgrave, 2001.

Schild, Georg. *Bretton Woods and Dumbarton Oaks*, New York: St. Martin's Press, 1995.

Schlesinger, Stephen C. *Act of Creation: The Founding of the United Nations: A Story of Superpowers, Secret Agents, Wartime Allies and Enemies, and Their Quest for a Peaceful World*. Boulder, CO: Westview Press, 2003.

Schoultz, Lars. *Beneath the United States: A History of U.S. Policy Toward Latin America*. Harvard University Press, 1988.

Service, Robert. *Stalin: A Biography*. The Belknap Press of Harvard University, 2004.

Sherwood, Robert. *Hopkins and Roosevelt: An Intimate Story*. New York: Harper, 1950.

Shills, Edward. "The End of Ideology?" *Encounter*, 5 (1955): 52–58.

Shills, Edward. "Ideology and Civility: On the Politics of the Intellectual," *Sewanee Review*, LXVI (1958): 459–480.

Silva, Charles. *Keep Them Strong, Keep Them Friendly: Swedish-American Relations and the Pax Americana, 1948–1952*. Stockholm: Akademitryck AB, 1999.

Smith, Jean E. *Lucius D. Clay*. New York: Henry Holt and Company, 1980.

Smith, Tony. *America's Mission: The United States and the Worldwide Struggle for Democracy in the Twentieth Century*. Princeton University Press, 1994.

Sofer, Sasson. "International Relations and the Invisibility of Ideology," *Millennium: Journal of International Studies*, 16, 3 (1987): 489–521.

Sørensen, Vibeke. *Denmark's Social Democratic Government and the Marshall Plan*. Museum Tusulanums Forlag: University of Copenhagen, 2001.

Steel, Ronald. *Walter Lippmann and the American Century*. New Brunswick, NJ: Transaction Publishers, 1999.

Steil, Benn. *The Battle of Bretton Woods: John Maynard Keynes, Harry Dexter White, and the Making of a New World Order.* Princeton University Press, 2013.

Stoler, Mark A. "George C. Marshall and the 'Europe-First' Strategy, 1939–1951: A Study in Diplomatic as well as Military History," *Journal of Military History,* 79, 2 (April 2015): 293–316.

Trachtenberg, Marc. *A Constructed Peace: The Making of the European Settlement, 1945–1963.* Princeton University Press, 1999.

Van Dormael, Armand. *Bretton Woods: Birth of a Monetary System.* New York: Holmes & Meier, 1978.

Wala, Michael. *The Council on Foreign Relations and American Foreign Policy in the Early Cold War.* Providence: Berghahn, 1994.

Wala, Michael. "Selling the Marshall Plan at Home: The Committee for the Marshall Plan to Aid European Recovery," *Diplomatic History,* 10, 3 (July, 1986): 247–265

Westad, Odd Arne. *The Global Cold War: Third World Interventions and the Making of Our Times.* New York: Cambridge University Press, 2005.

Westad, Odd Arne. "The New International History: Three (Possible) Paradigms," *Diplomatic History,* 24, 4 (Fall 2000): 551–565.

Westbrook, Robert B. *John Dewey and American Democracy.* Cornell University Press, 1991.

Whelan, Bernadette. *Ireland and the Marshall Plan 1947–1957.* Dublin: Four Courts Press, 2000.

Williams, William Appleman. *Empire as a Way of Life: An Essay on the Causes and Character of America's Present Predicament along with a Few Thoughts about an Alternative.* New York, Oxford University Press, 1980.

Williams, William Appleman. *The Tragedy of American Diplomacy.* Second Revised Edition. New York: W.W. Norton & Co., 1972.

Wood, Gordon S. *The Idea of America: Reflections on the Birth of the United States.* New York: The Penguin Press, 2011.

Zinn, Howard. *A People's History of the United States.* New York: Harper & Row, 1980.

Index

CPSIA information can be obtained
at www.ICGtesting.com
Printed in the USA
BVHW041109170422
634492BV00001B/6

9 781138 915718